Sentence Structure
and Characterization
in the Tragedies of Jean Racine

Sentence Structure
and Characterization
in the Tragedies of Jean Racine

A Computer-Assisted Study

Mary Lynne Flowers

Rutherford • Madison • Teaneck
Fairleigh Dickinson University Press
London: Associated University Presses

Associated University Presses, Inc.
Cranbury, New Jersey 08512

Associated University Presses
Magdalen House
136-148 Tooley Street
London SE1 2TT, England

Library of Congress Cataloging in Publication Data
Flowers, Mary Lynne.
    Sentence structure and characterization in the
tragedies of Jean Racine.

    Bibliography: p.
    Includes index.
    1.   Racine, Jean Baptiste, 1639-1699 — Style.
I.   Title.
PQ1909.F5   842'.4   76-50284
ISBN 0-8386-2056-6

PRINTED IN THE UNITED STATES OF AMERICA

Contents

List of Tables

(Appendix C)

Acknowledgments

I gratefully acknowledge assistance and supportive guidance in all phases of the project. The computer-readable texts for the Racine plays were supplied at a nominal charge by Professor Bryant C. Freeman and the University of Virginia Computer Center. Computer time was allocated by the Department of Romance Languages through the Instructional and Research Computer Center of the Ohio State University for use of the IBM 370/165. Special thanks go to Thomas Whitney of the IRCC for teaching me computer programming and especially for comfort and counsel when computer-related problems seemed insurmountable. Karen McCann, also of the IRCC, served as consultant for tape procedures and SPSS routines. Further computer time was provided at the University of Kentucky Computing Center as well as released time for research funded by a Summer Faculty Research Grant (1974) from the University of Kentucky.

Professors Eleanor Bulatkin, Robert Cottrell, and Robert Mills contributed personal insights and helped to broaden the base of the study. With a sense of humor and a fine critical mind, Professor Hugh M. Davidson assisted me in every phase of this study—from conceptualizing the problem to wording individual sentences. While gratefully acknowledging the encouragement and assistance of many people, I remain fully responsible for the study as it now stands.

M.L.F.

Introduction

Numerous critics, in developing approaches to dramatic literature, have focused their attention on the tragedies of Jean Racine; curiously, no one has studied in detail the dramatic aspects of Racine's sentence, the basic syntactic unit and a building block of his tragedies. A certain homogeneity of sentence structure in Racine can no doubt be identified as his style. Within that framework, however, principal characters or character types may distinguish themselves by their preferred patterns of sentence structure. The appropriate hypothesis, commonly called the null hypothesis, is actually the converse, that no significant differences in patterns of sentence structure exist in Racinian tragedies. Once the null hypothesis is discredited, factors other than simple distinctions among characters still remain. The larger context of the sentence, whether it be a monologue, a *tirade,* or a rapid exchange of dialogue, affects patterns of sentence structure. Characterization is dynamic; changing sentence patterns reflect changing situations for the characters and, therefore, some characters favor specific patterns in an emotionally charged situation, patterns different from those favored by the same characters in a relatively neutral state of affairs. Moreover, patterns of sentence structure are affected by the exigencies of the *alexandrin* as well. With these contextual and situational factors in mind and with the null hypothesis discredited, this study explores the literary implications of the hypothesis that the sentence, as a unit of the spoken language, is one of Racine's main instruments for characterization.

Implicit in studying one aspect of a literary work is the danger of becoming so engrossed as to lose sight of the totality of the work and to neglect the relationship of specific insights to that totality. In order to avoid the temptation of reveling in isolated phenomena of sentence structure, findings are periodically related to the play in question and to assumptions about tragedy. Approaching Racinian tragedy from one angle, certain recent critics have brought other disciplines to bear on literature and tragedy: the orientation of Roland Barthes to an-thropology, of Charles Mauron to psychoanalysis, of Lucien Goldmann to sociology and marxism, and of Raymond Picard to literary history and biography. While the insights of these critics are helpful in understanding Racinian tragedy, I intend to rely instead on the dramatic and poetic disciplines themselves. Using the computer to manipulate data is not equivalent to bringing another discipline to bear on literature in the sense implied above for reasons that will become clear in the next chapter. Other critics have isolated particular traits considered essential to Raci-nian tragedy: constraint and presence (John Lapp); characters' realiza-tion of their inability to attain the moral perfection they envisage (Judd Hubert); or "sacrifice, égarement et reconnaissance" (Eugene Vinaver).

While these critics deal specifically with Racinian tragedy, others ap-proach tragedy in more general terms and discuss the technical aspects of writing and performing dramatic literature. In the seventeenth century Pierre Corneille, as a highly successful practitioner of theater, deals in three discourses on theater both with his understanding of tragedy and with the technical aspects of writing and performing tragedy. A contem-porary of Corneille, l'Abbé d'Aubignac produced a handbook on the practical aspects of writing plays. A well-informed observer of the theater, d'Aubignac relies on Corneille to illustrate his many, detailed in-structions to would-be playwrights. In a particularly helpful modern work Jacques Schérer treats the technical aspects of classical French dramaturgy, drawing heavily on d'Aubignac as a theoretician and on Corneille as an innovator. In this perspective, Schérer sees Racine as a perfector of technical dramatic savoir acquired by his predecessors. As with approaches to tragedy through other disciplines and through essen-tial traits, I rely on discussion of technical matters to complement and to clarify this study, but look to another approach to clarify my assumptions about tragedy.

That other approach defines tragedy in terms of its underlying prin-ciples. An ancient approach through principles is found in Aristotle who describes tragedy in terms either so widely accepted as to become com-monplaces or so controversial as to become objects of heated disputes. A recent partisan of this approach, Bernard Weinberg, has studied the evolution and development of Racine's art by treating plot and character in Aristotelian terms. Weinberg envisages Racine as applying these prin-ciples as he writes his tragedies and improving his skill with each successive play. While Weinberg concentrates on Racine's use of Aristotelian principles, another contemporary critic, Elder Olson, in his *Tragedy and the Theory of Drama,* redefines the principles of tragedy and of drama in general. Olson works out a theory of tragedy with emphasis on specifically dramatic aspects; he concentrates on the whole work and relates constituent parts to that whole. While relying on Olson's helpful insights, I adopt the opposite perspective: concentrating on a part, sentence structure, and periodically relating it to the whole dramatic work through assumptions about tragedy.

Discussed in greater detail in chapter 1, these different approaches to tragedy serve as a frame of reference for understanding assumptions about tragedy, in much the same way that the latter serves as a frame of reference for discussion of sentence structure and characterization. The discussion of tragedy, while interesting and necessary, must not distract attention from the central issue, the stylistic one. A historical assessment of interest in style is clearly beyond the scope of this study. Marcel Cressot has recently, however, offered a place to begin a general consideration of language and sentence structure. In more literary terms, Leo Spitzer and R. A. Sayce offer contrasting but equally instructive methods. Narrowing the perspective even further to Racine himself, there is Jacques Cahen's work on Racine's vocabulary as well as the fine work of Peter France on his rhetoric. These approaches to style may all be termed traditional in contrast to computer-assisted research into style. In this new area it is valuable to know what the computer has already contributed to the study of literary language and what tasks the computer can reasonably be expected to perform. Against this double background of newer computer-assisted approaches to style and of the more traditional approaches outlined here along with the concept of tragedy, it is possible to set forth in detail my particular method of inquiry into style through sentence structure in Racine's dramatic works.

This study is designed to examine, manipulate, and categorize sentences and patterns of sentence structure by both manual and computer-assisted processes, with continual reference to the play in question and to specific notions about tragedy. I will, therefore, be attempting to answer such questions as the following. What is the relationship of language to serious dramatic literature? How does language, and sentence structure in particular, contribute to inference in Racine's tragedies? In specific plays, what does examination of these patterns contribute to understanding stable characterization? to assessing the emotional climate of particular situations and the resultant modifications of character or of our perception of character? to differentiating the particular forms of monologue, dialogue, and *tirade*? What evolution, if any, can be perceived in Racine's writing of tragedy as a result of this analysis? How does Racine's sentence structure differ from that of his contemporaries? How do requirements implicit in the verse form affect sentence structure?

These questions are applied first to the seven tragedies, from *Andromaque* to *Phèdre*. The computer-readable text is that prepared by Bryant Freeman for the Racine concordance; this text is based on the Mesnard edition (1885) with correction of typographical errors. Computer-readable texts of Corneille's *Tite et Bérénice* (Marty-Laveaux edition) and Pradon's *Phèdre et Hippolyte* (1677 edition) were prepared specifically for this study. In more specific terms, chapter 1 explores notions about tragedy in the light of numerous views and states my assumptions about tragedy relative to this study. More important, this first chapter deals with language and sentence structure and their relationship to dramatic literature. Chapters 2-6 present pertinent findings about sentence structure and characterization in each of the plays from *Andromaque* to *Phèdre* and relate these findings to the economy of the play in question. The distinctiveness of Racine's sentence structure is reinforced by comparison to two plays on the same subjects by Racine's contemporaries, Pierre Corneille and Jacques Pradon. Chapter 7 contrasts these findings to patterns in the two earlier plays, *La Thébaïde* and *Alexandre,* in the two late ones, *Esther* and *Athalie,* and in Racine's only comedy, *Les Plaideurs.* Chapter 8 relates sentence structure to versification. The conclusion then reviews the findings on a topical basis and discusses possible evolution in Racine's use of sentence structure as a tool for characterization in his dramatic works.

Sentence Structure and Characterization in the Tragedies of Jean Racine

1

From Tragedy to the Sentence as a Unit of Tragedy

Understanding the relationships between tragedy and the sentence as a unit of tragedy is crucial to proper perspective. Only in light of various approaches can this study delineate its specific approach to tragedy. One option stands out as appropriate: discussing tragedy by identifying its underlying dramatic principles. Using similar approaches as guidelines, it is possible to set forth point by point my own assumptions about the fundamental elements of tragedy. These assumptions constitute the first point of reference and are closely related to the function of language in tragedy and to the special significance of language in seventeenth-century French tragedy and in Racine. The second point of reference is style, beginning with general concepts of style, proceeding to literary style in both its traditional and computer-assisted aspects, and finally refocusing attention on Racine himself. With these two points of reference clearly in mind, the three phases of this investigation can be delineated, thereby launching this study of sentence structure and characterization in the tragedies of Jean Racine.

Assumptions about Tragedy

Attempts to prevent any particular authors or any particular works from meeting the qualifications of tragedy only perpetuate old disagreements and antagonisms rather than stimulating further exploration of the question. A number of familiar phrases about tragedy unfortunately correspond to preconceived notions or they provoke heated arguments. Moreover, these assumptions are not essential to discussion of sentence structure. Assumptions can be generated from another discipline brought to bear on the problem of tragedy. A number of contemporary literary critics are competent in fields of study different from

17

those traditionally associated with literature and bring with them the perspectives, methods, and vocabulary of disciplines such as biography, anthropology, marxism and sociology, and psychoanalysis. Raymond Picard, in *La Carrière de Jean Racine* (Paris: Gallimard, 1956), is the closest to discussing Racinian tragedy from a literary point of view, primarily because literary history and literary biography have long been adjuncts to the study of literature. In discussing the tragedies themselves, Picard delves into the circumstances under which each tragedy was written and first performed: the theater and its location, box office receipts, attendance and audience reaction, and subsequent publication of the play. These facts and figures do not, of course, constitute a definition of Racinian tragedy, but they do serve to support Picard's thesis that Racine's dramaturgy was a form of opportunism and that Racine's success as a playwright was only a means to an end. While this thesis explains Racine's abrupt departure from the theater to assume his new responsibilities as the King's historiographer, it also makes tragedy a mere function of Racine's social ambitions. Consequently, Picard treats the tragedies from an external and fixed perspective of time, place, audience, and purpose; while he may thus claim a great deal about Racine's goals in life, he says little about the plays themselves, about Racine's assumptions on tragedy, or about his own.

On the other hand, Roland Barthes deals directly with the plays in *Sur Racine* (Paris: Seuil, 1963) as an anthropologist searching for a species "l'homme racinien": "je me suis placé dans le monde tragique de Racine et j'ai tenté d'en décrire la population" (p. 9). This leads Barthes to talk about the primitive horde and the fundamental relationship, that of authority, in which the use of force and verbal aggression results in violence when applied to a context of love. The main solution — proposed by Racine and practiced by his characters — to this confrontation of an authority that cannot bring about love and compliance through the use of force is a solution of bad faith. The conflict is eluded altogether rather than solved and the tragic character is expelled from the scene so that the others may breathe freely in a domain outside the tragic (p. 60). This perspective provides valuable insights into the disposition of Racine's tragedies, a number of which are confirmed in this study. It also leads Barthes to generalize characters and character traits to the point that the individual characters are completely absorbed by the character type or "figure." The critic states this unequivocally: "Il n'y a pas de *caractères* dans le théâtre racinien . . . il n'y a que des situations, au sens presque formel du terme: tout tire son être de sa place dans la constellation générale des forces et des faiblesses" (pp. 24-25). The insights not-withstanding, Barthes's anthropological perspective and vocabulary tend to obscure the plays by his own superstructure instead of uncovering their foundations. Although this critic presents a coherent view of Racine's portrayal of fundamental relationships, Barthes so scrupulously puts boundaries on tragedy and the tragic that he threatens to stifle further inquiry along that line.

Whereas Roland Barthes draws his terminology and perspective from anthropology, Lucien Goldmann sees Racine's vision of the tragic in sociological terms in *Le Dieu caché* (Paris: Gallimard, 1955). Racine's tragic vision, like that of Pascal, is the individual expression of a collective mentality, that of Port-Royal: "toute grande oeuvre littéraire ou artistique est l'expression d'une vision du monde. Celle-ci est un phénomène de conscience collective qui atteint son maximum de clarté conceptuelle ou sensuelle dans la conscience du penseur ou du poète" (p. 28). Goldmann defines Racine's tragic vision as three main characters, man, the world, and God, involved in an essentially insoluble conflict. Man becomes tragic when he approaches the world with a demand for the absolute (the all-or-nothing approach), whereas the world operates on relatives (the better-or-worse approach). God is present as the transcendental demand for absolute values but is absent or hidden when it comes to aid and counsel to man.[1] While there is clearly some truth in what Goldmann says and great merit in his attempt to define the tragic vision of Racine, his assumptions about tragedy are not germane to language and his techniques for dealing with the subject and his vocabulary are almost insurmountable obstacles for the uninitiated.

Another modern field of study is psychoanalysis or, as applied to authors and literary works, psychocriticism. Charles Mauron in *L'Inconscient dans l'oeuvre et la vie de Racine* (Publications des Annales de la Faculté des Lettres, Aix-en-Provence, n.s. 16, 1957) gives priority to the expression of the subconscious structure in Racine's work and then, by extension, in his life. Mauron's premise is that great artists like Racine are capable of expressing their subconscious structure through conscious literary activity (p. 183). The familiar figure of the mother, sometimes generalized to include the possessive woman, and the simultaneous tendency to both incest and parricide are used to explain and to categorize Racine's characters. Racine's theater becomes a form of self-analysis and a symbolic expression of a subconscious conflict projected onto the various characters of the plays and evolving from one play to the next as shown by Mauron's intriguing diagram (p. 27). Here as with Barthes and Goldmann, there are valuable insights to be gained amid the technical terms. Since these critics deal almost exclusively with conceptual elements of tragedy, they completely neglect the dramatic implications of tragedy. It also seems that the problems encountered in the special perspectives and the technical vocabulary of these other disciplines outweigh the advantage they offer, not to mention the very real danger of reading into the text twentieth-century concepts that simply are not there.

Assumptions about tragedy are often an attempt to insure compliance in specifically technical matters such as number of acts or scenes, number of characters or incidents, unity of time or place, and degree of particularization or of generalization in circumstances presented. This last distinction is particularly powerful for purposes of exclusion. Shakespeare can be excluded by establishing criteria of generalized and universal characters and actions; Racine can be excluded by the opposite procedure, that of establishing criteria of localized and particularized characters and actions.[2] Other more specifically technical matters were of great concern in the seventeenth century, shown in part by the discourses of Pierre Corneille and *La Pratique du théâtre* of l'Abbé d'Aubignac; in recent years, Jacques Schérer used both Corneille and d'Aubignac extensively to discuss the technical aspects of classical French dramaturgy.

When Pierre Corneille published his collected plays in 1660, he included in that edition *examens* that relate specifically to the play in question. In that edition Corneille also published three discourses of a more theoretical nature.[3] In his first, *Le Discours de l'utilité et des parties du poème dramatique,* Corneille writes of the goals, of the moral utility, of the constituent parts, and of the quantitative divisions of the dramatic poem, without reference to generic distinctions. Two comments by Corneille in this discourse are of special interest here. Corneille reveals his "maxime infaillible" for the dramatic form: "il faut intéresser l'auditoire pour les premiers acteurs" (1:36). But he does not say how. He also seems to preclude character evolution: "conserver jusqu'à la fin à nos personnages les mœurs que nous leur avons données au commencement" (1:37).

The second discourse, *Le Discours de la tragédie et des moyens de la traiter selon le vraisemblable ou le nécessaire,* is for the most part a commentary and an elaboration on the principles of Aristotle, whose descriptive work in the *Poetics* becomes prescriptive in the hands of Corneille. For this reason I will come back to this discourse in discussing the approach through principles. The third discourse is *Le Discours des trois unités d'action, de jour et de lieu* where Corneille's perspective narrows appreciably. This section deals almost entirely with technical aspects of a play's construction. After discussing the exposition, *noeud*, and denouement, the division into acts and scenes, the various types of liaisons between scenes (1:103), as well as the technical problems involved in constructing them, Corneille discusses the three unities in terms of the rationale behind their usage and the liberties a playwright may take in observing them. He specifically emphasizes the supremacy of the principal action, which subordinates and orients all secondary actions; in tragedy, for instance, this unity of action is accomplished through the unity of peril for the hero (1:98). Corneille concludes his discourses by claiming the success of his plays to be the best proof for the efficacy of his theories: "Je serai tout prêt de les [meilleurs moyens] suivre lorsqu'on les aura mis en pratique aussi heureusement qu'on y a vu les miens" (1:122).

As a practitioner of theater, often highly successful, Corneille is keenly aware of the technical difficulties involved in the presentation of tragedy; this preoccupation is especially evident in the first and third discourses. Even in the second, which deals in prescriptions, Corneille is defending his own way of writing and presenting tragedy. Thus his presentation confronts very real problems of a technical nature, which must be resolved by the successful playwright; his prescriptive assumptions are primarily technical in nature.

Shortly before Corneille published his discourses in 1660, l'Abbé d'Aubignac had set down his guidebook for playwrights in *La Pratique du théâtre*.[4] The basis of d'Aubignac's observations and the source of most of his examples are the plays of Pierre Corneille. D'Aubignac deals with every imaginable ingredient in dramatic literature, from the use of the aside and of stanzaic form amid the *alexandrins* to the *liaisons des scènes* and to the appropriate set, props, and music. In this detailed study of the practical and technical aspects of the dramatic form, virtually every practice is accepted or discarded on the basis of its *vraisemblance*. Unfortunately, d'Aubignac does not effectively distinguish between *vraisemblance* and *bienséance* and therefore the latter is often included in the writer's notion of the former.[5] For understanding practical aspects of writing and performing plays from the seventeenth-century perspective, d'Aubignac's study is a valuable one indeed. As for tragedy itself, he comments specifically that separating tragicomedy from tragedy reveals the happy or disastrous nature of the denouement and is therefore an undesirable distinction. With the exception of this remark, d'Aubignac's specific discussion of tragedy and tragicomedy in book 2, chapter 10, is neither original nor very helpful in terms of his assumptions about tragedy.[6]

Jacques Schérer goes back to d'Aubignac, to Pierre Corneille, and to many others in his catalogue of the characteristics and difficulties of the classical French theater in La Dramaturgie classique en France (Paris: Nizet, 1950). He begins this descriptive and analytical work with the internal structure of the classical play: the characters along with the constituent parts of the play, exposition, noeud, and denouement. In discussing theater in seventeenth century France, Schérer examines both theoretical works and plays from the entire period. Here, and to a greater extent in his second section on external structure, Schérer deals with the practical aspects of classical dramaturgy. He emphasizes the limitations imposed on the playwright by the stage facilities, the troops of actors, and the audience. More important to the later development of this study, Schérer discusses the formal aspects of classical theater: the nature of acts and scenes, and the peculiar characteristics of récits and monologues and of such rhetorical devices as stichomythia, sentence, and repetition. In a third section, he examines the adaptation of the plays to the audience, dealing primarily with matters of vraisemblance and bienséance. Passing this wealth of information in review in his conclusion, Schérer emphasizes the evolutionary nature of seventeenth-century dramatic literature by characterizing each of three periods in that evolution, by pointing out the particular contributions of individual playwrights, and by underscoring three elements of ingredients in classical French dramaturgy: literary tradition, rules, and theatrical edifices and audiences.

The vigor of the classical French theater is found by Schérer to reside in the struggle to create the techniques of modern theater, a struggle in which Corneille was the great innovator and d'Aubignac the theoretician after the fact, and Jean Racine the talented playwright who assimilated their accomplishments and created a perfected and finished version of the product. Schérer's is a marvelously rich and useful study, complete and precise in matters of technique. Clearly, precise notions about tragedy in seventeenth-century France can be derived from careful examination of the technical aspects of writing and performing tragedy in that context. These notions, by the extensive nature of Schérer's work, are most appropriately a backdrop to the discussion in depth of language and characterization in a single writer.

Assumptions about tragedy sometimes isolate traits peculiar to Racinian tragedy which, therefore, serve to distinguish his vision from that of other serious playwrights. The title of John C. Lapp's *Aspects of Racinian Tragedy* (University of Toronto Romance Series 2 [Toronto: Toronto University Press, 1955]), promises assistance in the search for appropriate assumptions about tragedy. After discussing such standard subjects as themes, unities and other conventions, and Racine's symbolism, Lapp focuses in his fifth chapter on "The Essence of Racinian Tragedy." The critic describes the tragic setting as one where normal constraint is challenged by presence, "the electric effect of mere physical immanence" (p. 135). This dramatic situation is at the same time a mirror of life at court, replete with psychological deception and counterdeception as well as constant scrutiny of words, gestures, expressions, and even silences. In a second movement within this chapter on the essence of Racinian tragedy, Lapp examines Racine's limited affinity for each of the major Greek tragic playwrights and concludes that Racine's characters are not tragic in the traditional sense. Thus Racinian tragedy has two essential qualities: modernity as opposed to the Greeks, and constraint as revealed in a highly civilized and stylized life such as that experienced at the court of Louis XIV. The fatal momentum of Racine's plays comes from "the tragedy of modern man, trapped in a society of his own making, caught in the eternal tug between civilization and elemental emotion" (p. 192). These traits, though they rightly underscore the dramatic nature of tragedy, are not assumptions but conclusions about a specific playwright. The opposition of apparent outward control and inner chaos highlighted in the conflicts and confrontations on the stage is, however, an important aspect of Racinian tragedy that is pertinent to later chapters of this study.

For Judd D. Hubert in *Essai d'exégèse racinienne: les secrets témoins* (Paris: Nizet, 1956) the essential trait of Racinian tragedy is the way that his characters see themselves, ideally and in reality. On the one hand, the characters experience a narcissistic drive: "C'est le désir violent ressenti par le héros de créer une image si belle de lui-même qu'elle doive s'imposer d'office à l'admiration de l'univers et qu'il puisse la contempler sans aucun mépris" (p. 25). Coupled with this drive, however, is the bitter realization of their imperfection and of their inability to actualize this high vision of themselves. The tragic lies in the fruitlessness of the characters' attempts to bridge this gap, attempts that lead only to greater errors and greater crimes; they succeed only in widening the gap between themselves and their idealized selves, thereby falling into confusion and bewilderment and suicide and worse.

Eugène Vinaver in *Racine et la poésie tragique* (Paris: Nizet, 1963) seeks to isolate not particular traits but general movements within the plays of Racine while deliberately subordinating individual situations and characters represented to general ones: "Moins nous chercherons à connaître les individus, à les situer dans un cadre précis, et plus le dramaturge se sentira libre de nous les montrer dans une attitude universellement humaine" (p. 14). Vinaver strongly opposes as well the method of isolating the originality of a writer by subtracting elements borrowed from his sources, because this process destroys the organic unity of the work (p. 18). From this orientation Vinaver claims that Racine's great contribution to tragedy was rediscovery of "le pathétique." While his contemporaries were concentrating on the manipulation of action in tragedy in order to increase anticipation for the denouement, Racine was giving back to tragedy its affective function by attenuating the priority given to the denouement: "Il y a, nous rappelle-t-il, dans le théâtre grec, quantité de scènes inutiles au dénouement, mais indispensables à la tragédie" (p. 35). The theatrical representation of such "instants privilégiés" leads, according to Vinaver, beyond the emotion felt as we are confronted with the tragic fact or movement to the understanding of it and to the discovery of the poetic conditions under which it is produced (p. 20).

While critics like Lapp, Hubert, and Vinaver bring to the fore important aspects of Racinian tragedy as well as insights useful later in this study, a parochial vision is to be avoided in making assumptions at the beginning of a study. Notions about tragedy can come from a variety of sources: other disciplines, specific dramatic techniques, specific traits of Racinian dramaturgy. None of these is really germane to problems involving sentence structure and characterization. None makes broad, serious assumptions about the role of language in tragedy.

What is left? An approach to tragedy through identifying its underlying principles, the foundation on which tragedy is built, for tragedy has principles in much the same way that a building has a foundation. The stability of the edifice depends on the solidity of the foundation. Just as nothing added to a building after the foundation, whether it be func-

tional or ornamental, affects the general character of the building to the
extent that the size, shape, and solidity of a foundation affect it, so also
do the principles of a literary genre set the general character of that
genre. Other factors or additions may well affect the particular character
of the building and serve to distinguish it from other similar buildings;
nevertheless, it is the size and the nature of the foundation that determine
in large part the nature of the building. So also the principles of tragedy
are its foundation, marking both its point of departure and the general
character of the edifice to be built.

In the field of geometry, one begins with axioms and postulates. Axioms are self-evident truths which, although not subject to proof, must be
stated explicitly in the proof of theorems. Postulates, if not self-evident,
are at least established principles universally received and essential prere-
quisites to proceeding further. To speak in a nontechnical way, these axioms and postulates are the basic assumptions of geometry. In the same
way, tragedies are written on the basis of general assumptions and prere-
quisites that may or may not be self-evident but that, in any case, must be
listed and examined. Some of these principles are shockingly simple or
even self-evident, but they are thereby no less fundamental. Moreover,
they are often poorly understood for the very reason of their simplicity.

Before I develop my statement of principles of tragedy as the assumptions of this study, it is appropriate to examine other attempts to do so, in
order to avoid dangers inherent in this approach. The obvious first choice
is Aristotle, who in the sixth book of his *Poetics* offers a summary description of tragedy in long-familiar terms. It is not my purpose here to join
the multitude of critics who have attempted to explain precisely what
Aristotle meant in specific phrases of his definition. Clearly, Aristotle is
dealing with principles of tragedy, a list of basic ingredients that determine its general character. This is not to deny that he elaborates on his
definition and that in so doing he often deals in technical aspects of
tragedy. It is only to say that Aristotle gathers together, in a concise statement, the principles of tragedy, one of which mentions language.

Much later Pierre Corneille, as an avid seventeenth-century reader and
interpreter of Aristotle, tackles the principles of tragedy in his second
discourse, *Le Discours de la tragédie et des moyens de la traiter selon le
vraisemblable ou le nécessaire* (*OEuvres de P. Corneille*, 1:52-97). In going back to Aristotle, however, Corneille picks up only the last part of the
definition and attempts to explicate the notions of pity and fear and of

catharsis (1:62). Corneille goes on to divide tragedy into four kinds, based on the relationship of a character's will to cause the ruin and death of another character to his recognition of the true identity of that other character. Corneille claims, for the seventeenth century and for himself, the honor of having invented the fourth and most nearly perfect kind in which one character knows the true identity of another and yet persists in his attempts to bring death and destruction upon that other, but ultimately without success (1:66-70). In this same vein Corneille discusses the new type of hero, like Polyeucte, who represents "la force de l'exemple" (1:61). Then after discussing the liberties that an author may take with historical fact when adapting it to tragedy, Corneille discusses *le vraisemblable ou le nécessaire* of his title, to which I would add *le vrai*. It is evident that Corneille valued *le vrai* above all else when adapting history to tragedy, considered *le nécessaire* to be "le besoin du poète pour arriver à son but ou pour y faire arriver ses acteurs" (1:94), admitted *le vraisemblable* when it did not interfere with other principles like the unity of time, and regarded *plaire* as his primary motivation in writing tragedy. In sum, Corneille seems more intent on establishing the worth of his own work vis-à-vis that of the Greek writers than on confronting the principles of tragedy.

In recent years, Bernard Weinberg also returned to Aristotelian principles in *The Art of Jean Racine* (Chicago: University of Chicago Press, 1963). Weinberg, as he evaluates the overall effectiveness of each play, shows Racine in the process of developing and perfecting his art of tragedy by considering mainly the internal factors of probability and necessity in the areas of plot and character. While Weinberg uses some principles of tragedy and explicitly states the nature of those principles, probability and necessity, he does not admit the existence of other principles nor does he mention his debt to Aristotle. As his title indicates, Weinberg uses Racine exclusively, and so selects and adapts principles with only this author in mind.

Another recent critic, Elder Olson, struggles directly with the general principles of tragedy in *Tragedy and the Theory of Drama* (Detroit, Mich.: Wayne State University Press, 1966). Since Olson's insights form the basis of a later discussion, further comment on specifics is deferred until that time. Although I disagree with Olson's presentation of tragedy at several junctures, I nevertheless gratefully acknowledge his critical evaluation of the candidates for principles in the theory of drama.

From a long line of critics who have dealt with tragedy in terms of its principles I have chosen only a few, in order to illustrate what is meant by principles of tragedy and to ward off inherent dangers. The first danger is that of adopting Aristotle's statement and consequently of fighting preconceived notions (one's own and those of others) that are most difficult to dislodge, or of precipitating further controversy, thereby distracting attention from the purpose of making explicit assumptions. A second danger is represented by Corneille, who has a vested interest in establishing the value of his works and of seventeenth-century contributions to the art of tragedy. Weinberg represents a third danger noted in other approaches to tragedy in that he applies only certain principles to the development of one writer, limiting the general usefulness of the principles he discusses. Only Elder Olson talks in terms broad enough to encompass tragedy as a whole and fresh enough to avoid stereotyped notions. For these reasons Olson serves as a point of departure for establishing the relationship between tragedy and language as well as partial clarification of my assumptions about tragedy.

Tragedy is serious drama. While hardly earthshaking, the statement bears examination. Tragedy is drama. Because it is destined for the theater, tragedy is basically different from narrative fiction. The author's means of communication are not the same. The spectator's role is not that of the reader. Of course, plays may be read instead of viewed, but the role of the reader of narrative literature is not that of the reader of dramatic literature. The specific implications of this distinction become clear in the following section. Tragedy is serious. Beginning with Aristotle, nearly every critic and spectator has stated or assumed this principle. To avoid premature restrictiveness, I assume that seriousness refers to the general tonality of the drama and need not exclude nonserious moments or incidents as long as they do not alter the basic tonality of the drama.

Tragedy is serious drama in which the outcome is of great consequence and of great significance to the audience.[7] First of all, the outcome is of interest to the audience. In any play worthy of the name, either the individual characters or the situation presented is of interest. It is possible, however, for the outcome to be of no great interest. An abrupt, a contrived, or an artificial ending, a *deus ex machina,* is in fact an indication either that the outcome is of relatively little importance or that the playwright lacks the ingenuity to resolve a particular conflict. It is a sure indication that one is outside the realm of tragedy. The emphasis on the denouement in no way limits tragedy to outcomes of bloodshed or total annihilation. As stated earlier, d'Aubignac favored the option of a happy or disastrous outcome on the grounds that an unknown conclusion has greater dramatic effect. In his preface to *Bérénice,* a play whose denouement, if not happy, is not an unmitigated disaster, Racine defends himself by citing other factors that hold the audience's interest:

> Ce n'est point une nécessité qu'il y ait du sang et des morts dans une tragédie: il suffit que l'action en soit grande, que les acteurs en soient héroïques, que les passions y soient excitées, et que tout s'y ressente de cette tristesse majestueuse qui fait tout le plaisir de la tragédie.[8]

Second, the outcome is of great consequence. The characters must be liable to cause great harm or to fall prey to it (Olson, p. 163). Furthermore, the audience must be more than curious about the outcome, they must also care a great deal about it. This is not a matter of intellectually approving or disapproving of the outcome, but rather an emotional involvement in what Peter Nurse calls the "final alarmingness" of the situation.[9] Quoting A. P. Rossiter, Nurse further comments that the final alarmingness may be due not only to loss of life or to the injustice of excessive or too widespread retribution, but also to the threat of indignity, the loss of heroic existence, or to the mocking devaluation of those qualities by which the hero commands admiration.[10] It does not seem necessary that the audience develop a protective attitude toward any of the characters or to the situation, but only a concern to the point of active anticipation of the outcome.

Depending on the play and the audience, the specific reaction to the outcome may well not be that anticipated by the author, particularly when there exists a considerable time or cultural differential between the author and his audience. That is not important. What is essential, however, is that the audience actively anticipate the outcome and react to it. In the third place, the outcome must be of great significance to the audience. It must communicate at least a portion of the author's view of the world and of man's place in it.

Since the outcome is of such great importance in tragedy, it follows that the sequence of actions or events leading up to it must serve to orient the audience toward the denouement. Thus a corollary to this part of the definition is that *the whole tragedy must be carefully constructed.* The outcome can scarcely be of great consequence and of great significance unless the play is carefully structured; otherwise the outcome may not even have been clearly delineated and prepared. At this point I do not want to single out as superior any one method of achieving this careful construction; I want only to emphasize the need for achieving it.

Tragedy is serious drama in which understanding is based on a high level of inference. Inference is an integral part of all drama, just as it is in daily life. There is no omniscient and omnipresent narrator who can, if he chooses, reveal what someone is really thinking, what someone's real motives are, or what the precise implications of a situation are. The audience is restricted to inferring such things from what is seen and heard; even monologues seldom reveal everything a well-informed audience needs to know. There are, however, different levels of inference in different dramatic forms. To take an extreme case, the level of inference demanded in melodrama is low. Very little sophistication is needed to distinguish the hero from the villain or to discern motives. Therein lies part of the charm of melodrama. Tragedy lies at the other end of the spectrum; that is, it involves a high level of inference. Tragedy is demanding—demanding of the author, demanding of the actors, and demanding of the audience. It does not mean that tragedy is better than other forms of dramatic literature. It does mean that tragedy is different in the degree of inference necessary for its appreciation.

If one accepts the assertion that tragedy involves a high level of inference, it follows that tragedy is *serious drama in which careful use is made of language*. Although the language is often highly stylized, it can also be a carefully constructed version of normal speech. If tragedy must be carefully constructed and if language is part of tragedy, language must also be carefully constructed. I temporarily defer the discussion of the specific role of language in tragedy until the next section of this chapter, since that discussion leads away from consideration of the work as a whole. Here then are my working assumptions: tragedy is serious drama in which the outcome is of great consequence and of great significance to the audience, which therefore must be carefully constructed; in which a high level of inference is necessary for comprehension; and in which language is carefully deployed. The assumptions are purposely general in nature. They consist only of the essential ingredients of tragedy, not those supplemental elements which, whether functional or ornamental, are not strictly indispensable to tragedy. These assumptions, a point of departure for this study of sentence structure, furnish a periodic check on a perspective easily distorted by prolonged attention to details. It is, however, not yet clear precisely how language is related to tragedy.

From Assumptions about Tragedy
to Language in Tragedy

In the first chapter of *Tragedy and the Theory of Drama,* Elder Olson draws up a list of minimal requirements to constitute a play. This three-point list seems a fitting framework for moving on from the principles of tragedy to a sense of the place and function of language in tragedy:

(1) devise some sort of action, together with characters who can appropriately carry it out, (2) contrive a scenario which shows what actions are to be enacted on the stage in what order, and (3) compose the dialog, or at least indicate roughly what sort of thing shall be said by the actors. (p. 32)

The relationship of these three requirements for a minimal play must be clarified within the context of tragedy.

The etymon of the word *drama* is a Greek noun, δρᾶμα , meaning "action."[11] Drama differs significantly from narrative literature at this very point, for the latter term comes from the Latin *narrare,* meaning "to tell, relate," which in turn is derived from *gnarum,* "one who knows."[12] So it is that plot in drama is comprised of actions or, as Olson would have it, plot is a "system of actions."[13] The word *system* is important, because it indicates that plot is divisible into at least two activities and is organized into a pattern by a unifying principle.

The plot contains every action in this system, while the scenario selects from the plot those actions to be represented on the stage and sets them in the desired order. Here the characters come into play. Olson affirms that the audience comes to know characters in a play in much the same way that we know people in real life. We witness directly. We infer from what we see and from what we are told. We are dependent on the outer life for information about the inner life (p. 19). In other words, perception of character proceeds from action: what a character is is based on what he does. Or, at least from the finished play, the audience knows or infers what a character is through what he does. This argument is not intended to apply necessarily to the creative process whereby the playwright constructs his drama but only to the functioning of the finished product. William James goes even further in this direction by stating: "Sow an action and you reap a habit; sow a habit and you reap a character; sow a character and you reap a destiny."[14] Whether this is true in real life is of no concern here; if it is true in the theater, then it is a vital part of the audience's business to know characters through inference from their actions. This is accomplished, according to Olson, through signs (p. 21). These signs are outward actions and may be either natural, like tears or a pale and haggard face, or they may be artificial (or conventional in the particular classical French context), like funeral wreaths or black armbands. After his elaboration on the various categories of signs, complete or incomplete or multiple, common or special, ambiguous or clear, it is astonishing that Olson includes only actions as signs. One might add with John Lapp that mere presence is a sign; language also is a sign. Nevertheless, the essential and powerful function of the scenario is filtering the plot to let pass only those actions appropriate for representation on the stage with the desired effect.

As the third component of a minimal play, Olson proposes dialogue, but to him it is the least important of the three and may do no more than indicate roughly what sort of thing is said by the actors.

> It is a subsidiary part. Without it, certainly, a great number of subtle effects would be impossible; more than that, the profundity of great drama would be impossible; but these very considerations show that it is simply the medium through which these effects are achieved, under the gouvernance of plot. The dialog exists to give the plot its quality and power; therefore it is subordinate to plot. Since the representation determines when dialog is proper and when it is not, and what the nature of dialog shall be, the dialog is also subordinate to the representation. (p. 89)

Perhaps this concept is acceptable in Olson's hypothetical minimal play and in certain dramatic forms, but this limited appreciation of the role of language is clearly inadequate for tragedy. Besides, the author's writing of a play, when he may logically proceed from plot to representation to dialogue, is necessarily distinct from the audience's viewing of a play, when the process is reversed. Olson does not systematically distinguish the two processes. But with respect to tragedy, Olson himself indicates the right direction with comments like "subtle effects," "profundity of great drama," and "quality and power," all of which in the preceding quotation refer to the use of language in dramatic literature.[15] Language can be a powerful instrument of control over the performers and over the audience.[16] The performers are significantly limited in their characterizations by the written text, the language, of the play. They are not tyrannized, however, as is evident from the variety of interpretations of Racine's characters over the centuries.[17] Roland Barthes states flatly in "Dire Racine": "il n'y a plus à interpréter Racine une fois que l'on a choisi la façon de le 'dire' " (in *Sur Racine*, p. 139). Jean Vilar comments interestingly on the importance of the written text in his *De la tradition théâtrale* (Paris: Gallimard, 1963) when he recommends to actors and directors "de nombreuses lectures à l'italienne":

> Le tiers environ du nombre total des répétitions. Au moins. Manuscrit en main. Cul sur la chaise. Le corps au repos. Et la sensibilité profonde se mettant peu à peu au diapason voulu, quand l'interprète a enfin compris (ou senti) ce personnage nouveau qui un jour sera lui. (p. 25)

And more succinctly a few pages later, Vilar comments: "Le comédien digne de ce nom ne s'impose pas au texte. Il le sert. Et servilement" (p. 28). Language is also an instrument of control over the audience. The principal mechanism of drama is inference based, according to Olson, on the represented action (p. 136) and, I submit, in an equally significant way on the language of the play.

In daily life we can and do make inferences about people from what they say and especially from how they say it. As an audience also we can and do make inferences about characters from their actions, of course, but especially from their speech patterns. Language, like action, is a system of signs by which characters communicate with each other and through which the audience can know them. There are, admittedly, other factors involved in the successful process of inference: the ability and willingness of the audience to make inferences, their familiarity with conventional signs to be used in inference, and the quality of the performance. The main control reverts, however, to the author, who manipulates language as well as scenario in order to exercise his control over both the performers and the audience. While language may count as fine points of control for the author, Olson's "subtle effects," it remains one of two major avenues to the play for the performers and for the audience. This dual control may in part explain the potentially unsatisfactory experience of reading a play. The reader must be versatile indeed to be both performer and audience and thus to make appropriate inferences on both levels.

One note of caution is in order. I may seem to have implied that there is one and only one correct inference to be drawn from each action or from each bit of language. On the contrary, different inferences are often possible, and appropriate in some cases. The performers do in their own

way limit the possible inferences by the audience. While the author may
create intentionally or unintentionally ambiguous signs, other signs may
also be willfully distorted by performers, audiences, or critics.

I have thus far based my arguments on a hypothetical minimal play
with special restrictions in language for tragedy. To narrow the perspective for the moment to Racine's theater, the relative importance of
scenario and of language takes on even greater significance when based
not only on one's personal experience as audience but also on
seventeenth-century views. Imagine one of Racine's plays made into a
film and yourself watching it without benefit of the sound track. What
would you see? Except for rare moments like Phèdre's taking possession of
Hippolyte's sword, could you even infer what was happening? If not well
versed in Racinian tragedy, could you hope to discern which play it was?
Costumes and set would help, but would the represented actions tell you
much about the characters? Pierre Kohler recognized this problem of seeing and hearing Racine's plays. "Ceux qui reprochent à la tragédie
française sa monotonie et son défaut de mouvement sont, en général, des
gens qui jugent le drame avec les yeux et n'ont pas l'oreille assez exercée
pour percevoir la mélodie d'un discours poétique."[18] Jean Starobinski also
has remarked that in classical French theater and especially in Racine "les
gestes tendent à disparaître. Au profit du langage, a-t-on dit. Il faut
ajouter: au profit du regard."[19] Starobinski's emphasis is on "regard," but
his point is equally well taken with respect to language.

Still within the realm of personal experience looms the problem of
translation. Olson claims, and rightly so, that if a play survives translation as *Macbeth* does, its greatness must lie in what is translatable, in the
whole dramatic concept, not in the refinement of verses (p. 122). The
question is then whether Racine survives translation. In his chapter on
Phèdre (pp. 217-36), Olson deals almost entirely with plot and scenario as
he sets up useful comparisons between Racine and Shakespeare. While
this treatment is in line with Olson's point of view, it is not helpful in dealing with translations.[20] Francophiles have generally disclaimed any
evidence of Racine's survival after translation into English. The impressionistic Strachey compares a Racinian play to "an airy, delicate statue,
supported by artificial props . . . without them the statue itself would
break in pieces and fall to the ground."[21] More recently John Lapp explained the problem this way:

Perhaps indeed most Anglo-Saxon antipathy or indifference to our
dramatist is due to the fact that Racine, unlike the Greeks, really

doesn't survive translation. His poetry is so essential that when it is gone the work is no longer itself; in each play so delicate a balance prevails, so great is the interdependence of act, scene, and line, that to disturb a single element is to disrupt all. (*Aspects,* p. viii)

Translators themselves are cautious when approaching Racine. In his foreword to the Penguin Classics translation, *Iphigenia, Phaedra, Athaliah* (Baltimore, Md.: Penguin Classics, 1963), John Cairncross begins cautiously: "Racine, it is often said, is untranslatable" (p. 7). A page later Cairncross relates that fifteen years earlier his translation of *Phaedra* "was submitted to the B.B.C. who wrote back politely that it was somewhat 'staid' (i.e. dull) and 'a gallant effort' (i.e. a complete failure). It was submitted again to the B.B.C. early in 1957. That body's advisers sat on the translation for three months, and then came up with the sensational discovery that Racine was untranslatable" (pp. 8-9). And Robert Lowell's rendering of *Phaedra,* called an "English Version" but more properly termed an adaptation, radically modifies the tonality of the original.[22] It is Margaret Rawlings, the distinguished English actress and a French scholar, who produced a faithful version of *Phèdre* (New York: E.P. Dutton, 1961) that is "speakable and actable" (p. 9). Moreover, the translation, when it is not literal, has approximately the same tonality as the original. Despite the obvious appropriateness of her translation or perhaps because of it, Margaret Rawlings affirms the complete integrity of Racine's play: "Every word, in its order, and every line and Scene and Act, in their order, are irreplaceable in this unique dramatic poem" (p. 15). Clearly, there is a problem lying not in representational matters and scenarios, which are unaffected by translation, but in the language of Racine itself. For these two reasons — scarcity of action or even gestures in Racine's theater and problems revolving around translation — I submit that language is an important system of signs in Racine's plays, a system on which performers and audience alike depend as a basis of their inferences about character.

Can the seventeenth century add weight to the discussion at this point? Both Pierre Corneille and l'Abbé d'Aubignac, when they are not speaking in generic terms, refer to plays as "poèmes dramatiques." The very title of Corneille's first discourse reads *Le Discours . . . du poème dramatique;* in book 3 of d'Aubignac's *La Pratique du théâtre,* the first chapter treats "Des parties de quantité du poème dramatique et spécialement le Prologue." The term *poème dramatique* is significant in that it categorizes a play first as a poem; the adjective serves to distinguish this type of poem from others. The emphasis on the term *poème* is an emphasis on language. D'Aubignac frequently refers to the dramatist as "le poète." In the quarrel over *Le Cid,* one of many early seventeenth-century literary controversies relating to the theater, both Georges de Scudéry and Jean Chapelain, the latter writing on behalf of the newly formed Académie française, did in fact take Corneille to task over unities, *bienséances,* and *vraisemblance*; but the vast majority of the comments and criticisms were directed at Corneille's use of language. Furthermore, since *bienséances* severely limited what actions could be represented on the stage, writers of serious drama regularly reverted to *récits,* to language, in order to bring before the audience in verbal form information about events essential to the plot. D'Aubignac defends this use of discourse as a substitute for action in his famous phrase: *"Parler,* c'est *Agir"* (p. 282). D'Aubignac was neither inventing a concept nor defending the practices of a few, but was recommending the procedure by stating in maxim form one of the underlying assumptions of his age.[23] Nor is this concept restricted to the theater, for the emphasis on "beau langage" and concern for its appropriate use permeated the whole seventeenth century in France.

Although in the *Art poétique* Boileau's most famous lines deal with other matters, he nevertheless can be caught making assumptions about language in tragedy:

Ainsi, pour nous charmer, la Tragédie en pleurs
D'OEdipe tout sanglant fit *parler* les douleurs,
D'Oreste parricide *exprima* les alarmes
Et, pour nous divertir, nous arracha des larmes.[24]

After passing references that imply language, such as "discours" (v. 15), "raisonnemens" (v. 21), "rhétorique" (v. 23), "dès les premiers vers" (v. 27), and after an intervening survey of the history of the theater, Boileau returns to the matter of language and the need to diversify characterization through language:

Souvent, sans y penser, un écrivain qui s'aime,
Forme tous ses héros semblables à soi-même:
Tout a l'humeur gasconne en un auteur gascon;
Calprenède et Juba parlent du même ton.
La nature est en nous plus diverse et plus sage;
Chaque passion parle un différent langage:
La colère est superbe et veut des mots altiers;
L'abattement s'explique en des termes moins fiers.

(*Art poétique,* 3, 127-34)

Boileau continues by warning of abuses and the point is clear: language is important and differences in character and in mood should be evident from the language of the characters.

Jean Racine himself, on the other hand, is of no assistance. Nowhere in his prefaces does he deign to discuss his use of language or the place of language in tragedy. Since he is obviously on the defensive in these prefaces, parrying objections from contemporary critics, one can only assume that Racine was not generally criticized for his use of language and consequently felt no need to defend himself on that score. From the overwhelming evidence of seventeenth-century French writers and critics of tragedy, only a few of whom have been mentioned, it follows that language was indeed considered an important ingredient in tragedy, in some respects perhaps the most important.

I have departed considerably from Elder Olson on this point precisely because language, and sentence structure in particular, are a tool for characterization in Racine's tragedies and because examining Racine's use of sentences makes explicit the possible inferences about his various characters and their contributions to his theater. In conclusion, Olson sees scenario or representation and dialogue as two successive filters through which the author passes the plot. His scheme might look something like this.

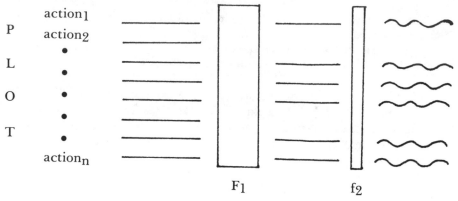

$$P \quad \begin{array}{l} \text{action}_1 \\ \text{action}_2 \\ \bullet \end{array}$$

$$L \qquad \bullet$$

$$O \qquad \bullet$$

$$T \qquad \bullet$$

$$\text{action}_n$$

$$F_1 \qquad\qquad f_2$$

The first filter (F_1) is the representation that lets pass only those actions (the parallel lines) to be presented on the stage, while filtering out the inappropriate ones. The second filter (f_2), smaller and thus less important than the first, is the dialogue that simply modifies the lines of action. The conception on which this study is founded differs significantly from

Olson's in this second phase and might be represented graphically as follows.

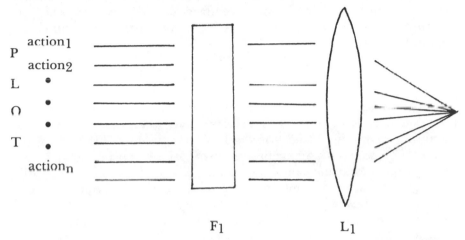

The first part of the diagram remains unchanged, whereas the second filter, the dialogue, has become a lens (L_1), whose function is to focus and clarify the represented action. It is at this focal point that the audience has primary access to understanding characterization and actions and thus the tragedy as a whole. While Olson's scheme is adequate for his hypothetical minimal play, the other scheme is a superior representation of tragedy in general and of Racinian tragedy in particular.

Style and the Sentence in Racine

In the preceding section the function of language in tragedy is shown to be that of signs by which both performers and audiences make inferences regarding the characters portrayed. Before outlining my method of inquiry into the nature of those inferences, I shall consider in this section general approaches to style and the sentence, the opposing approaches to literary texts of Spitzer and Sayce, and specific work on Racine's style. Alongside these more-or-less traditional approaches is the need to ascertain the direction and usefulness of computer-assisted literary studies. While it is not within the scope of this study to present a historical survey of stylistic studies, it is appropriate to clarify certain basic notions about style.[25] Dictionaries do little more than reinforce the vague notion that style is distinctive (modes of expression can be distinguished from each other) and that style is characteristic (writers and periods have typical modes of expression). A hint that there exists an accepted standard associated with style, perhaps a standard of elegance, by which to measure distinctive and characteristic modes of expression is still only a beginning.

Marcel Cressot's *Le Style et ses techniques* (Paris: Presses Universitaires de France, 1959) is an annotated catalogue of the distinctive elements of style and of the terms used to describe them. The author develops this catalogue in hierarchical order beginning with *le mot* and all its ramifications, building to the second and intermediate level, that of verbal and nominal constructions, and arriving finally at the top level, that of the sentence. Cressot, with an egalitarian bent, asserts that in oral and written expression everyone can and does have a style. Style is the result of a series of choices, unconscious ones for most writers, governing how one shall say what is said. The stockpile from which choices are drawn is the totality of words available for use in that language along with the structures for putting them together into sentences. If at any time one wishes permanently or temporarily to eliminate certain forms of expression as unacceptable or as inappropriate, then he is operating in a stylistic framework. This process of selection may, of course, be both an individual function and the collective function of a group. A special selection, for instance, is based on the limitations of the *alexandrin*. No two ways of saying "the same thing" are entirely equivalent. Style is, therefore, the result of a process of selection, both conscious and unconscious, both individual and corporate, operated on grammatically acceptable forms of expression in a language.

In more specific terms, Cressot calls the sentence "l'image de la pensée" and outlines these elements as contributing to the technique of the sentence: rhythm, *liaisons,* and volume. The last is essentially a measurement of length in the sentence, a characteristic that distinguishes short sentences from periodic ones and within the latter distinguishes types on the basis of the number of their elements: binary, ternary, and accumulative. *Liaisons* are the ways in which sentences, or clauses within sentences, are linked together and includes such topics as "organisation par masses croissantes," equilibrium, symmetry, and continuity. Rearrangement of these elements affects the rhythm of the sentence.

Frédéric Deloffre's little book on the sentence, *La Phrase française* (Paris: SEDES, 1967), is much like Cressot's in that Deloffre classifies sentence types and subtypes, showing how to distinguish one from the other. Most of Deloffre's book is devoted to straightforward grammatical categorizing of sentence types. Only briefly in his conclusion does he venture, and then only tenuously, into stylistic matters. Here the author divides sentences into two categories by means of pairs of criteria:

phrase liée	phrase morcelée
phrase linéaire	phrase à parallélisme
tendance intellectuelle	tendance affective
ordre logique	ordre expressif
	(pp. 194-97)

While it is evident from Deloffre's presentation that the series *liée / linéaire / intellectuelle / logique* is meant to contrast with the series *morcelée / à parallélisme / affective / expressif*, the author does not develop this fortuitous contrast beyond an embryonic stage.

These nonliterary perspectives offer basic orientation to style; the remaining questions seems to be matters of procedure and method. The late Leo Spitzer claimed that language is a "ready-made interpretation of the world" that can be used deliberately for an aesthetic effect.[26] The critic's job is to uncover the means by which the author moves from convention to personal expression. Spitzer's method, intuitive and quite personal, is called the philological circle. Struck by a particular characteristic of a passage, Spitzer makes an "observation hypothétique centrale"[27] that reveals some stylistique aspect of the passage. This observation is formalized in a general statement about the stylistic procedure in question. Spitzer then looks for repetition of the procedure in other passages by the same writer to determine whether it is in fact a stylistic constant. While many critics heartily endorse the dialectical movement from the part to the meaning of the whole and back again, Spitzer's point of entry, intuition, has proved difficult if not impossible for others to imitate.

In an effort to systematize work on style, R. A. Sayce proposes an alternative method, one that does not depend on an initial intuition as a point of departure. In *Studies in French Prose: A Method of Analysis* (Oxford: Clarendon Press, 1958) Sayce begins with the traditional parts of speech, moving on to figures of speech, clichés, and proverbs, and concluding with types of propositions. By applying this systematic examination to a number of passages from different authors and different periods, Sayce discusses period style, individual style, and good and bad style. All uninteresting data are eliminated from the final discussion, which revolves also around the meaning of the text and the reconstruction of the organic unity of the work of art (p. 135). Both Spitzer and Sayce have something to offer. The point of departure can be either an intuition or a systematic inventory of potentially interesting features. Both procedures can be adapted to computer-assisted research, in which the machine seeks to verify intuitions or to pass in review features selected by prior manual inventories made on a small scale.

In recent years the computer has found limited favor in analyzing literary texts, principally in concordances and in authorship studies. Concordances have become routine procedure, not because all the problems related to generating good concordances have been solved satisfactorily, but because the desirability of concordances is an established fact. Prose concordances are usually generated in KWIC (Key Word In Context) format, with the key word in the center of the page and context on both sides; poetry concordances, on the other hand, often give only the line in which the word occurs as its context. There are good reasons for generating KWIC concordances for poetic texts, as is the case for versification in chapter 8 of this study. At the same time, word counts are generated and words are listed separately in order of decreasing frequency.[28] Concordances are an invaluable aid in any study that keys on morphological elements.

The more intricate authorship studies are designed to answer the question: did "So-and-so" write this text? These studies depend on the existence of an undisputed text by the author(s) in question and text(s) of doubtful authorship. See, for instance, the computer-assisted resolution of the debate on the authorship of certain *Federalist Papers*.[29] The main problem is in choosing a set of good discriminators (p. 45). Since contexts vary and content words vary with the context, other elements are better discriminators. In the study just mentioned, sentence length is useless as a discriminator whereas the high-frequency function words do the best job. A serious note of caution is in order. First of all, statistical studies result only in probabilities of authorship. In that respect good discriminators function like fingerprints, which correctly identify the individual without revealing anything about his physical, intellectual, or emotional makeup. Relatively few attempts have gone beyond concordances and authorship studies into interpretative areas. One of the goals of this study is to explore new ways of profiting from the computer's peculiar capabilities.

The computer, however, does not replace the critic in interpretative work. Even a basic concordance demands extensive pre-computer work. Studies must be carefully conceived in advance so that the computer manipulates only potentially significant variables. The "let's-run-it-through-the-computer-and-see-what-we-get" approach results almost invariably in great quantities of worthless printout, the now proverbial "garbage in, garbage out." Even assuming careful statement of the problem and precise computer programming, the critic still must interpret the output data. The computer performs intermediate steps to save time and to improve accuracy on well-defined, repetitive tasks such as sorting, pattern-matching, and grouping data — and nothing more.

At first glance it may seem that computer-assisted research is essentially similar to critical approaches, decried earlier, that bring another discipline to bear on a literary text. Such is not the case. The computer is an electronic tool for manipulating data: the only differences between computer and manual manipulation (on index cards,for example) are speed and accuracy. Methodologically they are identical. The increased vogue for computer-assisted studies, which are still far from overwhelming literary studies by their number, is due in part to phenomenally increased speed and accuracy; in earlier times such studies demanded a lifetime commitment to the project — often an unrealistic demand. Manipulation of data, however, cannot replace and must not be used to replace interpretation of data. The computer is an intermediary left behind in later stages of analysis. For this reason, after the rejection of the null hypothesis, virtually all references to the computer, to statistics, and especially to their technical vocabularies can be abandoned in favor of literary analysis. Moreover, the computer furnishes neither basic insights nor basic assumptions to this study. Therefore, it does not have separate and methodologically critical status here, despite the obvious fact that this study would have been unthinkable without computer assistance.

A number of years before the advent of computer-generated concordances, Jacques G. Cahen very perceptively presented *Le Vocabulaire de Racine*, which constituted the *Revue de linguistique romane*, nos. 59-64 (Paris: Droz, 1946). At the beginning of his study, Cahen sees Racine's vocabulary as the result of a three-step, subtractive process: from the general lexicon of French to the literary vocabulary, then to tragic vocabulary, and finally to Racine's vocabulary, each vocabulary being a subset of the preceding one (p. 15). Cahen deals then with the nature of Racine's vocabulary, noting the taboos on physical functions and characteristics (p. 56). Also excluded from his vocabulary are most animals, vegetables, minerals, and colors, except for standard figurative usage. Of greater interest presently are Cahen's comments on verse, especially what he calls the "hémistiche racinien" (p. 213). Cahen also notes the internal divisions of the *tirade,* to which this study returns when discussing *Mithridate.* Invaluable also is the Racine concordance by Freeman and Batson, an admirable tool for research in Racine's style, particularly in isolating repeated morphological patterns.

Equally suggestive comments are made by Peter France in his *Racine's Rhetoric* (Oxford: Clarendon Press, 1965). In the course of discussing devices that are properly a part of traditional rhetoric, France makes a very useful distinction between functional and decorative ones. Functional devices are basically dramatic in nature, are associated with *l'art de persuader,* and are designed to elicit an emotional response from the audience. The decorative ones, on the other hand, are undramatic, are associated with *l'art de bien dire,* and are designed to elicit applause (p.35). In discussing period construction France poses a series of significant questions: "To what extent do Racine and his contemporaries construct or break up their periods for dramatic purposes? How much do they vary sentence length to convey different characters, moods or passions? On the answer to these questions depends to a great extent the relative success of the tragic writers of the time" (p. 144). Continuing along this same line, he comments in particular on Racine's use of short sentences as a distinguishing feature of his tragic style (p. 148). Following this discussion is an extended and convincing demonstration of Racine's use of the broken period in *Phèdre,* Act II, scene 5 (pp. 152-59). In speaking of rhetoric, France sees contrasts between the rhetoric of different characters (pp. 196-97). Could this not be as true of their sentence structure as it is of their rhetoric? In his conclusion, this critic goes even further by proclaiming the authenticity of the characterizations based on language: "In Racine sentence length varies constantly and the irregular alexandrine takes on the rhythm of the emotion expressed. . .The characters are real people; this may be due to Racine's superior knowledge of men, but in stylistic terms it is due to the real, living language which he puts into their mouths" (p. 241). These comments by Peter France on Racine's rhetoric appropriately return to the subject at hand: sentence structure and characterization.

Method of Inquiry and Topics of Discussion

What has been said thus far is crucial in providing proper perspective for what follows. The review of ways of looking at tragedy stresses the special perspective of this study and sorts out necessary assumptions about language in tragedy. The working hypothesis is that Jean Racine's use of language is not homogeneous throughout his tragedies: characters reveal something about themselves and about their immediate situations by the way they talk. Differences may depend on several factors: certain plays may have distinctive features; certain characters may; characters may have distinctive patterns under stress; certain formal contexts like *tirade* or rapid dialogue may reveal patterns peculiar to the context; versification may be a factor. Moreover, useful inferences about character and situations can be made on the basis of these differences in language.

For the purpose of testing the null hypothesis and exploring the working hypothesis, I have restricted the field of investigation to the sentence. First, as a limiting procedure: the sentence, taken as a whole, offers a wide range of features while at the same time limiting them in a logical way. Furthermore, the sentence forms an easily defined unit and, in Racine at least, the physical limits of the sentence contrast in remarkable ways with the physical limits of that more obvious poetic unit, the *alexandrin*. Finally, the sentence was chosen because my preliminary investigation and complementary indications by Peter France in *Racine's Rhetoric* point to rich and varied patterns of sentence structure.

The actual method of inquiry involves a three-phase study. Phase One consisted of all the preliminaries for background discussed earlier in this chapter plus careful, manual examination of the Racine texts. This phase broke the whole text of *Phèdre* into sentences to form preliminary conclusions about variations in sentence length, terminal punctuation, characteristic forms of subordination, use of repetition, and the like. This phase likewise included careful examination of the Racine concordance in order to determine which features of sentence structure could be linked to morphological elements and therefore would be suitable for computer assisted investigation on a large scale. Sophisticated analyses through transformational or generative grammar were not practical on this mass of data (over 25,000 lines of text in 14 plays). In addition, preliminary work in *Phèdre* indicated that characterization is probably not a factor at that level. Finally, it was logical to have the computer do only those repetitive tasks which cannot be performed by hand in a reasonable length of time. These features involving the sentence as a unit were retained for computer analysis:

1. terminal punctuation: is the sentence terminated by a period, a question mark, an exclamation point, or an ellipsis?
2. length of sentence: how many syllables does it contain?
3. type of sentence: how do the physical boundaries of the sentence compare with the boundaries of the *alexandrin*?

The following internal features were also retained for computer analysis:

1. internal punctuation: commas, semi-colons, colons, as well as internal question marks and exclamation points.
2. specific forms of subordination: *quand/lorsque, sans (que), puisque, tandis que, pour que.*
3. impersonal expression: *falloir.*
4. clauses introduced by *que.*
5. coordination: *et, ou, mais.*

In Phase Two these features of sentence structure were subjected to computer-assisted analysis.[30] As stated in the Introduction, the text is that of the Mesnard edition of 1885 as prepared in machine-readable form by Freeman and Batson.[31] Variants are not included in the primary analysis, because they interfere with division of the text into sentences. They are examined separately by hand and are mentioned in the study only when they affect significantly a feature under consideration. After altering the format of the text prepared for the concordance as explained in Appendix A, I divided the text into sentences, determining at the same time length in syllables and their type and noting the last results graphically. Then my computer program tested each sentence for all the characteristics listed above and associated this information with the particular sentence. In the new data file thus created, the computer stored on magnetic tape the tags[32] indentifying sentences along with the various sentence characteristics. From this data file, a standard computer program cross-tabulated the sentence features against the speaker, the act, and other criteria.[33] The purpose of this procedure was to determine distribution of particular features. Is a feature associated with a certain character or characters? with a certain act? with a formal context? with an emotional context?

The computer is a marvelous tool but only a tool whose function is manipulating data very rapidly and very accurately. The quality of the output is no better than the quality of the input, the programming, and the conceptualization of the problem to be investigated. In addition, the results of the computer-assisted intermediate phase must still be interpreted and applied to increase our understanding of the plays themselves This is the function of Phase Three. After studying the computer printout, I re-examine the Racinian texts, the original hypothesis, and supporting observations in order to correlate them to the additional information provided by the computer. But enough of preliminaries and generalities. It is time to see just what sentence structure can reveal about *Andromaque*.

Notes to Chapter 1

1.   See also the concise presentation by Goldman in "The Structure of Racinian Tragedy," in *Racine: Modern Judgments*, ed. R. C. Knight (London: Macmillan, 1969), pp. 101-16.

2.   See the discussion of differences between Racine and Shakespeare in the chapter on *Phèdre* by Elder Olson, *Tragedy and the Theory of Drama* (Detroit, Mich.: Wayne State University Press, 1966), pp. 217-36.

3.   All references and quotations are taken from *Œuvres de P. Corneille*, ed. Ch. Marty-Laveaux (Paris: Hachette, 1862), 1:13-122.

4.   Edition cited is that of Pierre Martino (Paris: Champion, 1927).

5.   See Jacques Schérer, *La Dramaturgie classique en France* (Paris: Nizet, 1950), Part 3, "L'Adaptation de la pièce au public," pp. 367-421.

6.   D'Aubignac lists these characteristics of tragedy: "vie des Princes, pleine d'inquiétudes, de soupçons. . .Les unes étoient funestes dans ce dernier événement. . .les autres avoient le retour plus heureux. . .une chose magnifique, sérieuse, grave et convenable aux agitations et aux grands revers de la fortune des Princes. . ."(pp. 142-43).

7.   "Drama which proposes the exhibition of an action of the utmost seriousness and the utmost significance" (Olson, p. 169).

8.   2:376. All quotations are from *Œuvres de J. Racine*, 10 vols., ed. Paul Mesnard (Paris: Hachette, 1885).

9.   "Toward a Definition of 'Le tragique racinien,'" *Symposium* 21 (1967): 218.

10.   A. P. Rossiter, "Shakespearean Tragedy," in *Tragedy: Modern Essays in Criticism*, ed. L. Michel and R. B. Sewall (Englewood Cliffs, N.J.: Prentice-Hall, 1963), pp. 196-97. Quoted by Nurse, pp. 218-19.

11.   Emile Boisacq, *Dictionnaire étymologique de la langue grecque*, 4th ed. (Heidelberg: Carl Winter, 1950), p. 199.

12.   A. Ernout and A. Meillet, *Dictionnaire étymologique de la langue latine: histoire des mots*, 4th ed. (Paris: Klinckseick, 1959), p. 278.

13.   P. 37. Olson goes on to distinguish effectively the various types of plot, pp. 41-45.

14.   Epigraph to *Psychology* (New York, 1915). Quoted by Peter Nurse, "Toward a Definition," p. 205.

15.   I use the term *language* where Olson uses *dialog*, to avoid confusion between dialogue meaning lines spoken by characters in a play and dialogue meaning rapid exchanges as opposed to *tirades* and monologues.

16.   Olson applies this statement to scenario but not to language (p. 89).

17.   See Maurice Descotes, *Les Grands Rôles du théâtre de Jean Racine* (Paris: Presses Universitaires de France, 1957).

18.   "Racine et la tragédie française," *Revue des cours et des conférences* 41 (1939-40): 521.

19.   "Racine et la poétique du regard," *L'Œil vivant* (Paris: Gallimard, 1961), pp. 73-74.

20.   His discussion of the *Agamemnon* of Aeschylus is no more helpful in this respect (pp. 171-94).

21.   Giles Lytton Strachey, *Literary Essays* (New York: Harcourt, Brace, 1949), p. 63.

22.   Published in *The Classic Theater, IV: Six French Plays*, ed. Eric Bentley (Garden City, N.Y.: Doubleday Anchor Books, 1961).

23.   See, for instance, Eugène Vinaver's discussion of this orientation to speech and the "cult of the spoken word," in which speeches become weapons and characters use a language made for battle. "Action and Poetry in Racine's Tragedies," in *Racine: Modern Judgments*, ed. R. C. Knight, pp. 151-53.

24.   *L'Art poétique* in *Œuvres*, ed. Georges Mongrédien (Paris: Garnier, 1961), cant. 3, vv. 5-8.

25.   In his introduction to *Stylistique et poétique françaises* (Paris: SEDES, 1970), Frédéric Deloffre offers a historical perspective on the word *style* as well as recent trends in stylistics, beginning with Charles Bally.

26.   "Language—the Basis of Science, Philosophy, and Poetry," in *Studies in Intellectual History*, ed. George Boas (Baltimore, Md.: Johns Hopkins Press, 1953), pp. 83-86.

27.   "Stylistique et critique littéraire," *Critique*, no. 98, p. 609.

28.   See, for instance, Bryant C. Freeman and Alan Batson, *Concordance du théâtre et des poésies de Jean Racine*, 2 vols. (Ithaca, N.Y.: Cornell University Press, 1968).

29.   Ivor S. Francis, "An Exposition of a Statistical Approach to the *Federalist* Dispute," in *The Computer and Literary Style*, ed. Jacob Leed (Kent Studies in English, no. 2 [Kent, Ohio: Kent State University Press, 1966]), pp. 38-78.

30.   The more technical aspects of this computer work are discussed in Appendix B.

31.   See the "Préface" and the "Préface du Programmeur" in their *Concordance*, pp. vii-xxii, for their discussion of the preparation of this text.

32.   The "tag" identifies the line and consists of play, speaker, act, scene, line number.

33.   See Appendix B, 4, for discussion of the procedure and examples of computer printout for *Andromaque*.

2
Andromaque:
Distribution of Basic Sentence Characteristics

Study of *Andromaque* as the first play under consideration involves only the basic characteristics of sentence structure: sentence length, sentence type, and terminal punctuation. That discussion, however, depends on determining what constitutes a sentence, defining its basic characteristics, and establishing norms within the play; it further depends on distribution of the basic characteristics, possible differences from character to character or from act to act, and differences that may depend on the nature of specific scenes. Finally, increased understanding of the play's basic movement comes from analysis and interpretation of significant differences in basic sentence characteristics.

What constitutes a sentence? A string of words beginning with a capital letter and ending with a terminal punctuation mark.

Vous me trompiez, Seigneur. (37)

T'ai-je jamais caché mon cœur et mes désirs? (39)

Oui, puisque je retrouve un ami si fidèle,
Ma fortune va prendre une face nouvelle;
Et déjà son courroux semble s'être adouci,
Depuis qu'elle a pris soin de nous rejoindre ici.(1-4)

Combien dans cet exile ai-je souffert d'alarmes! (13)

Ainsi tout trois, Seigneur, par vos soins réunis,
Nous vous. . .   (379-80)

This last string, though grammatically incomplete, is in fact terminated by the ellipsis; a new string begins immediately thereafter. Racine is consistent in this usage. Questions marks and exclamation points, on the other hand, cannot automatically be considered terminal.

Hélas! qui peut savoir le destin qui m'amène? (25)

Quoi? votre âme à l'Amour en esclave asservie
Se repose sur lui du soin de votre vie? (29-30)

If "Hélas!" and "Quoi?" are considered sentences, then "qui peut . . .m'amène?" and "votre âme. . .votre vie?" cannot by definition be sentences, since they do not begin with capital letters. Moreover, words such as *hélas, quoi, ah, hé,* and *ô* are not read or spoken as distinct and separate units, but as part of the string that follows (unless no string follows, as in the famous final "Hélas!" in *Bérénice*). It seems preferable to consider the marks following such interjections as internal punctuation and the composite units as sentences, although different in nature from "normal" sentences.[1] This string is also a sentence: "Ah! Madame, est-il vrai qu'une fois / Oreste en vous cherchant obéisse à vos lois?" (1147-48). Capitalization inherent in the word *Madame* does not mark a new sentence.

The first basic characteristic that distinguishes one sentence from another is length measured in syllables.[2] The second is terminal punctuation as illustrated above. The third I refer to as its "type." Type indicates where a sentence begins and ends as compared to the *alexandrin*. Thus a sentence whose end points coincide with the end points of the *alexandrin* is type "A" (*A*ll of a line, or *A*ll of a number of lines); one whose beginning coincides with it, but ends before the *alexandrin* is type "B" (*B*eginning of a line); one short sentence, neither of whose end points coincides with the *alexandrin* is type "M" (*M*iddle of a line); one whose ending coincides but that is shorter than one line is type "E" (*E*nd of a line). Type "M" always occurs alone. The other three types may occur in combination:

Type AB	*A*ll of a line + *B*eginning of a line
Type EA	*E*nd of a line + *A*ll of a line
Type EAB	*E*nd + *A*ll + *B*eginning
Type EB	*E*nd + *B*eginning

Hence there are four basic types and four combinations.

Type A: Oserai-je, Seigneur, dire ce que je pense? (165)

Hermione elle-même a vu plus de cent fois
Cet amant irrité revenir sous ses lois,
Et de ses vœux troublés lui rapportant l'hommage,
Soupirer à ses pieds moins d'amour que de rage. (115-18)

Type B: Il vient. (141)

Ah! qu'ils s'aiment, Phœnix: j'y consens. (253)

Type M: Allez. (623)

Type E: Je respire, je sers. (932)
                        Allons rejoindre mon époux. (924)

Type AB: Pour la veuve d'Hector ses feux ont éclaté:
                Il l'aime. (108-9)

Type EA: Parlez, et lui montrez
                Contre le fils d'Hector tous les Grecs conjurés. (135-36)

Type EAB: Mais je veux, Seigneur, l'assurer davantage:
                D'une éternelle paix Hermoine est le gage;
                Je l'épouse. (617-19)

Type EB: Hé bien! rien ne m'arrête:
                Allons. (433-34)

Although all sentence types occur in *Andromaque,* even a casual reading reveals that they do not occur with the same frequency or in the same distribution. Which type is the normal sentence, the neutral, regular, and inconspicuous one? The declarative sentence, terminated by a period, is clearly the least conspicuous in terminal punctuation. The declarative is also frequent, constituting more than sixty percent of the sentences in *Andromaque.*[3] The sentence of type A is inconspicuous since its physical limits coincide with the *alexandrin;* in quantitative terms, type A accounts for 68.8% of the sentences. Furthermore, a sentence consisting of a rhyming couplet or couplets would seem more regular or inconspicuous than other possibilities. Close examination of the text, however, shows that the 341 monostichs or one-line sentences decisively outnumber the distichs (240), but they do not occupy so much total space in the text. In sum, the "normal" sentence—one that constitutes a norm—is a declarative distich, or at least a declarative type A sentence. As the least personal and most expository of all subdivisions of the classical play, the *récit* can be immediately identified as a series of normal sentences. Most *récits* in Racine are not pure, because they contain an occasional change of terminal punctuation and of sentence type. The key word is occasional, and the *récit* remains the most nearly homogeneous sentence sequence. The first *récit* in this play, delivered by Oreste to Pylade in order to account for his activities in the interval since he has seen his friend, is a good example (vv. 37-104). Represented graphically, the sequence of sentence types and of terminal punctuation is as follows.

ORESTE: E A A A A A A A A A B E A A A A A A A A A A A A A A A A
         . . ? . . . . ! . . . ? . ? ?

The preponderance of the regular sentence of type A and of the period is evident. When an entire play is represented in this graphic fashion, the *récits* can be readily identified.[4]

Deviation from this normal sentence has possible implications for characterization. Do any of the four principal characters have typical patterns of deviation? Do any evolve during the play? Are the deviations more significantly linked to the presence or the absence on the stage of characters who could create emotional stress? Or do the deviations correspond to scenes that are emotionally charged as opposed to neutral ones? Establishing the existence of deviations is necessary, but attains only statistical significance, which means that deviations are probably not due to chance. Delineating meaningfully the precise nature of the relationship of deviations in sentence structure to characterization depends on a reexamination of the text itself in this light.

The Play Divided by Character and by Act

When sentences in *Andromaque* are associated with the speaker and those of the confidants are grouped together, only distribution of terminal punctuation is statistically significant.[5] It is thus probable that this distribution is not the result of chance and, consequently, merits further consideration.[6] Taken individually the period, question mark, and ellipsis attain an even greater level of significance.[7] Pyrrhus decisively exceeds the norm in use of periods, Hermione in question marks, Oreste and the confidants in ellipses. Since no mark of punctuation is consistently used in a single way, the affinity of a character for a particular terminal punctuation is a profitable point of departure rather than a conclusion.

Every character in *Andromaque* uses more declarative sentences than nondeclarative ones (61.7% of the average).[8] Pyrrhus averages roughly ten percent more than any other character. Also, his proportional use of sentences ending in a period increases with each act in which he appears, reaching 100% in Act IV.

Act I	59.7%
Act II	75.9
Act III	77.8
Act IV	100.0

In Pyrrhus's first appearance on the stage when Oreste confronts him on the subject of Astyanax (I, 2), Pyrrhus affects nonchalance and then plays the martyr. His first sentence shows this affected nonchalance: "La Grèce en ma faveur est trop inquiétée" (173). In fact, his nonchalance shows up even more in his questions to Oreste. Pyrrhus recites the siege of Troy and then, firmly and succinctly, states his refusal to take Astyanax's life: "Non, Seigneur" (217). This statement stands out as the first irregular sentence of the *tirade*.[9] After Oreste explains that the Greeks will not hesitate to take Astyanax by force, Pyrrhus plays the martyr in a series of four declarative sentences. Even the mention of Hermione fails to shake Pyrrhus.

> Non, non. J'y consens avec joie:
> Qu'ils cherchent dans l'Epire une seconde Troie;
> Qu'ils confondent leur haine, et ne distinguent plus
> Le sang qui les fit vaincre et celui des vaincus.
> Aussi bien ce n'est pas la première injustice
> Dont la Grèce d'Achille a payé le service.
> Hector en profita, Seigneur; et quelque jour
> Son fils en pourroit bien profiter à son tour.
>
> (229-36)

Later in the same act Pyrrhus fares less well in the role he plays opposite Andromaque. This scene is the source of the low proportion of declarative sentences for Pyrrhus in the first act (even slightly less than the average for the play as a whole), because he displays the least measure of control over himself. As a result it also shows the most movement within the character: Pyrrhus moves from communicating information about the situation regarding Andromaque's son to uttering threats and sarcasm, and finally to expressing outrage at Andromaque's reluctance to accept his offer, before regaining his composure. The whole central portion of the scene is marked by nondeclarative sentences, indicating that question marks, exclamation points, and ellipses can mark loss of control. Be that as it may, the beginning and the end of the scene where Pyrrhus imparts information, makes threats, and deals in sarcasm are entirely declarative in nature.

When Pyrrhus again confronts Oreste (II, 4), eleven sentences, all declarative, seem to indicate a calmness and single mindedness in his resolve to marry Hermione that his sentence types belie.

Oui. Mais je veux, Seigneur, l'assurer davantage:
D'une éternelle paix Hermione est le gage;
Je l'épouse. Il sembloit qu'un spectacle si doux
N'attendît en ces lieux qu'un témoin tel que vous.
Vous y représentez tous les Grecs et son père,
Puisqu'en vous Ménélas voit revivre son frère.
Voyez-la donc. Allez. Dites-lui que demain
J'attends, avec la paix, son cœur de votre main.

(617-24)

Presented graphically, the speech looks like this:

PYRRHUS: B EAB EA A B M EA

Five of the eight possible sentence types are here represented, including the rare EAB, with only one regular type A sentence. While distribution of sentence type over the play is not significant in and of itself, this situation demonstrates the powerful way in which it can interact with other factors to alter the total effect. Pyrrhus is concealing from Oreste, and perhaps from himself, what his real feelings are.

During the following scene (II, 5) and in the presence of his confidant, Pyrrhus attempts to convince himself to marry Hermione but keeps on talking about Andromaque. Finally Phœnix challenges him: "Vous aimez: c'est assez" (685). The punctuation of Pyrrhus's reply again reveals the tenuousness of his resolve.

PYRRHUS: ? . ? . . ! ! ! . .

Curiously though, when Pyrrhus meets Andromaque face to face in Act III, he fares better. He finally gets Andromaque's attention with a simple statement: "Allons aux Grecs livrer le fils d'Hector" (900). Pyrrhus seems in complete control. In the seventh scene, where he does all the talking, Pyrrhus works his way up to an ultimatum that leaves the choice to Andromaque. His sentences are all regular; the three questions interspersed among fifteen statements are calculated ones aimed directly at Andromaque. Thus they add to the total effect of the speech: shifting responsibility for the decision to Andromaque.

Throughout his brief appearance in the fourth act (IV, 5-6), as he meets Hermione on the stage for the first and only time during the play, Pyrrhus speaks entirely in declarative sentences, the majority of which are regular as well. Hermione's reaction is of course radically different. Pyrrhus retells the history of their "involvement," breaking the regularity of his *récit* with the significantly short sentence: "J'épouse une Troyenne" (1281). Missing the point of Hermione's veiled sarcasm, Pyrrhus mistakenly breathes a sigh of relief as he pronounces his second *tirade,* regular and declarative in its entirety. Hermione explodes in rage. In the light of this violent reaction, Phœnix tries in vain to get Pyrrhus to reconsider his course of action.

This then is the sequential effect of Pyrrhus's use of declarative sentences. For the most part, he conceals what he is thinking and feeling as he plays a role calculated to produce a desired effect on his interlocutor: nonchalance with a touch of martyrdom for Oreste; deals, threats, and an ultimatum for Andromaque; cool resolve for Hermione. He does not successfully play his self-appointed role in his first encounter with Andromaque and temporarily loses control because of her obstinateness. In the second encounter, however, Pyrrhus is in control and manages to shift to Andromaque the responsibility for the decision. When he finally meets Hermione in the fourth act, Pyrrhus knows Andromaque's decision and therefore dares to confront Hermione by rehearsing their situation historically, by inviting insults without recognizing their import when they are forthcoming, and by seeming to be generally oblivious to Hermione's imprecations. Here he is calmly revealing his perspective on the situation, whereas Hermione has lost control of herself. Except for the middle of his first encounter with Andromaque and for one slip with Phœnix (II, 5), Pyrrhus is in control of himself; this control manifests itself in part through the abundance of his declarative sentences. Understanding the nature of this phenomenon comes only from analysis of data and careful rereading of the text; the actual effect on the reader and the spectator comes from a direct experience of the play. The abundance of declaratives may explain difficulties actors have experienced in trying to incarnate Pyrrhus.[10] He often suffers by comparison with his interlocutors because of the formal, declarative nature of the role.

Whereas Pyrrhus has an untheatrical affinity for periods, Hermione favors question marks. Initially she uses them consciously for desired effects—suggestion, sarcasm, and attack. Later the questions come spontaneously and mirror the intensity of her emotions or the ambiguity of her feelings. During her first meeting with Oreste (II, 2), Hermione leads him to believe through a series of questions that she is glad to see him:

> Mais qui sait si depuis
> Je n'ai point en secret partagé vos ennuis?
> Pensez-vous avoir seul éprouvé des alarmes?
> Que l'Epire jamais n'ait vu couler mes larmes?
> Enfin qui vous a dit que malgré mon devoir
> Je n'ai pas quelquefois souhaité de vous voir?
>
> (523-28)

Hermione's composure is short-lived. When Oreste capitalizes on her leading remarks by commenting on Pyrrhus's indifference, Hermione's immediate outrage is revealed in an interrogative attack on Oreste.[11]

> Qui vous l'a dit, Seigneur, qu'il me méprise?
> Ses regards, ses discours vous l'ont-ils donc appris?
> Jugez-vous que ma vue inspire des mépris,
> Qu'elle allume en un cœur des feux si peu durables?
>
> (550-53)

Oreste is quick to perceive his error. Hermione, recovering her self-control, expounds in a long series of declaratives her duty and her willingness to follow Oreste. Questions are temporarily banished from her speech.

In her only scene with Andromaque (III, 4), Hermione strategically places one pointed question in her brief reply to her rival: "S'il faut fléchir Pyrrhus, qui le peut mieux que vous?" (884). Later she launches a full-scale attack of sarcasm on Pyrrhus, which he either misinterprets or chooses to ignore (IV, 5). The questions are prominent in this regular *tirade*. Momentarily, on two occasions in Act V, Hermione controls a series of rapid-fire regular questions to Cléone, a series of eight one-line questions (vv. 1441-48), and to Oreste, a series of eight regular questions, six monostichs, and two distichs (vv. 1545-54). The rest of Act V is another story altogether. Earlier in a moment of joy (III, 3), as she basks in the prospect of marrying Pyrrhus, Hermione deludes herself into thinking briefly that Pyrrhus is marrying her because he loves her. This interesting *tirade* can be represented in the following manner.

HERMIONE: B E A A A B EA B EB E A B
                ? ? ? . ? . ? ? @ ? . @[12]

Her emotional state is expressed both by the terminal punctuation and by the sentence types. With these exceptions, the losses of control occur entirely in the fifth act. Alone in the first scene, Hermione reveals the ambiguity of her feelings about ordering Pyrrhus's assassination. The uncertainty is expressed in the first fourteen lines of the *tirade* by questions and by exclamations and to a lesser degree by sentence type; the reaffirmation of her resolve occupies fourteen lines of regular declaratives; her doubt returns in the final nine lines with questions and an ellipsis. The complete and final breakdown occurs in the presence of Oreste as Hermione turns on him, unwilling to accept responsibility for the act.

Barbare, qu'as-tu fait? Avec quelle furie
As-tu tranché le cours d'une si belle vie?
Avez-vous pu, cruels, l'immoler aujourd'hui,
Sans que tout votre sang se soulevât pour lui?
Mais parle: de son sort qui t'a rendu l'arbitre?
Pourquoi l'assassiner? Qu'a-t-il fait? A quel titre?
Qui te l'a dit?

                                              (1537-43)

Racine uses the same technique to express the loss of orientation in Oreste. In the final scene of the play, Oreste dissolves in a flood of questions that mirror his confusion and derangement due to Hermione's reproof, her suicide, and especially the visions that he is himself experiencing.[13] More than any other single factor, the question furnishes clues to the developing character of Hermione: she may control her questions or they may control her. This richness in concealing and revealing herself, in attacking and succumbing, permits useful inferences about her character.

In contrast to Hermione, Andromaque is almost always in control of her sentences. She is, like Hermione, adept at sarcasm: "Et quelle est cette peur dont leur cœur est frappé, / Seigneur? Quelque Troyen vous est-il échappé?" (267-68). Whereas Hermione suggests to Oreste through questions the opposite of what she is thinking, Andromaque knows how to feign disbelief and astonishment when Pyrrhus offers to save Astyanax because of his love for her.

Seigneur, que faites-vous, et que dira la Grèce?
Faut-il qu'un si grand cœur montre tant de foiblesse?
Voulez-vous qu'un dessein si beau, si généreux
Passe pour le transport d'un esprit amoureux?

(297-300)

Andromaque also uses questions extensively in III, 8, to set before herself the choice of saving her son's life or of being faithful to Hector. But in every case, unlike Hermione, Andromaque is in control of her questions.

Exclamations are fairly evenly distributed, although Andromaque does lead in their use. In addition to exclamations for surprise (v. 1014) and for apostrophe (vv. 1045-46), Andromaque uses them for sarcasm and for reproach (vv. 907; 270). The ellipsis marks an incomplete sentence, incomplete either because a character is interrupted by his interlocutor or because he is simply unable to complete his utterance. Oreste accounts for more than one third of them in *Andromaque*, primarily because Hermione, as early as II, 2, can render him incapable of finishing sentences. In suggesting that Oreste assassinate Pyrrhus, Hermione renders him temporarily speechless four times (IV, 3).

Of the three criteria, only terminal punctuation is valuable in both quantitative and qualitative terms. In general, a series of irregular sentences underscores the emotional force produced by nondeclarative terminal punctuation or belies a façade of neutrality or control produced by a series of declaratives. Statistically speaking, Andromaque has the highest percentage of regular sentences (75.7%). Only she and Pyrrhus exceed the mean in that respect and therefore show the most control. Oreste and Hermione fall slightly short of the mean, whereas the confidants register the fewest regular sentences (63.8%).

Further examination, however, reveals qualitative differences in sentence types where quantitative ones are lacking. A well-placed short sentence makes the words it contains stand out from the general context of regular sentences. Type B sentences, ones that begin with the *alexandrin* and terminate prematurely, are the most frequent type after the regular sentence, comprising about 12% of the total number of sentences in the play. A number of these are taken up by imperatives: "Sortons," "Allez," "Retournez-y," "Va-t'en." While generally impersonal, imperatives are given specific content by Hermione: "Vengez-moi, je crois tout" (1157). "Courez au temple" (1172). "Chère Cléone, cours" (1269). All of these are directly related to the proposed assassination of Pyrrhus and occur in the space of slightly more than one hundred lines. The second common use of type B sentences is for exclamations: "Hé! Madame." "Ah Dieux!" Again it is Hermione who personalizes this form by giving it more specific emotional content: "L'infidèle!"(515). "Le perfide!" (1458). In addition to these commonly shared uses, each character has specific ways of using type B sentences. In the case of Andromaque when the exclamations and the imperatives are deleted, nearly all her type B sentences refer to Astyanax: "Hélas! il mourra donc" (373). "Mais il me reste un fils" (867). "Il a promis mon fils" (896). "Mais que ne peut un fils?" (932). Two others refer indirectly to her son, since they express her consent to marry Pyrrhus to save her son's life and her belief that Pyrrhus will honor their agreement after her own death: "Oui, je m'y trouverai [à l'autel]" (1064). "Je sais quel est Pyrrhus" (1085). Prominent in the text because of their unusual length, these sentences emphasize that Astyanax is the one factor that interferes with her preferred course of action.

Pyrrhus uses this special sentence type to express his growing resolve to marry Andromaque. To Oreste on the subject of surrendering Astyanax: "Non, Seigneur" (217). To Andromaque: "Je vous offre mon bras" (293). As he is rebuffed by Andromaque: "J'abandonne son fils" (695). And finally, Pyrrhus expresses clearly his resolve to Hermione and to his confidant Phœnix: "J'épouse une Troyenne" (1281). "Andromaque m'attend" (1392). The other personalized use of these short sentences belongs jointly to Oreste and to Hermione. The sentence type combines in the fifth act with terminal punctuation to translate emotions out of control. Some are remarkably similar and reinforce the impression of interrogative contagion.

Hermione	Oreste
Il est mort? (1495)[14]	Elle meurt? (1604)
Quel transport me saisit? (1394)	Quelle horreur me saisit? (1627)

Hermione is more prolific in her use of them and precedes Oreste by a scene or two; she directs them at Oreste, whereas he tends to internalize his questions. Although there are common impersonal uses of the form, each character personalizes it and, in so doing, reveals his or her preoccupations or emotional distress.

The third criterion, sentence length as measured by the number of syllables per sentence, does not offer great insights. Mean sentence length by character, from the highest number of syllables per sentence to the lowest, is as follows:

Pyrrhus	20.197
Oreste	19.884
Andromaque	19.421
---MEAN--------	19.012---
Hermione	18.327
confidants	17.412

Certain trends are worth remembering for comparison with later tragedies: the most emotional character and the confidants show average sentence lengths shorter than the mean for the play. They, along with Oreste, also fall short on percentage of regular type A sentences.

At the same time that characters were cross-tabulated against the basic characteristics of sentence structure, similar cross-tabulations of acts against the criteria were performed to check for unusual distribution throughout the play. Generally results were inconclusive or could be attributed to specific characters. For instance, the high frequency of questions in Act V is due to Hermione and to Oreste. Several items are of interest, however. The relative frequency of type A sentences decreases from act to act, except for Act II, which is slightly low for its position. The decreasing proportion of regular sentences is understandably linked to the growing emotional tension of the play. It is surprising that this phenomenon cannot be attributed to any particular character, but is a cumulative effect to which all contribute. In contrast, the mean sentence lengths for Acts I and IV are high: 23.273 and 21.607 syllables per sentence respectively. The other acts are in the 16-17 syllable-per-sentence range. These differences are more radical than those encountered earlier with characters. The longer sentence length in Act I is due to expository material. Act IV is not so easily explained. In addition to long sentences, Act IV claims the high in periods as well as the low in question marks. For every other division of the play, by characters or by acts, the most frequently occurring sentence length is 12 syllables, a monostich. In Act IV it is 24 syllables, a distich. These unexpected characteristics in Act IV are due to the cumulative effect of resolutions made and expressed—Andromaque's to marry Pyrrhus, Hermione's to have Pyrrhus assassinated, plus several *récits*. The effect created is one of slight détente before the disasters of Act V are precipitated; it also increases the contrast between Acts IV and V. Furthermore, these disasters are a direct result of the very factors that had previously created the détente.

The other question is a combination of the two previous ones: is there a significant change or perceptible evolution within characters from act to act? The answer for Hermione is a clear affirmative, based on the data itself and on the qualitative study of her questions. While Pyrrhus shows an increasing proportion of declaratives during the course of the play, he is reaffirming his initial course of action rather than changing it. Oreste is swept along to a certain extent by Hermione; his sentences tend increasingly to mirror hers. Andromaque is the same person throughout, although she uses a large number of declaratives (29 of 31) in Act IV as she communicates her decision to marry Pyrrhus and to die.

The Play Divided for Emotional Charge and for Presence of the "Enemy"

The emotional charge carried by scenes varies greatly: scenes that are mostly expository are neutral; others are highly charged; still others lie in the middle range. Each scene was assigned to one of four categories: neutral, doubtful, charged, or highly charged. The same cross-tabulations were performed in an attempt to use present criteria to discriminate among these categories. The results are disappointing. Neither by statistics nor by observation could I discriminate among categories either through terminal punctuation, the most powerful criterion thus far, or through sentence type. When a single character causes a scene to be highly charged, another's calmer sentences neutralize that effect, and the net result does not show quantitative evidence of the emotional charge of the scene.

The only useful criterion in this area was mean sentence length.

neutral	22.161
doubtful	19.266
---MEAN--------------	19.012---
charged	18.630
highly charged	18.182

The mean of the play falls conveniently between the "doubtful" and the "charged" and the descending order is intact. While it confirms a previous conclusion, the information adds little to our understanding of the total effect of the play.

Another possible division within the play is suggested by John Lapp.[15] He claims that mere physical presence of certain people challenges constraint in others. Theoretically, Hermione's presence would thus affect Oreste, Pyrrhus's would affect Hermione, and Andromaque's would affect Pyrrhus. This is not necessarily the case. In *Andromaque* characters are not necessarily affected adversely by the presence of the others. In fact, quite the opposite seems to be true; characters may function reasonably well in the presence of the "enemy" and less well when left alone or with a confidant to reflect on the situation. After dividing the play into those scenes which contain a potentially volatile pair and those which do not, the cross-tabulations were again performed. In the area of terminal punctuation, use of the question mark was identical. While not statistically significant, the relative frequency of periods was high and that of exclamations was low in the presence of the enemy. That is quite the opposite of what one might expect, since periods are "normal" and exclamations are "abnormal." On the other hand, regular sentences were frequent and short ones were infrequent in such situations. The sentence lengths were high (20.309) for presence and low (17.929) for absence.

These findings seem to indicate that by and large the characters in *Andromaque* are able to conceal their feelings in the presence of the enemy but feel free to reveal them in other circumstances. Only late in the tragedy do Hermione and Oreste lose that constraint. Instances of the shock produced by physical presence are strategically placed throughout the Racinian canon. They are not, however, perceptible in quantitative terms. For that reason, the enormous task of separating scenes on this basis is not justifiable.

Cross-tabulations based on emotional charge in a scene or on presence of an "enemy" do not contradict earlier findings, but otherwise make only a minimal contribution to interpreting *Andromaque*. These cross-tabulations are therefore not performed on the rest of the plays. Differences from character to character, on the other hand, are far more finely tuned and lead directly to the basic issues of the tragedy.

Conclusion

The characters in *Andromaque* exercise a basic option in their speech: they may conceal their thoughts, desires, and motives, or they may reveal them. The general tendency, clearly evident in the first few acts, is to conceal in public and to reveal in private with only a confidant present. Within the concealing register, there exist several possibilities. Silence is one. Making nontruthful utterances is the other possibility, in which a character may dispassionately hide real thoughts or may speak with feeling, using sarcasm in particular. At this point a character is perilously close to revealing his feelings to his interlocutor. Hermione and Andromaque are adept at sarcasm, marking it by well-placed questions and exclamations. The revealing register, on the other hand, offers more modes of expression to the characters. In *récits* and the like, the character narrates events in a neutral, impersonal way. Related to this are the times when a character speaks freely and dispassionately. These two modes are characterized by high percentages of declarative and regular sentences, many of which are attributable to Pyrrhus. Or a character may speak frankly but with feeling. Oreste expresses his love for Hermione to Pylade early in the play. Andromaque uses sarcasm in rejecting Pyrrhus's advances. In turn, Pyrrhus increasingly threatens Andromaque. The extreme in the revealing register, however, is the expression of outrage in Hermione and derangement both in her and in Oreste. In one sense there is a continuum from silence as extreme concealment to outrage and derangement as equally extreme revelation.

Along the concealment-revelation continuum, characters are operating either voluntarily or involuntarily. The losses of control in language occur toward the extremes of the continuum. When characters do not know what they desire or what they think, then by their silence they involuntarily conceal that fact; they may even be unaware of the nontruths and half-truths that they do utter. At the other extreme in outrage and derangement, characters' language is out of control as they involuntarily reveal their great distress. Pyrrhus usually operates within the voluntary range: he calculates and manipulates other characters, especially Andromaque. Although she takes quite a while to devise a way to protect Astyanax while remaining faithful to Hector, Andromaque also stays within the voluntary range. Hermione mistakenly affirms that she desires the death of Pyrrhus and then is outraged when her orders are carried out: loss of control on both counts. In the fifth act, Oreste also falls prey to derangement, involuntary revelation of his state of mind. Just as he had misread Hermione's sarcastic remarks in Act II, Oreste is taken in by what Hermione says she wants in Act IV.

Another dimension to these two registers, concealment and revelation, and voluntary and in certain cases involuntary expression of their relations with one another, is the audience's perception of them. This perception, based in large part on inferences drawn from language, also heightens involvement in the denouement, anticipating and fearing possible turns of events. The careful reader and the attentive spectator suspect early that Hermione does not really want Pyrrhus dead and know that Oreste lacks the ability to read between her lines. Pyrrhus is harder to figure since he is so cool and calculating, so completely in control of himself and of his language. Andromaque suffers mental anguish until she can arrange events to her satisfaction. Pyrrhus effectively shifts the decision to Andromaque, assuming that the denouement will then hinge on her decision. But for all his calculating self-assurance, Pyrrhus does not realize the possible violence of Hermione's reaction. The reins pass to Hermione once Andromaque has made her decision. Force of emotion, coupled with Oreste's demonstrated inability to understand Hermione, spells death for Pyrrhus and Hermione and derangement for Oreste.

This analysis has been based entirely on the interpretation of the most basic of sentence characteristics. In summary, Racine's technique in *An-*

dromaque at this level includes unequal distribution of terminal punctuation among characters as a sign of basic stance or of evolution; use of irregular sentence types as a sign of emotional distress; interaction of terminal punctuation and sentence type for reinforcement or contradiction; beginning of a trend in which sentence length is roughly proportional to the emotional stability of characters. As anticipated, these basic sentence characteristics have proved to be signs through which important inferences about characterization can be made. Their assimilation, whether intuitive or analytical, also contributes significantly to the focus on and the anticipation of the denouement of the tragedy. It remains to be seen to what extent these basic patterns inform Racine's later plays and it is time to introduce gradually other features of sentence structure potentially as significant in the analysis of techniques of characterization through language.

Notes to Chapter 2

1. The ramifications of these internal marks of punctuation are discussed in the following chapters. See Appendix B for a description of the SPITBOL routine used to distinguish these internal marks of punctuation from their terminal counterparts.

2. See Appendix B for a discussion of the computer-assisted method for counting syllables.

3. All statistics are based on the text of the 1697 edition unless stated otherwise. Careful examination of the variants for *Andromaque* reveals nothing of statistical significance. Several tendencies resulting from modifications and deletions are perhaps worth noting: reduction in differences between length of characters' sentences results from decrease for Andromaque and increase for Hermione; sentence types of deleted passages are distributed in the same way as for the text as a whole; modifications result in fewer distichs and slightly reduced number of irregular sentences.

4. This task is easily accomplished by a SPITBOL program once the sentences are classified according to the relevant data. See Appendix B.

5. Except in rare instances, considering confidants as separate characters for this purpose proved unsatisfactory because they speak relatively few sentences, making statistical inference unreliable. Moreover, interesting distinctions among confidants are rare on the level of sentence structure.

6. The level of rejection used is .01. This means that there is one chance in a hundred, or less than one, that this distribution was arrived at by chance. There are therefore 99+ chances out of 100 that this distribution is deliberate. The null hypothesis can be rejected at this point although much more evidence is forthcoming (see Introduction).

7. Level of rejection here is .001 or one chance in a thousand.

8. Since the period is the basis of my assertion that a sentence is declarative, imperatives are also included in this category automatically. When imperatives are of special interest, they are singled out for discussion. See, for instance, my discussion of Mithridate's use of imperatives in chapter 4.

9. Irregular sentences are all types except type A.

10. See Maurice Descotes, *Les Grands Rôles du théâtre de Racine,* pp. 48-52.

11. This reaction on the part of Hermione foreshadows her interrogative attack on Oreste following the assassination (V,3).

12. The symbol @ replaces the ellipsis, which in this diagram could not be distinguished from three periods.

13. It is perhaps a matter of interrogative contagion, for as early as II, 2, when Hermione attacks him in a series of questions for suggesting that Pyrrhus might be indifferent to her charms, Oreste replies in a series of questions (vv. 555-59). See also my discussion of type B sentences in chapter 3.

14. The earlier version of this sentence reads: "Quoi? Pyrrhus est donc mort?" The change could have been made in order to reinforce this parallelism.

15. *Aspects of Racinian Tragedy,* chapter 5. See my comments above in chapter 1.

$$\left[\begin{array}{c} 3 \\ \textit{Britannicus} \text{ and } \textit{Bérénice} \end{array} \right]$$

Racine's next two tragedies are both set in Rome, but *Britannicus* and *Bérénice* are as different from each other as they are from *Andromaque*. In each case the young Emperor has a decision to make that can affect the whole course of his reign. How the decision is made and what consequences are endured as a result are basically different. How the decisions are made is revealed through the structure of the sentences in these two tragedies.

Britannicus

In this tragedy, set during the early years of Néron's reign, the scenes of confrontation are numerous. The first meeting of Junie and Britannicus, for instance, occurs under most inauspicious circumstances (II, 6). Néron has just made clear to Junie that Britannicus's young life depends on her dismissing him from her presence without explanation. Junie speaks a mere six sentences, all of them regular and declarative. Britannicus, already alarmed by the news that Néron has abducted Junie in the middle of the night, begins by questioning her on that subject. His first few sentences, mostly questions, convey astonishment at seeing her at all.

BRITANNICUS: A A A A A B M E A B E A A A A B M E A B E A A
? ? ! ? ? ! ! ? ? ? ? ? ? ? ? ! ! ? . . .

After a flood of nine questions in this *tirade*, Britannicus realizes that Junie has not answered. "Vous ne me dites rien? Quel accueil! Quelle glace! / Est-ce ainsi que vos yeux consolent ma disgrâce?" (707-8). In contrast, Junie speaks three colorless lines, hoping to make Britannicus understand that they must not speak openly. Undaunted, Britannicus reproaches Junie for her fear of Néron and cites the support of Agrippine against him. When Junie replies in terms complimentary to the eavesdropping Emperor, Britannicus mistakenly assumes in a new series of questions that Junie is attracted to Néron. Both sentence type and terminal punctuation are again affective.

BRITANNICUS: A A A A A B E B E B E A B E
    . . ? ? ? ? ? ? ? @ . . ?

In this scene neither Junie nor Britannicus reacts naturally to the other. The cause of Junie's constraint is hidden only from Britannicus; thus he moves from confusion to confusion, first because of the unexpected abduction and then because of Junie's coldness toward him. This scene is largely responsible for Britannicus's high proportion of questions (24 out of 40 sentences here) used to express confusion and anger.

Junie spends most of their next scene together (III, 7) trying to explain what had happened. She uses a subtle approach, only to be rebuffed by Britannicus (vv. 961-66). On her second attempt to explain, the impetuous young man interrupts her in mid-sentence.

Seigneur, sans m'imputer . . .

Ah! vous deviez du moins plus longtemps disputer.

(969-70)

In an insulting tone Britannicus continues a "this-is-the-last-straw" speech. Impatient with him, Junie divulges that Néron had been listening to their previous conversation. Not easily satisfied, Britannicus reproaches her for not showing the truth in her eyes. By the time they finally come to an understanding, Néron appears and understands just as fully. As they meet again at the beginning of the fifth act (V, 1), Britannicus appears confident of his future, whereas Junie trembles at the prospects of the proposed reconciliation.

In the only scene in which Néron and Britannicus face each other (III, 8), they engage in a verbal battle reminiscent of Corneille. After preliminary remarks by Néron regarding the tender scene that he has just interrupted between his rival and Junie, Britannicus challenges Néron's claim to respect and obedience and thus to the throne (vv. 1037-40). About ten lines later they fall into rapid exchange of one-line and two-line type A sentences, commonly called stichomythia. The pattern continues until Britannicus unwisely comments that at least he does not spy on Junie. Néron abruptly has him taken captive: "Je vous entends. Hé bien, gardes!" (1069).

As Emperor, Néron frequently issues such orders. He handles even Junie with address at the end of this particular scene. When he tires of verbal exchanges with Britannicus, Néron terminates the discussion by taking him prisoner. Normally he has little difficulty with his advisers, Narcisse and Burrhus, managing to listen when he so desires or to cut the discussion short. It is thus not surprising that Néron accounts for a disporportionately high number of the declarative sentences (77.8% of his sentences, almost ten percent above the average for the play), just as Pyrrhus had done in *Andromaque*. Néron deals that way with everyone, except where Agrippine is concerned. It is true that in the early acts he lacks total control when talking about Junie. A substantial number of his short sentences deal with his new love for her: "Dis-moi: Britannicus l'aime-t-il?" (427). "Je la suis" (753). "Il faut que j'aime enfin" (778). "Adieu. Je souffre trop, éloigné de Junie" (799). He manages to play his role well, however, when talking to her. With regard to his mother, Néron fails on both counts, talking about her and talking to her.

Twice Narcisse causes the Emperor to demonstrate the power his mother still holds over him. As early as II, 2, Narcisse probes Néron's hesitation to take Junie as his wife. Néron first claims that everything stands in his way. "Tout: Octavie, Agrippine, Burrhus, / Sénèque, Rome entière, et trois ans de vertus" (461-62). As Narcisse probes further, Néron finally admits the control that, by her presence, Agrippine is able to exert over him (vv. 496-510). Nothing in the sentence structure of the *tirade* itself, whose regular sentences are abnormally long (three, eight, and four lines respectively), and very little in the sentence structure of the scene point to a loss of composure: Néron simply admits what he knows to be true.

When Narcisse approaches Néron to report that the poison is ready (IV, 4), the Emperor informs him of the proposed reconciliation. Arguments regarding Britannicus and Junie fail. But Narcisse knows what argument cannot fail to arouse the Emperor's anger. "Agrippine, Seigneur, se l'étoit bien promis: / Elle a repris sur vous son souverain empire" (1414-15). Néron immediately explodes: "Quoi donc? Qu'a-t-elle dit? Et que voulez-vous dire?" (1416). "De quoi?" (1418). Unquestionably, Narcisse knows how to unnerve Néron by showing the Emperor that his mother has again exerted her control over him and, what is worse, is telling everyone about it.

The situation is also clear on the two occasions when Agrippine and the Emperor meet face to face in confrontations dramatically postponed until Act IV. Agrippine shows nothing quantitatively unusual in her sentence types or terminal punctuation, which throughout *Britannicus* lie near the average for the play. Her sentences are, however, among the longest; she even favors the distich over the one-line sentence. In her first meeting with Néron (IV, 2), she dominates the scene by talking most of the time. From her first sentence, "Approchez-vous, Néron, et prenez votre place" (1115), she does not permit him a word until she has finished. Her lengthy *tirade* of 108 lines is for the most part a *récit*. She makes clear to her son what she had done to place him on the throne (vv. 1119-94), ending appropriately: "C'est le sincère aveu que je voulois vous faire: / Voilà tous mes forfaits. En voici le salaire" (1195-96). Only one question and one ellipsis break the declarative pattern of the *récit*. Agrippine uses short type B sentences or clauses to underscore the progress of her strategy and its final results:

> Vous régnez. (1119)
> Je fléchis mon orgueil, (1129)
> Le sénat fut séduit: (1136)
> Ce n'étoit rien encore. (1143)
> Je fis plus: (1159)
> Il [Claudius] connut son erreur. (1175)
> Il mourut. (1183)
> On vit Claude [mort]; (1193)
> Voilà tous mes forfaits. (1196)

Having impressed upon Néron what she has done for him in the past, Agrippine lists what Néron is doing in return: letting Burrhus and Narcisse turn him against his mother, abducting Junie, possibly repudiating Octavie his wife, banishing Pallas, and preventing Agrippine herself from seeing the Emperor at will.

In the light of these accusations, Néron begins cautiously. He dares to question her motives only by quoting in an interrogative format what others are wondering:

"Tant d'honneurs, disoient-ils, et tant de déférences,
Sont-ce de ses bienfaits de foibles récompenses?
Quel crime a donc commis ce fils tant condamné?

Est-ce pour obéir qu'elle l'a couronné?
N'est-il de son pouvoir que le dépositaire?"

(1231-35)

Gaining courage, Néron intimates and then states openly that Agrippine
has been aiding Britannicus, intending to present him to the army, but
he knows immediately, by his mother's reaction, that he should not have
said it (vv. 1258-86).

AGRIPPINE: B E A A A A A A A B E A B E A A A
         ? ? ? ? ? . . . . ! ? . ? . .

From outrage expressed by irregular and regular questions, Agrippine
passes on to hurt feelings: "Que je suis malheureuse!" (1275). She is bold
enough to suggest sarcastically to Néron that he might as well take her
life, too. Néron, unable to withstand the onslaught, agrees to a reconciliation with Britannicus and other considerations. His mother has
scarcely left the stage, however, when Néron declares to Burrhus his intention to free himself from Agrippine's control by assassinating Britannicus.

When the deed has been done, Néron faces Agrippine again. She ac-
costs him in no uncertain terms.

  Arrêtez, Néron; j'ai deux mots à vous dire.
Britannicus est mort, je reconnois les coups;
Je connois l'assassin.

(1648-50)

Outraged at Narcisse's justification of the Emperor's action, Agrippine
addresses Néron, using for the first time the familiar form. Her short
sentences in particular erupt in sarcasm. "Poursuis, Néron, avec de tels
ministres" (1672). "Poursuis" (1674). "Adieu: tu peux sortir" (1694). Up
to the very end of the tragedy, Agrippine hopes to bring Néron around to
her way of thinking (vv. 1765-67).

The conflicts within the play develop on two levels: Néron versus
Agrippine, and Britannicus versus Junie. The conflict between the
Emperor and his mother is a long-standing one, whereas the other is a
temporary misunderstanding. Néron's desire for Junie is not the central
issue, but only serves to precipitate renewed conflict on an old bat-

tlefront. Néron is in fact preoccupied with Junie early in the tragedy but, as the tragedy progresses, he is more and more exclusively concerned with freeing himself from his mother's power. The struggle for power and control involves the Roman Empire only peripherally; the characters are struggling for control over Néron's person and over his actions. Narcisse and Burrhus are important parties to this struggle, pulling the Emperor in opposite directions. Narcisse ultimately prevails by taking advantage of Néron's desire to be freed from his mother's control. If this is not, strictly speaking, a political struggle, it is even less the struggle for physical possession. Néron's desire to possess Junie is soon subordinated to his desire to subjugate his mother. Despite brief encounters with the Emperor, Britannicus and Junie, hoping primarily for a peaceful existence together, are mere pawns rather than parties to that other struggle. These two levels are mirrored in the relative sentence lengths of the two groups:

Burrhus	23.847
Agrippine	22.688
Narcisse	21.857
Néron	21.493
---MEAN---------	21.403---
Albine	21.300
Junie	18.796
Britannicus	18.606

Variants that represent passages deleted before the 1697 edition affect only the composite sentence lengths of Burrhus (25.343) and Néron (21.224). The variants do not, however, affect the overall configuration. Burrhus's lengthiness would simply be more pronounced and, although Néron's average would fall slightly below the mean of the play, it would by no means approach the average sentence lengths of Britannicus and Junie. The implications of the two groups operating on different levels remain intact. The dramatic effect of the deletions is far more important. Deleting the section from III, 1 removes Burrhus's elaborate references to the inappropriate posture of Narcisse between the Emperor and Britannicus as well as eliminating a *récit* of past events. The latter must originally have taken much of the impact out of Agrippine's *récit* to Néron in the second scene of Act IV which, while similar in content, is radically different in intent. Deleting the other passage removes Junie from V, 6, and focuses the final scenes on the conflict between Néron and Agrippine.

The basic trends from act to act in the play are interesting if not surprising. As in *Andromaque,* the gradually decreasing sentence length reverses itself in Act IV, to peak at an average this time even longer than that of Act I.

Act I	22.600
Act II	20.961
Act III	19.132
Act IV	24.249
Act V	20.329

Coupled with the absence of Britannicus and Junie from the stage in Act IV is a détente; only here is there talk of reconciliation with Britannicus. Regular type A sentences are frequent in Acts I and IV, as might be expected; the high percentage of short sentences and the doubling of the number of exclamations mark the astonishment, confusion, and outrage that in Act V follow the announcement of Britannicus's death.

Internal Punctuation: Question Marks
and Exclamation Points

Internal question marks and exclamation points occur almost exclusively with a few expressions: "Quoi?", "Mais quoi?", "Hélas!", "Ah!", and "Hé bien!" Agrippine uses exclamations occasionally and with most of her interlocutors except Junie. Britannicus and Junie use them almost exclusively with each other. With one exception, all of Britannicus's utterances of "Quoi?" are directed at Junie. Four of them occur in II, 6, where they convey his confusion at the coolness of Junie's reception. Six of them occur in their third and final meeting (V, 1) where "Quoi?" first conveys his surprise and pleasure at the prospect of being free to love Junie and then his surprise at Junie's distrust of Néron's motives. His "Ah!" and "Hélas!" serve much the same function. Junie concentrates her exclamations in the second and third scenes with Britannicus, when she is free to express her feelings. They are all but absent from the first encounter. Nor are hers addressed exclusively to Britannicus: five are addressed to Néron. In the final analysis, their specific use is not as important as their distribution. They express an emotional reaction, notably surprise or confusion; they betray a person caught offguard. Britannicus employs these internal marks of punctuation to express surprise and confusion at Junie's attitude toward Néron. Junie's exclamations (she has very few internal question marks) are the result of Britannicus's or Néron's statements. Agrippine's exclamations occur with regard to Néron's unexpected actions and vice versa. The function remains basically the same, but Agrippine and Néron use the device much less frequently. These features of sentence structure belong primarily to Britannicus and Junie, clearly those characters in the play who rely most heavily on their feelings. Through this feature also, they distinguish themselves from the other characters in the play, demonstrating once again that they function on a different level. They are motivated by love, whereas the other characters are caught up in the struggle for possession of Néron's soul.

Subordination: *Si* clauses

With the exception of Narcisse, who utters only one conditional sentence, this characteristic is rather evenly distributed. Repetition of the *si* clause invariably betrays the major preoccupation of the speaker. In attempting to convince Junie how important he considers their marriage, Néron compares having her to having the Empire:

En vain de ce présent [l'Empire] ils m'auroient honoré,
Si votre cœur devoit en être séparé;
Si tant de soins ne sont adoucis par vos charmes;
Si tandis que je donne aux veilles, aux alarmes
Des jours toujours à plaindre et toujours enviés,
Je ne vais quelquefois respirer à vos pieds.

(589-94)

In addition to the repetition of *si* clauses, the tortured syntax of this sentence is significant. Shortly thereafter Burrhus impresses upon Néron that one does not love involuntarily:

Mais *si* dans son devoir votre cœur affermi
Vouloit ne point s'entendre avec son ennemi;
Si de vos premiers ans vous consultiez la gloire;
Si vous daigniez, Seigneur, rappeler la mémoire
Des vertus d'Octavie, indignes de ce prix,
Et de son chaste amour vainqueur de vos mépris;

Surtout *si* de Junie évitant la présence,
Vous condamniez vos yeux à quelques jours d'absence:
Croyez-moi, quelque amour qui semble vous charmer,
On n'aime point, Seigneur, *si* l'on ne veut aimer.

(781-90)

In his lengthy, contrary-to-fact clauses, Burrhus touches on three reasons (duty, reputation, wife) to avoid an involvement with Junie, and on one way (absence) to reduce his interest in her. His last line in the present tense generalizes Burrhaus's point. Both Néron and Burrhus intend their conditional sentences to have persuasive force. Agrippine, more sarcastic than persuasive, expresses her displeasure to Néron:

Ah! *si* sous votre empire on ne m'épargne pas,
Si mes accusateurs observent tous mes pas,
Si de leur empereur ils poursuivent la mère,
Que ferois-je au milieu d'une cour étrangère?

(1261-64)

The present tense emphasizes the factual nature of the accusations, while putting them in a series of subordinate *si* clauses attenuates slightly the sharpness of her accusations.

Si clauses usually occur as a series of parallel constructions in long regular sentences. Persuasion and sarcasm are the typical modes of expression. No preference either as to interlocutor or as to tense can be attributed to specific characters. Content likewise varies, except in the case of Agrippine, all of whose thirteen conditional sentences deal with Néron.

Most of the characters in *Britannicus* know what they want or whom they want. Although, much to the Emperor's dismay, Britannicus can match Néron verbally in their single encounter, Britannicus and Junie both willingly admit a preference for an undistinguished existence together to the struggles of the Roman court. Agrippine reveals early in the tragedy her desire to be as influential a figure in directing the course of Néron's reign as she had been in procuring the throne for him. Burrhus and Narcisse, the young Emperor's advisers, are clearly pulling him in opposite directions. Only the Emperor's true motives and desires are in doubt. Why he abducted Junie is not clear. When he reveals his love for her, he has mixed emotions about taking her as his wife. Taking this and other of the Emperor's recent actions as a personal affront, Agrippine moves quickly to shift the focus of the play from Britannicus/Junie to Agrippine/Néron. Junie does not enter directly into Néron's decision to have Britannicus poisoned. It is Agrippine who tries to impose a reconciliation by overpowering her son. Once she is out of his presence, however, Néron reverts almost violently to the desire to kill Britannicus. Although Burrhus stems the tide temporarily, Narcisse is able to reverse Néron's thinking; the Emperor cannot abide the thought of his mother's power over him. The final confrontation of the play is again between Agrippine and Néron. The abduction of Junie brings to a crisis a long-standing conflict between the Emperor and his mother.

The registers of concealing and revealing one's thoughts and feelings are not predominant here as they were in *Andromaque*. Nor is love the cause of disorder and disaster. In the conflict only Néron is moved to physical violence. Yet opposing forces are fighting for control over him. The character who effectively perceives and utilizes the Emperor's involuntary subjugation to his mother's will has the force to determine finally Néron's course of action. Possession of Junie is, in the final analysis, a secondary consideration; the great battle of *Britannicus* is for the possession of Néron's soul.

Bérénice

Viewing *Bérénice* as a whole, it is apparent that its sentence structure is substantially different from that of *Britannicus*. In striking contrast to *Britannicus,* where sentences averaged over twenty-one syllables in length, in *Bérénice* they average less than nineteen (18.941). Among the main characters, Titus maintains the longest sentences, averaging between 20 and 21 syllables; Bérénice and Antiochus fall in the 17-18 syllable range. On the other hand, Paulin, whose function is to instruct the new Emperor with regard to duty, honor, and precedent, averages over 24 syllables per sentence (24.460). This puts him in the company of Burrhus (23.847), who performs a similar function vis-à-vis Néron. The occurrence of seven percent fewer regular type A sentences than in the two preceding plays reinforces the effect of generally shorter sentences.

A speech of the *récit* type, composed of regular, declarative sentences,

is a rarity in *Bérénice*. There are none in the first two acts, although Antiochus almost achieves declarative regularity in I, 4, when he declares his
intention to leave Rome. Titus does almost as well in his discussion with
Paulin (II, 2). But only when the Emperor instructs Antiochus in what to
tell Bérénice does he achieve composure marked by regular, declarative
sentences (III,1). Hence, exposition in the early acts is not made in the
impersonal terms of the earlier plays. In effect, before the final scenes of
the play (V, 5-7), only Titus demonstrates composure, and that composure is short-lived. There is also a slight increase in the use of internal
questions and exclamations.

  The decided increase in the number of one-sentence exchanges between characters is especially evident in two rapid-fire exchanges between
Titus and Bérénice, one early and one late in the play. In both instances
Bérénice dominates the exchange. In the first (II,4), she presses Titus in
vain for a satisfactory answer regarding her situation:

Titus: Mais . . .
Bérénice: Achevez.
Titus: Hélas!
Bérénice: Parlez.
Titus: Rome . . . l'Empire . . .
Bérénice: Hé bien?
Titus: Sortons, Paulin: je ne lui puis rien dire.

                                                (623-24)

Seven sentences in a mere two lines! Titus is capable neither of lying to
Bérénice nor of telling her the truth. Instead, he flees her presence. In a
similar exchange (V,5), Bérénice again dominates the situation and
thereby prevents Titus from speaking to her:

Titus: Mais, de grâce, écoutez.
Bérénice: Il n'est plus temps.
Titus: Madame,
              Un mot.
Bérénice: Non.
Titus: Dans quel trouble elle jette mon âme!

                                                (1307-8)

Although Bérénice finally relents and lets Titus have his say (V,6), she
does not lose control. These rapid-fire exchanges are radically different

from the one between Britannicus and Néron discussed earlier in this chapter. That exchange, an example of stichomythia, is typical of seventeenth-century tragedy in general and is frequently used by Pierre Corneille.[1] The exchanges in *Bérénice* are internal to the *alexandrin,* breaking each verse into several sentences given to two or more characters.[2] This procedure is more typical of seventeenth-century comedy than of tragedy. The fact that Racine wrote *Les Plaideurs* (where such exchanges are common) between *Andromaque* and *Britannicus* suggests that writing a comedy made Racine aware of a flexibility in the *alexandrin* that he transferred sparingly in the six exchanges in *Britannicus* and realized fully here in *Bérénice.*

The cumulative effect of these features, shorter and more irregular sentences with more frequent internal questions and exclamations along with irregular rapid-fire exchanges, is to cast the tragedy in nuances rather than in sharp contrasts. As Maurice Descotes has observed, critics often consider *Bérénice* far removed from the tragic atmosphere of *Andromaque* and *Britannicus.* Examining further the sentence structure of *Bérénice* should clarify this and Descotes's own intuition that the expressions here are "plus proches de la langue courante que du style tragique" (*Les Grands Rôles,* p. 84).

In contrast to the pattern of mean sentence length from act to act in *Andromaque* and *Britannicus,*[3] mean sentence length in *Bérénice* plunges abruptly in Act III and recovers only slightly in Act IV before climbing in Act V.

Act I	21.337
Act II	20.816
Act III	16.655
Act IV	17.252
Act V	19.019

At the same time, interrogative sentences increase sharply to 34.3% in Act IV, nearly eight percent above the average. In Acts III and IV Titus's intentions are finally revealed to Bérénice first by Antiochus and following his own struggle by Titus. Thus the first four acts are taken up with the discussion of what Titus will do and how he will tell Bérénice. In the fifth act multiple resolves of suicide are averted by Bérénice, who rises to the occasion and displays her greatest composure in the play as she resigns herself to the separation.

Unlike other characters in this play, or characters in Racine's preceding plays for that matter, Titus concentrates his conditional sentences in only three important scenes, containing four to six such sentences each. Each scene produces a major confrontation with another character — Paulin, Antiochus, and finally Bérénice herself — and marks a step in Titus's decision to send the Queen away. In II, 2, Titus and Paulin discuss frankly the implications of Titus's marrying Bérénice. These conditional sentences reveal (a) his unwillingness to face the situation, (b) his knowledge of the consequences, and (c) his apprehension about Bérénice's reaction. The first three are contrary to fact, whereas the last is part of his experience.

(a)   J'ai même souhaité la place de mon père,
      Moi, Paulin, qui cent fois, *si* le sort moins sévère
      Eût voulu de sa vie étendre les liens,
      Aurois donné mes jours pour prolonger les siens:
      Tout cela (qu'un amant sait mal ce qu'il désire!)
      Dans l'espoir d'élever Bérénice à l'Empire,
      De reconnoître un jour son amour et sa foi,
      Et de voir à ses pieds tout le monde avec moi.

                                        (431-38)

      Combien mes tristes yeux la trouveroient plus belle,
      S'il ne falloit encor qu'affronter le trépas!

                                          (500-501)

(b)   Quelle honte pour moi, quel présage pour elle,
      Si dès le premier pas, renversant tous ses droits,
      Je fondois mon bonheur sur le débris des lois!

                                        (468-70)

(c)   Encor *si* quelquefois un peu moins assidu
      Je passe le moment où je suis attendu,
      Je la revois bientôt de pleurs toute trempée.

                                        (537-39)

In the first example the conditional sentence is wholly embedded in a relative clause and seems almost incidental. Its purpose in this syntactically complicated sentence is to point up contradictions within Titus, who desired his father's throne and frequently thought himself willing to sacrifice his life for his father's. All for Bérénice. The interpolated exclamation functions semantically to express Titus's lack of awareness of consequences and metrically to break the rhythm of the *alexandrin*. What appears at first glance to be a regular eight-line declarative sentence is both in form and in content a subtle mirror of Titus's indecisiveness.

After an unsuccessful attempt to tell Bérénice of his decision, the Emperor summons Antiochus (III,1). Only the first of four conditional sentences is contrary to fact, again emphasizing the Emperor's reluctance. "Ah! qu'un aveu si doux auroit lieu de me plaire! / Que je serois heureux, *si* j'avois à le faire" (711-12). The second reveals Bérénice's precarious position with respect to the Roman people (vv. 732-34). The others occur in a single complicated sentence in which the two conditional clauses frame the sentence.

> *Si* l'espoir de régner et de vivre en mon cœur
> Peut de son infortune adoucir la rigueur,
> Ah! Prince, jurez-lui que toujours **trop fidèle**,
> **Gémissant** dans ma cour, et **plus exilé** qu'elle,
> **Portant** jusqu'au tombeau le nom de son amant,
> **Mon règne** ne sera qu'un long bannissement,
> *Si* le ciel, non content **de me l'avoir ravie**,
> Veut encor **m'affliger** par une longue vie.
>
> (749-56; emphasis added)

A tortured sentence, to be sure! The two conditionals are not parallel, since the first depends on the main clause, "Jurez-lui . . . ," whereas the second depends on the noun clause, "que . . . mon règne ne sera qu'un long bannissement." Only the first two lines apply to Bérénice; in the other six lines Titus concentrates on himself, as seen in the italicized expressions, the first four of which, incidentally, should modify a first-person-singular subject but in fact appear to modify *mon règne*. Once again Titus's syntax mirrors his state of mind.

In his second scene with Bérénice (IV, 5), Titus confronts the Queen with the arguments developed earlier in private:

> S'ils [les Romains] parlent, *si* les cris succèdent au murmure,
> Faudra-t-il par le sang justifier mon choix?
> S'ils se taisent, Madame, et me vendent leurs lois,
> A quoi m'exposez-vous?
>
> (1140-43)

Titus, more sure of his decision, substitutes a present/future pattern for the hypothetical imperfect/conditional of earlier sentences.

Bérénice distinguishes herself not by the occasions on which she employs conditional sentences (nine such sentences in six different scenes), but rather by the tense format she chooses. With one exception her conditional sentences begin in the present tense. When Phénice, her confidante, offers to help the Queen arrange her hair and veils in preparation for Titus's visit, Bérénice refuses in a series of conditionals the assistance of "ces vains ornements." Repetition emphasizes the force of her emotions.

Si ma foi, si mes pleurs, si mes gémissements,
Mais que dis-je, mes pleurs? Si ma perte certaine,
Si ma mort toute prête enfin ne le ramène,
Dis-moi, que produiront tes secours superflus,
Et tout ce foible éclat qui ne le touche plus?

(974-78)

Her other conditional sentences, while less interesting in and of themselves, also delineate Bérénice's orientation in time and her preoccupations by the repeated use of the present tense.

As in their conditional sentences, and also in other areas of sentence structure, the characters in Bérénice do not by and large distinguish themselves from one another in quantitative terms. Specific use of certain features does vary significantly. Bérénice, for instance, uses her quota of questions in a revealing way. Understandably, her questions show surprise when Antiochus speaks so unexpectedly of his departure from Rome and then of his love for her (I,4). When Antiochus returns later to speak for Titus, the Queen shows in short type B and type E questions her impatience to hear the Emperor's message to her. "Et qu'a-t-il pu vous dire?" (859). "Quoi? Seigneur . . ." (861). "Que vous a dit Titus?" (880). When Antiochus finally reveals the message, Bérénice cries out in disbelief: "Nous séparer? Qui? Moi? Titus de Bérénice!" (895). Four sentences in a single alexandrin! Only by refusing to believe Antiochus does Bérénice recover her calm, declarative self-composure. At the beginning of the fourth act Bérénice shows her impatience for Phénice's return from Titus in two identical questions four lines apart. "Phénice ne vient point?" (953 and 957). In the following scene, as Phénice describes the state in which she found the Emperor, the Queen can think of only one thing. "Qu'a t il dit? Viendra-t-il?" (963). "Vient-il?" (966).

In the actual encounters with Titus, Bérénice adds to her repertoire of questions used for surprise and impatience. In Act II, scene 4, as they meet on the stage for the first time, Bérénice takes control of the situation and rebukes Titus for his recent silence. Absorbed in affairs of state, did he at least think of her?

> Tous vos moments sont-ils dévoués à l'Empire?
> Ce cœur, après huit jours, n'a-t-il rien à me dire?
> Qu'un mot va rassurer mes timides esprits!
> Mais parliez-vous de moi quand je vous ai surpris?
> Dans vos secrets discours étois-je intéressée,
> Seigneur? Étois-je au moins présente à la pensée?
>
> (579-84)

Titus does not lie well. Although his words affirm his love for Bérénice, two cold declarative distichs tell her just the opposite. When Titus is unable to respond to her questions about his coldness,[4] she suggests an excuse for him, his father's recent death. It is in fact characteristic of Bérénice to invent excuses for Titus and thus to deceive herself. Moreover, she recognizes that fact: "Hélas! pour me tromper je fais ce que je puis" (918). Titus is finally driven from the stage as Bérénice presses him in rapid-fire imperatives for an explanation that he is not ready to give (vv. 623-24, discussed above).

By rebuking Titus, Bérénice is using questions coupled with regular declaratives to draw the truth out of him, or rather to obtain a declaration of love. Titus is at her mercy. After his two neutral sentences, the rest are almost all irregular ones containing affective terminal punctuation.

TITUS:		
	A A	. .
	B	@
	A B	! !
	E B E A	? ? . .
	B EA B	. . @
	M	!
	E	@
	E	.

Only after the Emperor's precipitous exit does Bérénice permit her emotions to come to the surface (II,5).

BÉRÉNICE:	A A B M E
	? ! ? ? ?
PHÉNICE:	A A A B
	. . ? .
BÉRÉNICE:	EA B E B E B EA A A B EAB EA A B EA A A A AB
	EA A A A A
	. . . . ? ? . ? . @ @ . ? . . . . . . ! . . . .

Later in his monologue (IV, 4) Titus reveals his indecision about Bérénice; the proportion of questions is extraordinarily high, attaining almost seventy percent.

| TITUS: | ? . ? ? ? ? . ? ? ? . ? . ? ? ? ? . ? . . @ ! ? ? . ? ? ? ? . ? ? . ? ? |
| | ? ? ? ! @ |

Up to the first ellipsis (@) Titus's internalized questions probe his feelings about sending Bérénice away. "Tes adieux sont-ils prêts? T'es-tu bien consulté? / Ton cœur te promet-il assez de cruauté?" (989-90). He wonders whether he will be able to tell her, having already failed to do so on one occasion. He wonders why he is preparing to send her away when no one, not even the senate, has demanded her departure. Just as he is beginning to believe his delusions, Titus breaks his rhythm with an ellipsis. "Rome sera pour nous. . . . Titus, ouvre les yeux!" (1013). Coming to himself and taking a historical approach to the situation, Titues rebukes himself and expresses his duty through questions again directed inward (vv. 1014-20). Just as Titus reaffirms his choice of honor and duty (vv. 1029-32), Bérénice appears and interrupts him.

Titus takes control of the situation by telling the Queen that they must separate (IV, 5). Here Bérénice's questions are also rebukes. Why didn't you tell me long ago? How can you do this now? Can't I stay? Are the Romans already up in arms about it? While it would be an exaggeration to suggest that Bérénice has completely lost control of herself as Hermione does, she is obviously disturbed and angered.

Only in the final scenes of the tragedy does Bérénice add a touch of sarcasm to her repertoire of questions.

Non, je n'écoute rien. Me voilà résolue:
Je veux partir. Pourquoi vous montrer à ma vue?
Pourquoi venir encore aigrir mon désespoir?
N'êtes-vous pas content?

                                                        (1303-6)

        Vous m'aimez, vous me le soutenez;
Et cependant je pars, et vous me l'ordonnez!
Quoi? dans mon désespoir trouvez-vous tant de charmes?
Craignez-vous que mes yeux versent trop peu de larmes?

                                                        (1345-48)

In keeping with the subdued tone of the play, her sarcasm is born more of
sorrow than of bitterness. Then uttering only one word, *Hélas!*, for nearly
a hundred lines, Bérénice lets Titus and Antiochus speak their minds.
Finally putting an end to their threats of suicide, she bids them both
adieu with almost perfect composure. After a long series of declarative
and regular sentences, only a few short sentences as a final remonstrance
reveal the difficulty with which she speaks. "Tout est prêt. On m'attend.
Ne suivez point mes pas. / Pour la dernière fois, adieu, Seigneur"
(1505-6). Although Bérénice last addresses Titus, it is ironically Antiochus who finishes the tragedy, with a final despondent "Hélas!"

Subordination: *Quand* and *Lorsque*

Numerically, *quand* predominates over *lorsque* (20 occurrences as opposed to 14). Their respective distribution seems, however, to be determined by metrical and phonological exigencies.[5] In fact, they occur side
by side three times in the more elaborate sentences of this type. The best
example is the following:

Je n'aurois pas, Seigneur, reçu ce coup cruel
Dans le temps que j'espère un bonheur immortel;
Quand votre heureux amour peut tout ce qu'il désire,
Lorsque Rome se tait, *quand* votre père expire,
Lorsque tout l'univers fléchit à vos genoux,
Enfin *quand* je n'ai plus à redouter que vous.

                                                        (1081-86)

As with her conditional sentences, Bérénice speaks in the present tense. The first clause of this type expresses in general terms the freedom of choice that Titus has recently attained; the second and third detail the reasons for his freedom; the fourth reemphasizes the power accompanying his new position; and the final one places the responsibility squarely on the Emperor's shoulders. Bérénice never uses a future in this construction and reverts to a past tense on only two occasions. The first occurs early as she recites past events to Antiochus. The others occur as she confronts Titus with his past behavior. "Ignoriez-vous vos lois, / *Quand* je vous l'avouai pour la première fois?" (1065-66). "Ne l'avez-vous reçu, cruel, que pour le rendre, / *Quand* de vos seules mains ce cœur voudroit dépendre? (1071-72). It is clear that the Queen is working toward a present tense and specifically to the elaborate sentence cited above (vv. 1081-86). By contrast, Titus speaks primarily in past or in future terms. The past tenses are related either to precedents of his case or to his former attitude toward Bérénice; the future ones are related to his reputation or to his inability to speak frankly to the Queen.

Impersonal Expressions: *Falloir*

Impersonal expressions as a group are not common in Racine's tragedies. Those constructed with *être* + adjective are completely lacking except for *il est vrai* (37 occurrences), *il est juste* (3), and *il est nécessaire* (1). The other impersonal expressions are almost equally rare, except for *il suffit* and *il faut*. The former occurs a total of 25 times in seven tragedies, hardly enough to warrant sustained interest. On the other hand, the impersonal verb *falloir* in its various forms occurs 47 times in *Bérénice* alone. Unlike features already studied, *falloir* has intrinsic meaning. From this point of view it is not surprising that Titus leads decisively in the use of this expression (accounting for nearly half of them, or 22 out of 47), that Antiochus follows next, and that Bérénice uses it the least of all the characters (5).[6] Antiochus uses the expression primarily in Act I, as he explains the necessity for his imminent departure. By the same token, Titus shows a particularly high frequency in Act IV, where he makes his final decision in private and then confronts Bérénice with the necessity for their separation. So obvious, in fact, are the connections, that it must be presumed that this distribution is primarily a function of semantics and that therefore it would be inappropriate to discuss this impersonal expression as if it were a feature of sentence structure.

Comparison to Corneille's *Tite et Bérénice*

The particular sentence structure described above is Racine's choice for *Bérénice*: the sentence structure is not automatically predetermined either by the subject matter or by some all-pervasive style of the period. Such a statement is usually based on intuition; in this case, however, Pierre Corneille has provided us with a good comparison, his *Tite et Bérénice*, a play written in the same year on the same subject. Yet his sentence structure is clearly distinct from that of Racine in all features studied thus far.[7] Sentences are consistently and significantly longer in Corneille's play, both for the play as a whole and for characters who appear in both plays.

Tite	29.467	Titus	20.548
confidants	28.810	confidants	18.972
--MEAN-----	28.421	----------MEAN--------	18.941---
Bérénice	28.404	Bérénice	17.703

Domitie (28.117) and Domitian (27.304), while a bit shorter than the others, still cluster near the mean for the play. A quick glance at Table 3 in Appendix C shows these figures to be elevated in comparison to all of Racine's plays, including his first two, *La Thébaïde* (24.714) and *Alexandre* (26.088).

The frequency of regular sentences is similarly elevated (82.2%), nearly twenty percent above that of *Bérénice* and comparable only to *La Thébaïde* and *Esther* (Table 2). As could be anticipated from sentence length, the proportion of short sentences, those less than twelve syllables in length, is extremely low and comparable only to *Alexandre*. Other types are within the range established for Racine.

	A	B	E	M
Bérénice	63.2%	13.9%	9.4%	2.6%
Tite et Bérénice	82.2	6.5	4.0	1.9

In Corneille's play internal questions (1.6%) and exclamations (3.6%) are rare in comparison to Racine's use of them, but *quand /lorsque* and especially conditional *si* are much more frequent.

	quand/lorsque	si
Bérénice	3.3%	4.4%
Tite et Bérénice	5.4	18.8

The limited scope of this study prevents a digression into the interesting qualitative differences between sentence structures of *Bérénice* and of *Tite et Bérénice*. It is even doubtful that Corneille used sentence structure specifically for characterization. In any case, even this rapid quantitative survey of *Tite et Bérénice* makes it obvious that Racine's use of sentence structure is individual insofar as it differs significantly in many points from that in contemporary work by Pierre Corneille, the other great tragedian of the seventeenth century.[8]

Bérénice is, with respect to sentence structure, a tragedy written in nuances. A number of factors contribute to the conversational tone of the play. The basic characteristics show a predominance of shorter and more irregular sentences combined with more frequent use of affective internal and terminal punctuation. Also, the revealing register in *Andromaque* and in *Britannicus* extended from *récits* to violence and threats of violence. A truncated register in *Bérénice* displays fewer impersonal *récits* and no threats of violence to others. It is true that each of the three principal characters at one time or another contemplates suicide. These are, however, not always convincing threats; particularly those of Titus and Antiochus seem to be made in the hope of obtaining a more animated response from their interlocutor. By the same token, the concealing register lacks bitter sarcasm and, for the most part, lacks half-truths and nontruths promulgated with any conviction. Titus's difficulty stems more from inability to face Bérénice with his decision for separation than from inability to make that decision. Once his decision is made, Bérénice must decide her fate and that of Titus and Antiochus as well.

Conclusion

It is apparent that *Britannicus* and *Bérénice* are quite different tragedies. Even quantitatively their sentence structures differ significantly. The range of emotions is much greater in *Britannicus,* where characters are in violent conflict with each other: several lives are at stake; characters throw themselves into passionate struggle to control Néron. He himself seems to have seized Junie as much to assert himself as for any other reason. The assassination of Britannicus is nothing other than Néron's attempt to free himself from his mother's grasp. Britannicus and Junie, if not innocent bystanders, are pawns sacrificed to this struggle for control over Néron and his destiny. It is not a struggle for political power, but rather a struggle to possess his person and to direct his actions. There is considerable doubt as to the specific outcome and as to how much blood will be shed. But given the violence of the emotions and the characters involved, there can be no doubt that some will be shed.

On the other hand, Titus and Bérénice function at a level not unlike that of Britannicus and Junie, except that Titus has some measure of control over their destinies. The similarity of sentence structure is striking. The range of emotions is restricted: none of the characters is in violent conflict with any of the others. Titus is pulled in one direction by an almost mythical Rome and his adviser, Paulin, and in the opposite direction by Bérénice and Antiochus. Ultimately, Titus prefers his image as the dutiful Emperor to that as the devoted lover. Only his ability to tell Bérénice the truth and her reaction to it are in doubt. Consequently, no life is in danger at others' hands. Three suicides are threatened. By renouncing her own, Bérénice is able to prevent the other two; the denouement is bloodless. *Bérénice* does lack the violent conflicts and bloodshed of other plays by Racine. Its drama is played out in nuances and thereby attains "cette tristesse majestueuse" that its author attributes to it.[9] By its very nature also, the drama of *Britannicus* is played out in violent conflict and death.

In addition to pursuing the analysis of the three basic features of sentence structure as elaborated in relation to *Andromaque,* discussion of other features was begun with *Britannicus* and *Bérénice.* Internal punctuation for questions and exclamations proved significant for interpreting *Britannicus,* as did qualitative differences in the use of conditional *si* clauses. Both features are, therefore, systematically investigated in later plays and discussed wherever they shed light on Racine's technique. Tenses used with *quand/lorsque* were more interesting than the actual distribution of this particular type of subordination; the feature is retained. Distribution of impersonal expressions and especially *falloir* is apparently based on semantic considerations and therefore is not suited for characterization; the feature is not retained. Finally, comparison of

Bérénice to Corneille's *Tite et Bérénice* established the individual quality of Racine's style. That assurance, along with specific features capable of discriminating among characters, provides the foundation for study of later plays and paves the way for discussion of other techniques of characterization related to sentence structure.

Notes to Chapter 3

1. See the discussion by Jacques Schérer in *La Dramaturgie classique en France*, pp. 302-16.

2. Other rapid-fire exchanges are discussed in later chapters, Chapter 4 on *Bajazet;* Chapter 5 on *Iphigénie;* and Chapter 6 on *Phèdre.*

3. Mean sentence length decreases from Acts I through V except for Act IV, where the count equals or exceeds that of Act I. See Chapter 2 for discussion with regard to *Andromaque* and the present chapter with regard to *Britannicus.*

4. Britannicus received a similarly cold response from Junie but for different reasons.

5. See discussion of this aspect of versification in chapter 8.

6. The verb *devoir* has a similar distribution in this tragedy.

7. The computer-readable text is based on that of Ch. Marty-Laveaux in *OEuvres complètes de Pierre Corneille* (Paris: Hachette, 1862), 10:201-76.

8. Statistics for *Tite et Bérénice* are listed in all tables of Appendix C in order to facilitate comparisons of all features with Racine's other plays as well.

9. Préface de *Bérénice. OEuvres de J. Racine*, 2:376.

$$\left[\begin{array}{c} 4 \\ \textit{Bajazet} \text{ and } \textit{Mithridate} \end{array}\right]$$

After *Bérénice* Racine returns to the representation of more violent conflicts in *Bajazet* and in *Mithridate*. The settings also become what may be loosely called Oriental and in *Bajazet* contemporary. In both plays Racine presents a contest among several characters for the possession of another: Roxane and Atalide use different methods to compete for Bajazet; Mithridate and his two sons, Xipharès and Pharnace, compete for Monime. Political considerations are more positively correlated to amorous considerations in *Bajazet* than in *Mithridate*. Mithridate is torn between love or jealousy on one hand and political and military ambitions on the other; Roxane vainly hopes to fulfill both desires at the same time.

Bajazet

In terms of basic sentence characteristics, *Bajazet* falls generally within the normal range. Percentage of sentences ending in periods (66.5%) is slightly higher than in *Andromaque* and *Bérénice* but lower than in *Britannicus*. The relative proportion among the affective terminal punctuation marks, question marks (24.6%), exclamation points (5.7%), and ellipses (3.2%) is also roughly that of the preceding tragedies. Internal questions and exclamations are, however, noticeably fewer in *Bajazet* than in *Bérénice* or in *Britannicus*. The frequency of regular type A sentences falls between that of *Bérénice* on the one hand and those of *Britannicus* and *Andromaque* on the other. Each irregular type accounts for a similar proportion of sentences, the highest going to type B (13.8%), followed by type E (8.9%). Thus *Bajazet* does not distinguish itself quantitatively in these two areas.

The mean sentence length for the tragedy is 19.966 syllables per sentence and is thus within the normal range. Its distribution, however, is unusual, both with respect to individual characters and with respect to the five acts. Bajazet himself attains an average of 24.177 syllables, a level previously reserved for royal counselors like Burrhus and Paulin. Acomat, the Visir, as well as the confidants, are in the 21-22 syllable range, well above the mean for the play. In contrast, both Roxane and Atalide find themselves in the 17-18 syllable range. Thus there exists an average three-syllable-per-sentence gap between the two women rivals and the two men and the confidants.

Bajazet	24.177
Acomat	22.103
confidants	20.924
---MEAN------	19.966---
Atalide	18.533
Roxane	17.770

In preceding plays characters possessing average sentence lengths in the 17-18 syllable range (and thus falling below the mean of the play in question) tend to be those whose existences are emotionally oriented. Nevertheless, clear distinctions will have to be made between these two women, for they are not so similar as this feature might indicate. Whereas the basic trend from act to act within Racine's tragedies is gradually decreasing sentence length, each play has an anomaly in the third or fourth act. *Bajazet* is no exception. Act I contains an unusually high proportion of expository material, due possibly to the fact that this contemporary and Oriental material was less familiar to Racine's first audiences than was the ancient Greek and Roman material. Thus Act I of *Bajazet* averages 23.009 syllables per sentence, and the distich is here more frequent than the monostich. The levels of Act II and III drop to the more common 19-21 syllable range. But Act IV plunges an average of four syllables per sentence to an unprecedented level of 15.853 syllables. Can this radical decrease be attributed to the absence of Bajazet? He is also absent from Act I and contributed no more than ten to fifteen percent of the sentences in Acts III and V. Only in Act II, where he contributes almost forty percent of the sentences, is he a significant factor.

Roxane dominates this fourth act by uttering 106 sentences, about forty-six percent of the total. It is not so much Roxane's dominance *per se* as it is her uncertainty and insecurity that lower the average sentence length. Here in Act IV she receives a letter from the victorious Emperor Amurat, who is returning to the city; hence urgency to act. Here also she discovers the letter from Bajazet to Atalide in which he makes clear his feelings about Atalide. In addition to Roxane's problems there are other uncertainties and emotional traumas: Atalide receives Bajazet's letter and worries more than before about his ability to feign love for Roxane and to save himself thereby; she faints upon hearing the news of Amurat's imminent return as well as Roxane's alleged intention to surrender; Acomat offers to kill Bajazet and, after Roxane's refusal to authorize it, he also hesitates and then resolves to do what he can to save Bajazet. In Acts I through III characters have only their cherished desires, their doubts, and their fears. In Act IV most of their worst fears are realized. The effects of these various discoveries in the course of Act IV are shown in part by the radical reduction of sentence length.

It is also significant that there are no rapid exchanges between characters prior to Act IV. The entire third scene of that act is composed of quick exchanges of two lines or less, most of which are single sentences. Without knowing the true nature of the relationship between Atalide and Bajazet, Roxane shows Atalide the letter from Amurat. The diagram on the following page shows how few regular sentences there are in this scene as well as how seldom a character manages more than two sentences in a row. As a matter of fact, Atalide's series of five regular declarative sentences (vv. 1184-92) is due solely to the fact that she is reading aloud the letter from Amurat.

ROXANE:	A A	. ?		ROXANE:	B	?
ATALIDE:	A A	. .		ATALIDE:	E	.
ROXANE:	A	.		ROXANE:	B	?
ATALIDE:	B	@		ATALIDE:	EAB	@
ROXANE:	EA B	. .		ROXANE:	E AB	?@
ATALIDE:	M	!		ATALIDE:	M	?
ROXANE:	EA	.		ROXANE:	E	.
ATALIDE:	A	?		ATALIDE:	B	!
ROXANE:	B E	. .		ROXANE:	E B	? .
ATALIDE:	A	!		ATALIDE:	EA	!
ROXANE:	A	.		ROXANE:	B E	. .
ATALIDE:	B	!		ATALIDE:	B	.
ROXANE:	E A	. .		ZATIME:	E	.
ATALIDE:	B	?		ROXANE:	A A	. .
ROXANE:	E A	. .				
ATALIDE:	A A A A A	. . . . .				

(N.B.: Read down the first column and then down the second.)

Based on terminal punctuation, it is clear that Roxane is in control of

the situation. Nineteen of her 25 sentences are declarative while five are
interrogative and one sentence regarding Bajazet trails off in an ellipsis.
Her deliberate questions are calculated to put Atalide on the defensive:
"De tout ce qui s'y passe êtes-vous informée?" (1166). "Hé bien?" (1193).
"Que vous semble?" (1194). "Moi, Madame?" (1198). "Et que faire en ce
péril extrême?" (1201). Discounting the reading of the letter, Atalide has
only fourteen sentences: four declarative, three interrogative, five exclamatory, and two elliptical. She is both surprised and fearful; even her
declaratives can be emotionally oriented: "Je me meurs" (1205). Twice
she tries to regain control of the situation by making the kind of suggestion that had previously worked on Roxane (vv. 1177-78; 1194-98). Her
protestations are to no avail; the scene draws to a close as Atalide faints,
unable to face the prospects outlined by Roxane.

In Act V two rapid, emotionally charged exchanges precede two *récits,*
the first of which describes the death of Roxane and the second, the death
of Bajazet.

Acomat:	Crains mon juste courroux [à Atalide].
	Malheureuse, réponds.
Zaïre:	Madame!
Atalide:	Hé bien, Zaïre?
	Qu'est-ce?
Zaïre:	Ne craignez plus: votre ennemie expire.
Atalide:	Roxane?
Zaïre:	Et ce qui va bien plus vous étonner,
	Orcan lui-même, Orcan vient de l'assassiner.
Atalide:	Quoi? lui?

(1664-69)

Osmin:	....
	Et vengé dans son sang la mort de Bajazet.
Atalide:	Bajazet?
Acomat:	Que dis-tu?
Osmin:	Bajazet est sans vie.
	L'ignoriez-vous?
Atalide:	O ciel!

(1692-94)

Another remarkable aspect of the final scenes of Act V is the rapidity with
which characters appear on the stage to announce a new development in
the denouement.

V, 7 (8 lines):	Zatime enters to announce that Acomat has taken over the palace.
V, 8 (20 lines):	Atalide asks Zatime for news of Bajazet.
V, 9 (10.5 lines):	Acomat enters asking Bajazet's whereabouts.
V, 10 (9.5 lines):	Zaïre enters to announce the death of Roxane.
V, 11 (46 lines):	Osmin enters to describe the battle and to announce the death of Bajazet.
V, 12 (28 lines):	Atalide realizes the import of these *récits* and kills herself.

Rapid-fire exchange of responses within a scene is here transposed to rapid-fire exchange of information as the entire denouement unfolds in the space of slightly over one hundred lines constituting six scenes.

Atalide is the most frequent user of *quand / lorsque*. Most of her sentences of this type are constructed with past-tense verbs; one other is in the present tense; the remaining one, a future tense, is part of her false confession to Roxane (V, 6). One sentence contains four clauses of this type, all in the imperfect. Atalide is talking to Zaïre, her confidante, just after receiving news of the impending marriage of Bajazet and Roxane. Although she had encouraged, even forced, Bajazet to enter into this arrangement, Atalide reveals here how uncertain she is of Bajazet's intentions.

Cependant **croyois-tu,** *quand* jaloux de sa foi
Il s'alloit plein d'amour sacrifier pour moi;
Lorsque son cœur, tantôt m'exprimant sa tendresse,
Refusoit à Roxane une simple promesse;
Quand mes larmes en vain tâchoient de l'émouvoir;
Quand je m'applaudissois de leur peu de pouvoir:
Croyois-tu que son cœur, contre toute apparence,
Pour la persuader trouvât tant d'éloquence?

                                                  (907-14; italics added)

The subordinate clauses are framed by two occurrences of **croyois-tu,** the first as if it were broken off by the *quand / lorsque* clauses. These clauses, two regarding Bajazet and two regarding herself, contain information that Atalide knows to have been accurate in the past. Taking that into account, she is uncertain as to how Bajazet found the eloquence to persuade Roxane of his sincere love for her and of his willingness to marry her. In her other sentences of this type Atalide is simply recounting past events (vv. 927-28; 1050-51; 1435-36). The other characters use the construction sparingly and without noteworthy implications.

One factor is of special interest from the perspective of the whole play: the marked increase in use of conditional sentences. In *Bajazet* one sentence out of every twelve is conditional in nature, whereas only one in twenty was in *Britannicus* and in *Bérénice*. Nearly every character uses them, but Bajazet leads proportionately since approximately one out of every eight of his sentences is conditional. Atalide has the greatest number, with a total of 25, averaging about one for every eleven sentences. Bajazet concentrates his conditional sentences in four scenes, two with Atalide (II, 5, and III, 4), one each with Acomat (II, 3) and with Roxane (V, 4). The only pattern that emerges from these sentences is that they occur only in scenes where Bajazet is saying what he really thinks. He takes a resigned attitude with Acomat, but indicates that he is willing to be rescued by force of arms if his life is precious to them and if it is necessary (vv. 627-30). With Atalide, Bajazet's greatest concern is what may happen to her, even claiming that he would have told Roxane everything if he had not feared dangerous consequence for Atalide (vv. 701-2; 749-52). In a later interview with Atalide, Bajazet again reveals his misgivings and his inability to forgive himself for what he is about to do.

Vous n'avez plus, Madame, à craindre pour ma vie;
Et je serois heureux, *si* la foi, *si* l'honneur
Ne me reprochoit point mon injuste bonheur;
Si mon cœur, dont le trouble en secret me condamne,
Pouvoit me pardonner aussi bien que Roxane.

             (942-46)

When Roxane confronts him with the letter to Atalide written in his own hand, Bajazet immediately capitulates. Emphasizing the temptation of the Empire, Roxane's unwillingness to take no for an answer, and his own silence, Bajazet claims that he would have rewarded Roxane properly if things had worked out.

Et *si* l'effet enfin, suivant mon espérance,
Eût ouvert un champ libre à ma reconnoissance,
J'aurois par tant d'honneurs, par tant de dignités
Contenté votre orgueil, et payé vos bontés,
Que vous-même peut-être . . .

             (1521-25)

By interrupting him Roxane demonstrates her disbelief, or at least her disinterest in that kind of compensation. When Roxane then indicates that Bajazet can redeem himself by sanctioning Atalide's death, he pleads with her in vain and she again interrupts him, this time signaling his death in a single word.

> Bajazet: Ajoutez cette grâce à tant d'autres bontés,
>   Madame; et *si* jamais je vous fus cher . . .
> Roxane: Sortez.
>
>   (1563-64)

By the same token, Atalide uses conditional sentences when she is revealing her thoughts and feelings; half of them are addressed to her confidante, Zaïre. But the ones addressed to Roxane are designed to persuade her to defend the seraglio against Amurat (v. 1198) or, in the false confession, to persuade her that she, Atalide, is alone responsible for deceiving her (v. 1586). Acomat alone restricts himself to conditional sentences, eight of them, based in the present tense. None is contrary to fact; he apparently has no illusions.

Roxane, however, often uses conditional sentences to threaten others directly or indirectly in the hope of obtaining desired responses. Her threats toward Bajazet become shorter and more explicit as they become more intense and violent. In general terms she explains first to Atalide what assurances she expects of Bajazet.

> Peut-être trop d'amour me rend trop difficile;
> Mais sans vous fatiguer d'un récit inutile,
> Je ne retrouvois point ce trouble, cette ardeur
> Que m'avoit tant promis un discours trop flatteur.
> Enfin *si* je lui donne et la vie et l'Empire,
> Ces gages incertains ne me peuvent suffire.
>
>   (281-86)

When Atalide asks naively what assurances Roxane has in mind, the latter replies in no uncertain terms: "S'il m'aime, dès ce jour il me doit épouser" (288). Roxane then launches into a *tirade* on the Sultans and their customs. Near the end of the *tirade* Roxane repeats her demand and adds an ultimatum:

> Malgré tout mon amour, *si* dans cette journée
> Il ne m'attache à lui par un juste hyménée,

S'il ose m'alléguer une odieuse loi;
Quand je fais tout pour lui, s'il ne fait tout pour moi:
Dès le même moment, sans songer si je l'aime,
Sans consulter enfin si je me perds moi-même,
J'abandonne l'ingrat, et le laisse rentrer
Dans l'état malheureux d'où je l'ai su tirer.

(317-24)

These are truly conditions imposed on Bajazet. Extra force is attained through the opposition in "*When* I do everything for him, *if* he doesn't do everything for me" and by her use of present tense rather than future in the main clause: "J'abandonne l'ingrat et le laisse rentrer. . . ."

Two scenes later (II, 1) Roxane confronts Bajazet personally with the conditions and only slightly veiled threats.

Mais avez-vous prévu, si vous ne m'épousez,
Les périls plus certains où vous vous exposez?

(503-4)

S'il m'échappoit un mot, c'est fait de votre vie.

(542)

        Ah! crois-tu, quand il [Amurat] le voudroit bien,
Que si je perds l'espoir de régner dans le tien,
D'une si douce erreur si longtemps possédée,
Je puisse désormais souffrir une autre idée,
Ni que je vive enfin, si je ne vis pour toi?

(547-51)

The two *si* clauses, although separated, are parallel in the last quotation. The clause introduced by *quand* is significant also, since it too could have been conditional. It is not and thus represents an assumption, an enormous one; it has the force of *quand même* (even when, or even if). Assuming that Amurat is willing, Roxane is sure that she herself could not live with the idea. In Act V, this time talking to Zatime, Roxane reemphasizes Bajazet's precarious position in explicit terms: "Je puis le retenir. Mais *s*'il sort, il est mort" (1456). The concentrated expression of Roxane's all-or-nothing approach to Bajazet in her final conditional sentence at the same time prepares the fatal "Sortez."

Subordination: *Sans* + Infinitive

The construction of *sans* + infinitive appears in thirty-six of the 1050 sentences in *Bajazet* (3.4%). All major characters use this construction, but Roxane leads with twelve such sentences. There does not seem to be any special pattern to their use, although Atalide's examples occur only when she is talking to her confidante (4 times). Roxane uses the construction with most of her interlocutors, but concentrates half of them in one scene with Atalide. (See, for instance, vv. 321-22, quoted above.) This is the scene in which Roxane reveals to Atalide her hesitation as well as her determination to make marriage with Bajazet the deciding factor; with one exception these sentences deal with Bajazet. Unfortunately, however, these bits of information add little to the total understanding of the characters in *Bajazet*.

Two names recur repeatedly in opposition to each other: Atalide and Roxane. It has already been shown that (1) they both have decisively shorter sentences on the average than do the other characters; (2) they both show uncertainty and hesitation in carrying out a course of action; (3) Roxane deals in threats aimed at promoting a marriage with Bajazet; (4) in their third encounter Roxane manages to put Atalide on the defensive. It is also true that (5) Atalide specializes in lies aimed at preserving Bajazet's life. Is this rivalry over Bajazet the driving force behind the tragedy? Perhaps this conflict deserves a more systematic approach to its evolution.

Early in the play (I, 3) Roxane declares her basic plan: to marry Bajazet and to take over the reins of power. Assuming Atalide to be trustworthy, Roxane first declares this plan to her. By her questions Roxane reveals uncertainty about Bajazet's intentions; it is in her conditional sentences that Roxane sets forth the ultimatum regarding Bajazet. Atalide says little in this scene except to reassure Roxane of Bajazet's affection. She does let slip one astonished remark: "Vous épouser! O ciel! que prétendez-vous faire?" (289). Roxane, however, passes over the remark, apparently assuming that Atalide is shocked by the breach of the law and customs that such a marriage would entail.

Only after Roxane has gone does Atalide fully reveal her dismay. The

four short sentences of type B that break the rhythm of her *récit* reveal
fear that Bajazet will not be able to lie to Roxane so effectively as she
herself had. "Et moi, je ne puis rien" (383). "Hélas! tout est fini" (389).
"Bajazet va se perdre" (395). "Il se perdra, te dis-je" (402).

In their second encounter (III, 6) Roxane wonders about Bajazet's recent cool responses. Atalide attempts in vain to reassure Roxane and thus
to regain control over the situation. When Atalide lies, her sentences are
regular and declarative; on this occasion she does introduce one long
question to suggest an explanation for Bajazet's actions (vv. 1049-56).

ATALIDE: A A A A A
         . . . . ?

The second time that Atalide attempts to explain away Bajazet's attitude,
Roxane interrupts her.

Roxane: Vous parlez mieux pour lui qu'il ne parle lui-même.
Atalide: Et quel autre intérêt . . .
Roxane: Madame, c'est assez.
                                                        (1058-59)

As Roxane becomes more and more suspicious, she begins to take over
control of the situation from Atalide. In the monologue that immediately
follows, Roxane reveals all her uncertainties. The frequency of questions
is overwhelming, although the monologue is fairly regular.

ROXANE: A A A A B E A A A A A A A A A B E A A A A A A A A B E B
        ? ? ? ? ! ! ? ? ? . . ? ? . ? ? ? ? ? ? ? ? ? ? @ ? ?

The three sets of short sentences are, of course, significant.

Bajazet interdit! Atalide étonnée! (1069)
Quel seroit son dessein? Qu'a-t-elle fait pour lui? (1083)
Que de justes raisons . . . Mais qui vient me parler?
Que veut-on?   (1095-96)

By the third encounter Atalide completely loses control because of
Roxane's decision to obey the returning Amurat. Another monologue
follows this encounter; here Roxane has fewer questions, because her

uncertainty regarding Atalide has been resolved. She reproaches herself for facilitating meetings between Atalide and Bajazet. Her decision is to wait and see what Bajazet does. However regular and declarative her final sentences may be, they are born of violent intent.

Je saurai bien toujours retrouver le moment
De punir, s'il le faut, la rivale et l'amant.
Dans ma juste fureur observant le perfide,
Je saurai le surprendre avec son Atalide;
Et d'un même poignard les unissant tous deux,
Les percer l'un et l'autre, et moi-même après eux.
Voilà, n'en doutons point, le parti qu'il faut prendre.
Je veux tout ignorer.

(1243-50)

Her apparent calm is shattered (IV, 5) as Zatime brings her Bajazet's letter of reassurance to Atalide. Caught up in (a) the tension, and then in (b) the actual discovery, Roxane uses many short sentences:

(a)   Ah! que viens-tu m'apprendre,
          Zatime? Bajazet en est-il amoureux?

(1250-51)

          Donne. Pourquoi frémir? (1263)
          Il peut même . . . (1266)

(b)   Qu'il meure. Vengeons-nous. (1277)
          Tu pleures, malheureuse? [à elle-même] (1308)
          Ah! traître, tu mourras. Quoi? tu n'es point partie?
          Va.   (1314-15)
          Va, retiens-la. Surtout garde bien le silence.
          Moi . . . Mais qui vient ici différer ma vengeance?

(1329-30)

Despite her transports, Roxane, like Hermione, is not sure that she wants Bajazet's death. When Acomat offers to assassinate him, Roxane hesitates. Later she gives Bajazet another chance to redeem himself, but only if he will sanction Atalide's death.

The fourth and final meeting between Roxane and Atalide occurs in V, 6. This is Atalide's final attempt to regain control over Roxane and to prevent her doing harm to Bajazet. In this false confession she attempts to spare Bajazet by assuming all the guilt and by offering to commit suicide. Consisting entirely of lies, the confession is basically regular and declarative.

ATALIDE: A A A A A A A A A A A B E A A A A A A B EA
. . . . ! . . . . ? . . . .

Roxane hears her out but is unconvinced: ironically, she has just sent Bajazet to his death.

Bajazet is little more than a pawn caught between Atalide and Roxane. Although his main concern appears to be protecting Atalide, Bajazet is basically a rational, rather than an emotional character; at least that is the way he talks. His whole sentence structure indicates that he maintains emotional equilibrium as he is buffeted back and forth. In this respect Bajazet is quite unlike Britannicus. Political considerations are important, probably more central to this tragedy than in previous Racinian tragedies. Acomat is motivated almost completely by political considerations. Although precipitated in large measure by Amurat's return, the denouement depends primarily on the resolution of the conflict between Roxane and Atalide over possession of Bajazet.

Atalide is on the defensive during the entire play, trying to prevent something from happening. By lying to Roxane about Bajazet's amorous interests, Atalide is able to postpone Bajazet's death at the hands of Roxane. On the other hand, Roxane has been trying to cause something to happen. By offering him the throne, Roxane is able to delude herself about Bajazet's intentions. She discovers the truth and ultimately wills Bajazet's death. Although control passes from Atalide to Roxane, the latter is unable to maintain control because of Bajazet and because of Amurat's messenger Orcan. Thus both women fail to obtain what they want and, more important, the person whom they want. Both die as a result. This denouement is in fact the bloodiest since *La Thébaïde*. Although other characters contribute to the atmosphere of violent conflict, it is Roxane's all-or-nothing approach to Bajazet that most significantly contributes to setting the violent tone of this tragedy. Atalide appears to have a calming effect, but in fact her deception, once uncovered, pushes Roxane to violence and death.

Mithridate

Comparison of *Mithridate* to the four tragedies of Racine already examined shows that distribution of both terminal punctuation and of sentence type is here well within Racine's normal range. The number of ellipses is, however, fairly high. Conditional sentences remain frequent but do not reach the level of Bajazet; the sentences using *quand / lorsque* are about as infrequent as might now be expected. Internal questions are again relatively few in number, as are internal exclamations. Alongside these nondistinctive features, it is surprising to discover the highest mean sentence length thus far: 21.928 syllables per sentence, about 0.5 syllables per sentence above the level of *Britannicus*. Even Monime, who averages the shortest sentences in *Mithridate*, is in the 20-21 syllable range, a far cry from the 17-18 minimum of the four previous plays. The span of mean sentence length is less than three syllables from Xipharès to Monime; this split is not unlike that between Bajazet and Atalide:

Xipharès	23.246
confidants	22.991
Pharnace	22.000
---MEAN------------	21.928---
Mithridate	21.777
Monime	20.692

The level from act to act also varies in an interesting way. Acts I and V have the highest levels (23.365 and 23.429 respectively). Acts II and III are not far below, in the 21-22 syllable range. In Act IV the level drops off to a surprising 19.853, surprising because even Monime averages nearly one syllable per sentence above that level. A similar phenomenon was observed in *Bajazet*. What then happens in Act IV to cause characters to shorten their sentences? Nothing obvious. It is true that passions and emotions dominate the act; political considerations are temporarily forgotten. The consequences of Mithridate's ruse make themselves felt on Xipharès and Monime. Mithridate again confronts Monime with a marriage proposal and is greeted with surprise and refusal. Only in the brief scenes that close the fourth act do political considerations come again to the fore as Arbate and Arcas announce the arrival of the Romans and Pharnace's complicity. Accompanying the relatively long mean sentence length in the play is the noticeably increased number of distichs. In fact, they predominate over the monostichs in Acts I and V, as well as in the sentences of Xipharès, Pharnace, and the confidants.

At the same time, the number of rapid exchanges between characters has diminished. They would be nonexistent except for critical moments when a piece of news is brought, almost breathlessly, to the characters on the stage. In Act I (4), Phœdime brings news of Mithridate's imminent return.

PHOEDIME:	A	.
MONIME:	B	!
XIPHARÈS;	M	!
PHARNACE:	E	?
PHOEDIME:	A	.
XIPHARÈS:	B	?
MONIME:	M E	. !

The two parts of Phœdime's message (three-line regular and declarative sentences) are followed by the brief reactions of those present. A similar pattern occurs when Arcas arrives to announce Pharnace's treason and the arrival of the Romans (IV, 7) and when Arbate arrives in time to prevent Monime from taking the poison (V,3).

Coordination: *Et, Ou,* and *Mais*

The conjunction *et* can of course link any parallel elements of a sentence: nouns, adjectives, main clauses, dependent clauses, etcetera. In a series of parallel elements, the conjunction *et* normally occurs only before the final member of a series. As such, this conjunction is an approximate measure of a sentence's complexity or, more precisely, its compoundness. It is not illogical to suppose that this feature would be more likely to occur in longer sentences than in shorter ones. A positive correlation exists between the use of *et* and mean sentence length: the longer a character's sentences, the more frequently he uses this conjunction. In *Mithridate* the percentages of sentences containing *et* are as follows:

	confidants	37.7%
	Xipharès	36.0
	Pharnace	35.2
-------(MEAN)---------	Mithridate---------	33.5---
	Monime	29.2

The major characters fall into the same order as they did for sentence length. The confidants admittedly show a higher frequency of *et* than might be expected. The case is approximately the same with regard to *Bajazet*. (Tables 5 and 9 in Appendix C summarize these features for all plays.)

Acomat	33.5%
Bajazet	32.3
---MEAN------------	26.5---
confidants	25.2
Roxane	24.0
Atalide	22.1

Moreover, the averages for the plays are correlated: longer sentences in *Mithridate* correspond to greater frequency of *et*. A note of caution is in order. Correlation means that these two variables, frequency of *et* and mean sentence length, change at the same time and in the same way: when one increases, the other increases; when one decreases, the other decreases. This does not necessarily imply a causal relationship between the two features. The variation from act to act, for instance, does not correspond so neatly.

	Bajazet	*Mithridate*
Act I	32.4%	32.3%
Act II	27.0	33.8
Act III	22.4	30.4
Act IV	20.8	32.5
Act V	30.4	11.3

The general trend in *Bajazet* is similar for the two variables: decreasing through Act IV with a marked increase in Act V. In *Mithridate* Acts I-III correspond reasonably well, but the frequency of *et* is far too high in Acts IV and V to match the mean sentence length. At this time it is risky to affirm more than the basic correlation. Chapter 8 demonstrates that the conjunction *et* has an important function in versification. In any case this feature of sentence structure substantiates useful information already gleaned from mean sentence length, but offers no new insights into characterization.

The conjunction *ou* is almost equally distributed among the characters and acts of these two plays; it appears in up to five percent of the sentences in any category. The average frequency for the two plays is quite close: *Bajazet* has 2.7% and *Mithridate* 1.9%. This difference is insignificant, particularly when compared to the seven percent spread with *et*. The same is true with *mais*, although it occurs more frequently than *ou*: *Bajazet* has 9.2% and *Mithridate* 7.6%.

Because of the long sentences and the long series of sentences in *Mithridate* and because of the nondistinctive nature of most other features of sentence structure, this section examines instead the variations in the *tirade*: the *récit*, which abounds in this tragedy, the varied formats for *tirades*, based on terminal punctuation and sentence type, and the situations in which the *tirade* is used by Mithridate himself.

The *récit*, as previously defined, is a series of regular and declarative sentences with only an occasional departure from that format. A *récit*, as its name indicates, is expository and is designed to provide information on background and on important happenings off stage. After preliminary exchanges with Arbate, Xipharès launches the tragedy in I, 1, with a *récit*.

XIPHARÈS: EA A A A A A B EA A A A A A A A B EA A A A A
A A A A A A A A A A A A
. . . ? . . . . . ! . ! . . . .

The breaks in regularity show that Xipharès is not disinterested in the events that he is relating: he is talking about his love for Monime, the history of their involvement, Pharnace, Mithridate, in short the present situation. His shortest sentence contains three syllables, "Je la vis," and his longest 72. These are, however, neither his shortest nor his longest in the tragedy. The mean sentence length here is 28.824, considerably higher than even his average. Here the sentence forming a quatrain is as frequent as both the monostich and the distich (eight occurrences of each). Several sentences contain *quand* constructions; none is conditional. The same is basically true of other *récits* in *Mithridate*.

	Mithridate (III,1)	Arbate (V, 4)	Xipharès (IV, 2)
Mean sentence length	28.174	33.273	25.714
Monostichs	6	6	2
Distichs	19	8	10
Quatrains	8	2	2
Range of sentence length	6-108	12-96	12-48

With regard to basic features, the *récit* is one type of *tirade*, consisting of neutral terminal punctuation (period), neutral sentence type (type A), and unusually long sentences, especially distichs and quatrains. Within the first two categories, different combinations produce different formats for other *tirades*; either one or the other, or both, categories may be affective rather than neutral. All three of these possibilities occur in *Mithridate*. In I, 3, for instance, Monime refuses Pharnace's advances in a *tirade* consisting entirely of declarative sentences. Her sequence of sentence types belies the apparent neutrality of the terminal punctuation.

MONIME: E A B EA A AB EA A B EA A AB EA

. . . .

Here Monime emphasizes her obligations to Mithridate and her hatred for all things Roman through her type B sentences in particular: "Mithridate me vit" (251)., "Il fallut obéir" (255)., "J'y vins: j'y suis encor" (261)., "Enfin, je n'ai qu'un cœur" (271). Mastering her utterances, Monime makes clear to Pharnace that she is offended by his offer of marriage. Mithridate uses the same format in his second monologue (III,6), in which he ponders the fate of Xipharès.

MITHRIDATE: B E B E B EA A B EA

. . . .

The King's short type B sentences are significant here as well. 'Ils s'aiment" (1117)., "Ah! fils ingrat" (1118)., "Tu périras" (1119). This time anger, resentment, and desire for revenge cause Mithridate to shorten sentences and to break the rhythm of the *alexandrin.*

On the other hand, sentence types can be regular while the terminal punctuation is affective. Following his father's *récit* of plans to march on Rome, Pharnace first "admires" Mithridate's plan and then suggests appeasement as an alternative (III, 1).

PHARNACE: A A A A A A A A A A A A A A A
. . . ? ? . ? ? ? ? . ? ? ? . @

His questions are carefully calculated to throw doubt on both the possibility and the necessity of such a campaign (vv. 869-70; 881-86). Phœdime argues in similar fashion with Monime that Mithridate would not stoop to subterfuge in order to obtain a confession from her (IV, 1).

PHŒDIME: A A A A A A A
? ? . ? . . ? ?

Phœdime, like Pharnace, uses questions to convince her listener of the truth in what she says (vv. 1147-49; 1151; 1159-60).

One other possibility exists, that of modifying both terminal punctuation and sentence type. This is the case in Mithridate's first monologue (III, 4). Here the King is tempted to believe what Pharnace has just told him about Xipharès and Monime, and debates the appropriate course of action to uncover the truth.

MITHRIDATE: B E A A A A A A A A AB E A A B E B E A A A A AB EA
? ! . ? ? ? ? @ ? ! . @ . . . . . ? . . @ .

These two features conspire to convey Mithridate's uncertainty as well as his anger. Obviously, all possible combinations of neutral or affective terminal punctuation and sentence types actually occur in the *tirades* of *Mithridate.* Radical modification of sentence type alone indicates either loss of control or effort to maintain control in a difficult moment. Modification of terminal punctuation, primarily the use of questions here, indicates that a character is trying to produce a desired reaction in his interlocutor: information and emotional reactions freely given or extorted. Disturbances in both features simultaneously indicate violent emotion and often loss of control.

Another way of looking at the *tirade* emphasizes the context: the interlocutor, the topics of discussion, and the general situation. Mithridate is the best example. Not counting the short transitional scenes, Mithridate appears on the stage in thirteen scenes out of a total of 29. Mithridate also accounts for 34.3% of the sentences. On one occasion he talks to Arbate; on three he discusses the present situation with one or both of his sons, the third occasion being a series of three scenes; on three occasions he confronts his fiancée, Monime; three times the King reflects alone on recent developments; and in the final scene of the tragedy Mithridate addresses the characters assembled for the denouement. The basically military discussions with his sons occur early in the play, so that by the beginning of Act III Mithridate is ready to detail to Xiphares and Pharnace his plan of attack on Rome. Thereafter his scenes alternate between monologue and confrontation in dialogue:

III, 4: MONOLOGUE on the possibility of love affair between Xiphares and Monime.

III, 5: DIALOGUE with Monime in which Mithridate tests his hypothesis by suggesting to Monime that she marry Xiphares.

III, 6: MONOLOGUE on the implications of what Monime has revealed and on his proposed plan of action.

IV, 4: DIALOGUE with Monime in which Mithridate reaffirms his desire to marry her.

IV, 5: MONOLOGUE on the alternatives open to him.

V, 5: DIALOGUE with remaining characters in which Mithridate reviews his conquests and generously pardons Monime and Xiphares, urging them to carry on the war with Rome.

The two elements of politics or war and love are only occasionally discussed separately by Mithridate. Regardless of where he begins a conversation, the other topic is present in his mind and eventually in his speech.

In his only scene with Arbate (II, 3) Mithridate recites his recent military difficulties before interrogating Arbate about the presence of his two sons in Nymphée. These are real questions.

Mais tous deux en ces lieux que pouvoient-ils attendre?
L'un et l'autre à la Reine ont-ils osé prétendre?
Avec qui semble-t-elle en secret s'accorder?
Moi-même de quel œil dois-je ici l'aborder?

(475-78)

By his concise imperatives to Arbate, Mithridate emphasizes his urgent
need to know the facts. "Ecoute" (463)., "Parle" (479). Then Mithridate
momentarily loses control of himself, pouring out his apprehensions.
"Qu'est-ce qui s'est passé? Qu'as-tu vu? Que sais-tu? / Depuis quel temps,
pourquoi, comment t'es-tu rendu?" (481-82). Monime appears, however,
before the King can get satisfactory answers from Arbate. His initial tone
with her is that of the gallant lover finally proposing marriage; it is
characterized by regular and calculated statements.

MITHRIDATE: A A A A A A A
             . . . .

In light of Monime's cool resignation to her fate, the King's tone changes
to reproach, indicated by regular and calculated questions.

MITHRIDATE: A A A A A A A A A A
             . ? ? ? . ? ? ? . .

That one lone declarative sentence amid the questions is a long (twelve
full lines) and complicated one, in which Mithridate delineates the
esteem in which others would continue to hold him if he were completely
defeated.

Ah! pour tenter encor de nouvelles conquêtes,
Quand je ne verrois pas des routes toutes prêtes,
Quand le sort ennemi m'auroit jeté plus bas,
Vaincu, persécuté, sans secours, sans États,
Errant de mers en mers, et moins roi que pirate,
Conservant pour tous biens le nom de Mithridate,
Apprenez que suivi d'un nom si glorieux,
Partout de l'univers j'attacherois les yeux;
Et qu'il n'est point de rois, *s*'ils sont dignes de l'être,
Qui, sur le trône assis, n'enviassent peut-être

Au-dessus de leur gloire un naufrage élevé,
Que Rome et quarante ans ont à peine achevé.

(559-70)

Even under those dire conditions, hypothetical of course, kings and princes would envy the glory of Mithridate; how can Monime not be eager to marry him under the present and considerably more favorable circumstances? Monime repeats that she will obey. From ineffective reproaches, the King moves on to accusations that her alleged interest in Pharnace prevents her from consenting wholeheartedly to marry the King. Mithridate's agitation is all the more apparent when he summons Xipharès and expresses the same accusations to his son. While the *tirade* is regular and declarative except for one exclamation, Mithridate reveals his anger and his determination in other ways. Through a series of verbs the King ascribes infamy to Pharnace.

Venez, mon fils, venez, votre père est trahi.
Un fils audacieux *insulte* à ma ruine,
Traverse mes desseins, *m'outrage*, *m'assassine*,
Aime la Reine enfin, lui *plaît*, et me *ravit*
Un cœur que son devoir à moi seul asservit.

(606-10)

After assuring Xipharès of his confidence in him and briefly sketching his military projects, Mithridate issues a series of imperatives to his son.

Vous cependant ici *veillez* pour mon repos;
D'un rival insolent *arrêtez* les complots.
Ne *quittez* point la Reine; et s'il se peut, vous-même
Rendez-la moins contraire aux vœux d'un roi qui l'aime.
Détournez-la, mon fils, d'un choix injurieux.

(625-29)

At the beginning of Act III, Mithridate returns to his military projects in order to develop them fully in the presence of his two sons. The King begins with a *récit* that is unusual in that it narrates future events rather than past ones. It projects Mithridate's general plan to conquer Rome along with the stages of the conquest, as if the actions had already been realized. Having outlined the project and the strategy, Mithridate issues a call to arms, ostensibly to both sons, in a series of first-person-plural imperatives.

> *Marchons*; et dans son sein *rejetons* cette guerre
> Que sa fureur envoie aux deux bouts de la terre.
> *Attaquons* dans leurs murs ces conquérants si fiers;
> Qu'ils tremblent, à leur tour, pour leurs propres foyers.
> Annibal l'a prédit, *croyons*-en ce grand homme,
> Jamais on ne vaincra les Romains que dans Rome.
> *Noyons*-la dans son sang justement répandu.
> *Brûlons* ce Capitole où j'étois attendu.
> *Détruisons* ses honneurs, et *faisons* disparaître
> La honte de cent rois, et la mienne peut-être;
> Et la flamme à la main *effaçons* tous ces noms
> Que Rome y consacroit à d'éternels affronts.

(831-42)

In the next section of his *tirade* Mithridate adroitly separates Pharnace from this project in a series of second-person imperatives that send him off to a politically expedient marriage. Mithridate illustrates once again that declarative sentences are not necessarily so neutral as they might seem; his imperatives give this *tirade* its special vigor.

Lofty plans trail off as Pharnace tries to dissuade his father and as Xipharès offers to go in his father's stead, his offer based on Monime's insistence that Xipharès flee her presence. When he has heard enough, Mithridate cuts Pharnace off and then adds a threat in the form of a conditional sentence reminiscent of Roxane: "Prince, vous m'entendez, / Et vous êtes perdu *si* vous me répondez" (965-66). Suddenly accusations fly. Mithridate accuses Pharnace of stalling because of Monime; Pharnace immediately accuses Xipharès.

Alone shortly thereafter, Mithridate expresses in a series of first-person-plural imperatives his intention of testing Monime by deceiving her. Here he includes only himself in *"voyons, examinons," "trompons," "feignons."* These imperatives are less noble than the previous ones, a distinction that serves to underscore the two aspects of his personality: noble warrior and jealous scheming lover. Nevertheless, even in his noble military projects, Mithridate is not above scheming.

Face to face with Monime (III, 5) Mithridate resorts to sarcastic imperatives in the hope of unnerving her.

Hé bien! n'en *parlons* plus, Madame.
Continuez: *brûlez* d'une honteuse flamme.
Tandis qu'avec mon fils je vais, loin de vos yeux,
Chercher au bout du monde un trépas glorieux,
Vous cependant ici *servez* avec son frère,[1]
Et *vendez* aux Romains le sang de votre père.
Venez.

(1083-89)

When he has finally pushed Monime into telling all, Mithridate is clearly
unnerved himself.

MITHRIDATE: B M E B M E A B
. . . .

Non, Madame. Il suffit. Je vais vous l'envoyer.
Allez. Le temps est cher. Il le faut employer.
Je vois qu'à m'obéir vous êtes disposée.
Je suis content.

(1113-16)

Beneath the King's apparent control, even Monime perceives the truth:
"O ciel! me serois-je abusée?" (1116). In his next scene with Monime (IV,
4) Mithridate uses imperatives in vain to promote their marriage. In fact,
Monime picks up the technique in her responses: "*Jugez*-en . . ." (1362).
"Après cela, *jugez*. *Perdez* une rebelle; / *Armez-vous* du pouvoir qu'on
vous donna sur elle" (1371-72). "*Croyez*. . . ." (1375). The state of mind
in which Monime leaves the King is evident in the monologue that follows
(IV, 5):

MITHRIDATE: B EA A B M E A A A A A A A B E A A A A A B EA
A A A A A A A A A
! ? ? ? ? ? . , ... ? ! ? ? ? ? ? . ? . ! @ . ? ? ! ! . ! ?

His surprise and confusion are complete. How could this be happening to
him? "Qui suis-je? Est-ce Monime? Et suis-je Mithridate?" (1383). This
line is reminiscent of one in his early conversation with Arbate (v. 481) as
well as of Hermione's famous "Où suis-je? Qu'ai-je fait? Que dois-je faire
encore?" (*Andromaque*, 1393). The King hastily outlines three murders,
using first-person-plural imperatives. Coming to himself, he recalls how

important Xipharès is to his military ambitions and resolves rather to work around the situation. "*Songeons* plutôt, *songeons* à gagner sa tendresse: / J'ai besoin d'un vengeur, et non d'une maîtresse" (1399-1400). This is one of two brief preparations for the denouement.[2] Nevertheless, the King hesitates to hand Monime over to his son. Mithridate does not reappear until the final scene of the tragedy. Wounded and dying, he returns with Xipharès to assure the continuity of the struggle against Rome. Only after passing in review his own victories for the benefit of all those assembled does Mithridate praise Xipharès. The King instructs his son through a series of imperatives on fighting the Romans. As his father dies, Xipharès adopts the imperative form in a subdued call to arms and to vengeance.

> Ah! Madame, *unissons* nos douleurs,
> Et par tout l'univers *cherchons*-lui des vengeurs.
>
> (1697-98)

The whole tragedy revolves around Mithridate, for on him depends the fate of all the other characters. Two sides of his nature are in conflict. He is a resolute warrior determined to continue fighting against Roman aggression; this primary concern eventually takes precedence. Unable, however, to ignore the domestic situation, Mithridate seems several times to be on the verge of giving that situation priority by seeking vengeance for his sons' amorous interest in Monime. Maurice Descotes comments, and rightly so, that these two aspects of Mithridate's character are not well integrated; that fact makes the role a difficult one to play and to analyze (*Les Grands Rôles*, pp. 116-17). Not only that, but his petty schemes for forcing information out of Monime are not commensurate with his lofty dreams of conquest. This difference is most clearly represented in his use of imperatives.

In a larger perspective, the *tirade* is a flexible tool. Differences produced by change of situation and interlocutor are significant: to Xipharès and Pharnace the King reveals his military plans; to Arbate and in monologues he reveals his uncertainty, his anger, and his indecision; with Monime he plays roles designed to discern her state of mind. Variations of basic sentence patterns are even more significant, since they actually reveal to the audience what Mithridate is doing and how he schemes, as well as how much control he is exercising over himself and over the situation.

Conclusion

Roxane and Mithridate have several traits in common. They share the same uncertainties regarding the person they love and are treated with the same coolness when they propose marriage. Both have absolute power over the fate of that one person. They both reveal extensively their thoughts and feelings in monologues and to other characters. But Roxane manages to integrate her political and amorous interests. Everything hinges on Bajazet, however, in a way that matters in *Mithridate* do not hinge on Monime. And Bajazet has shown himself to be reluctant on both political and amorous accounts. Roxane's most distinctive mode of expression is the threat, both direct and indirect, particularly evident in her conditional sentences. Her threats are real: she has the power of life and death over Bajazet and, although she does hesitate, Roxane is quite capable of sending him to a certain death when other plans fail. The level of violence in this tragedy is extraordinarily high, whether measured physically by the number of bloody deaths or emotionally by Roxane's menacing attitude. She schemes to the extent that, as her suspicions grow, she has Bajazet and Atalide watched more and more closely. She discovers the letter, however, as if by accident. There is no development in her character, only a growing realization of Bajazet and Atalide's love for each other and therefrom a growing violence and directness in her threats.

Mithridate, despite his military conquests and ambitions, is a less violent person than Roxane. Perhaps this is true in part because his political ambitions and his love interests are always working at cross purposes; the situation is such that the King must choose between the two. His suspicions are also divided between his two sons. Once they discover that their father is not dead as had been reported, Xipharès and Pharnace cease to compete actively for Monime, whereas Atalide continues to compete for Bajazet. Mithridate does not deal in threats but rather in imperatives: a call to arms for Xipharès or to obedience for Pharnace, and sarcasm for Monime. In the course of the tragedy Mithridate is unable to integrate his two aspirations. The general trend shown by studying the *tirades* is from preoccupation with military problems and lofty plans of conquest to preoccupation with jealousy and revenge, petty schemes, and ruses. As the play draws to a close Mithridate finally chooses at the end of Act IV to give priority to fighting the Romans, thus giving Monime up to Xipharès and at the same time redeeming his image of himself. In this respect Mithridate is reminiscent of Titus; as in *Bérénice*, the King's choice is the one that he must make as king. Like Titus, Mithridate lacks Roxane's singleness of purpose and to that extent her momentum. This distinction is reflected in the level of violence of the tragedies as well as in the mental state of the characters. In *Bajazet* the violence and conflicts are highly charged and physical; in *Mithridate* violence and conflict are mainly verbal. And as Mithridate dies, the young lovers, Xipharès and Monime, are united at the final curtain, for they have succeeded in integrating the two opposing preoccupations of Mithridate.

Previously introduced features of sentence structure take on new importance in *Bajazet* and *Mithridate*. Roxane is the first and only Racinian character who completely integrates the conditional sentence as the expression of her basic stance in *Bajazet*. Not only do rapid-fire exchanges recur but they are also transformed into rapid-fire scenes that present the denouement of *Bajazet* in whirlwind fashion. Study of the *tirade* in *Mithridate* reveals new flexibility in the interplay of terminal punctuation and sentence type as well as the special use of imperatives by Mithridate himself. On the other hand, newly introduced features, *sans* + infinitive and the conjunctions *et*, *ou*, and *mais*, fail to add significantly to the analysis of *Bajazet* and *Mithridate*, although they do not contradict interpretations based on other features. It is becoming increasingly clear that Racine's technique of characterization through language depends on selected features of sentence structure, each used to a different degree.

Notes to Chapter 4

1. The first hemistich of verse 1087 is identical to that of a verse quoted above: "Vous cependant ici *veillez* pour mon repos" (625). See also my comment in Chapter 8 on this hemistich in relation to versification.

2. The other occurs later in this same monologue and deals with Mithridate's extraordinary resistance to poisons (vv. 1413-16).

$$\begin{bmatrix} 5 \\ \textit{Iphigénie} \end{bmatrix}$$

With *Iphigénie* Racine returns to ancient Greek sources. It is a difficult tragedy to discuss, since interest is concentrated neither in one character, as it will be in *Phèdre*, nor in a situation of violent conflict as it had been in previous tragedies, but is distributed among a number of characters, several of whom are more passive than might be expected in the face of a situation involving Iphigénie's very life. In fact, the whole situation lacks forcefulness, since only Achille actively seeks to orient the denouement. Iphigénie, the submissive victim, and even Agamemnon the king are mere spectators to what happens. Violent only in her verbal opposition to the plan, Clytemnestre puts the King in a bad light with her sarcasm and threats and urges Achille to oppose the sacrifice actively. Only the intrepid Achille throws himself into the conflict.

Nevertheless, the general distribution of basic sentence characteristics in *Iphigénie* is not unusual. Given the expository nature of his role, Ulysse understandably leads in the use of declarative sentences (76.1%), a full thirteen percent above the mean; in type A sentences (79.1%) and in mean sentence length (26.746) Ulysse possesses the highest level yet attained by a Racinian character. Ériphile, the other functional character, also has usually long sentences. At no time does Ulysse influence the action; representing in the first act the attitude of the Greeks, he urges Agamemnon to proceed with the sacrifice of his daughter; he does not reappear until the fifth act, where his function is to relate the denouement to Clytemnestre. Ériphile, on the other hand, appears in Acts II through IV and, unlike Ulysse, actually influences the action. From Act II to Act IV her resentment increases against Achille and Iphigénie; her sentences become more and more irregular as the tragedy progresses until in Act IV her type A sentences account for only 45.7% of her utterances. She opens Act IV by reflecting on recent turns of events with her confidante, Doris. Despite the ominous oracle, Ériphile doubts that Iphigénie's death is imminent, especially because of Achille's active opposition to it. She often uses short sentences: "Favorables périls! Espérance inutile!" (1093). "Et tu la plains, Doris?" (1103). "Mais que dis-je, expirer?" (1106). "Tout le camp n'en sait rien" (1117). "Et que fera-t-il donc?" (1119). "Ah! *si* je m'en croyois . . ." (1127). Considering how unlikely the proposed sacrifice is, Ériphile begins to formulate a plan to turn the Greeks' attention away from Troy by promoting a rift between Agamemnon and Achille (vv. 1133-40). Ériphile does not appear again until the end of the act, where she decides to put into action this hypothetical plan. Her function *per se* is to inform Calchas of Iphigénie's departure and then to replace Iphigénie as victim for the sacrifice.

Whereas these two functional characters have unusually long sentences, the other characters in *Iphigénie* are found in the more familiar 17-20 syllable-per-sentence range.

Ulysse	26.746
Ériphile	25.109
Iphigénie	20.337
---MEAN------------	20.170---
Achille	19.804
Agamemnon	19.085
confidants	17.867
Clytemnestre	17.701

Clytemnestre seems to be the most volatile of the group. Although Achille uses the interrogative forms statistically more frequently than she (40.7% versus 28.0%), careful analysis of the text reveals that Achille's questions are for the most part real ones directed at a character who should have an answer. Clytemnestre, like Hermione, often uses them as weapons. The most striking example occurs in Act IV, 4, where the Queen all but buries Agamemnon under an avalanche of sarcastic interrogatives.

Quoi? l'horreur de souscrire à cet ordre inhumain
N'a pas, en le traçant, arrêté votre main?
Pourquoi feindre à nos yeux une fausse tristesse?
Pensez-vous par des pleurs prouver votre tendresse?
Où sont-ils, ces combats que vous avez rendus?
Quels flots de sang pour elle avez-vous répandus?
Quel débris parle ici de votre resistance?

Quel champ couvert de morts me condamne au silence?
Voilà par quels témoins il falloit me prouver,
Cruel, que votre amour a voulu la sauver.

(1255-64)

Interrogatives are frequent in this fourth act, where 31.1% of the sentences are questions as compared to the play's average of 27.1%. By a sort of contagion, a number of characters participate in the interrogative mood of Act IV.

Achille	54.8% (of his sentences)
confidants	38.5
Clytemnestre	34.0
Agamemnon	27.5

The figure for Agamemnon is all the more astonishing when compared to his interrogative tendencies in other acts: Act I (12.5%), Act II (6.7%), and Act III (6.3%). The frequency of questions in Agamemnon's speech is the result of confrontations with Clytemnestre and with Achille in Act IV after their discovery of his plan to sacrifice Iphigénie. On the other hand, it is equally striking that Iphigénie does not use a single interrogative in this act—or any other affective terminal punctuation in her eighteen sentences there.

Distribution of sentence length from act to act is unusual. After the first two acts the mean sentence length stabilizes in the 18-19 syllable-per-sentence range.

Act I	24.712
Act II	20.958
Act III	18.980
Act IV	18.333
Act V	18.612

While preceding plays characteristically have a high mean sentence length in the first act, that of *Iphigénie* is the highest thus far. It is a "masculine" act, for Agamemnon has as yet faced neither his wife nor his daughter. Much essential information is reviewed and Agamemnon's initial effort to spare Iphigénie by forestalling her arrival is both planned and thwarted. Despite the basically expository nature of Act I, nearly all the potential *récits* are here punctuated with questions and exclamations.

Even the declarative Ulysse poses numerous questions to Agamemnon (I, 2) and to Achille (I, 3), designed no doubt to encourage Agamemnon to proceed with the sacrifice and to persuade Achille to defer temporarily his marriage plans.

Internal exclamations are decisively more frequent than internal questions. Despite that tendency Clytemnestre uses effectively repetition of the internal question *quoi?* to convey her astonished outrage that Ériphile has revealed to Calchas and to all the Greeks Iphigénie's secret departure from Aulide.

Ô monstre, que Mégère en ses flancs a porté!
Monstre, que dans nos bras les enfers ont jeté!
Quoi? tu ne mourras point? *Quoi?* pour punir son crime . . .
Mais où va ma douleur chercher une victime?
Quoi? pour noyer les Grecs et leurs mille vaisseaux,
Mer, tu n'ouvriras pas des abîmes nouveaux?
Quoi? lorsque, les chassant du port qui les recèle,
L'Aulide aura vomi leur flotte criminelle,
Les vents, les mêmes vents, si longtemps accusés,
Ne te couvriront pas de ses vaisseaux brisés?

(1679-88)

Iphigénie herself uses the internal exclamation predominantly; most of these exclamations express to Achille her reluctant resignation, as in *Ah!* and *Hélas!*

Use of conditional sentences and of *sans* + infinitive continues to decline from their peak level in *Bajazet*. There is a slight resurgence of *quand/lorsque*. Most of Agamemnon's conditional sentences, for instance, are concentrated in the first act, where to Arcas he quotes the oracle and reveals that if Iphigénie sets foot in Aulide she is dead (vv. 134-35); to Ulysse in the fourth scene Agamemnon tries first an "if it were your son destined to be sacrificed" approach. When that argument fails Agamemnon, concealing his scheme to prevent Iphigénie's arrival, states that *if* his daughter comes, he will consent to sacrifice her. Iphigénie's conditional sentences deal almost exclusively with her resignation to her father's will, culminating in Act V, where she attempts to persuade Achille that her death is necessary for his future glory in the Trojan War (vv. 1543-44; 1558-60), and where she begs her mother not to reproach her father for her death. "Surtout, *si* vous m'aimez, par cet amour de mère, / Ne reprochez jamais mon trépas à mon père!" (1653-54). Achille's conditionals concentrate increasingly on Iphigénie as the level of his violence increases.

Si de sang et de morts le ciel est affamé,
Jamais de plus de sang ses autels n'ont fumé.
. . . .
Et *si* dans les horreurs de ce désordre extrême
Votre père frappé tombe et périt lui-même,
Alors, de vos respects voyant les tristes fruits,
Reconnoissez les coups que vous aurez conduits.

(1603-4; 1609-12)

In brief, most characters use conditional sentences to reveal their thoughts and feelings. Clytemnestre, on the contrary, uses them as a means to persuade and to threaten. On two occasions she begs Achille to help them.

Oubliez une gloire importune;
Ce triste abaissement convient à ma fortune.
Heureuse *si* mes pleurs vous peuvent attendrir,
Une mère a vos pieds peut tomber sans rougir.

(929-32)

Tout est perdu, Seigneur, *si* vous ne nous sauvez.

(1048)

She toys briefly with Agamemnon (vv. 1161-62), suggests an alternative (vv. 1269-70), and finally dares the King to take Iphigénie from her. "Venez, *si* vous l'osez, la ravir à sa mère" (1314). While conditional sentences offer insights, they unfortunately do not lead to the key features of the tragedy. The same comment is even more applicable to *quand / lorsque* constructions.

Absent from Act I, true *récits* occur primarily in the fifth act as Arcas arrives to announce Achille's intervention on Iphigénie's behalf (V, 5).

ARCAS: A A B E A A A A A A B
. . . .

As usual, the two type B sentences are significant. "Achille est à l'autel" (1703). "Ne craignez rien" (1716). It is Ulysse, however, who in scene 6 brings news of Iphigénie's safety. Although nearly half of Ulysse's sentences were interrogative in Act I (16 out of 33), here in Act V they are all declarative. This fact reinforces the impression that Ulysse is purely a functional character and that his sentence structure is a reflection of his function and not of his character.

ULYSSE: A A A A A A A A A A A A A A B EA A A A A A A A A A
       B EA A B EA

. . . .

Rapid exchanges between characters are infrequent in *Iphigénie*. Only in his first encounter with Iphigénie does Agamemnon display any real difficulty in verbalizing his plan to sacrifice her.

Iphigénie: Que va-t-elle [Épriphile] penser de votre indifférence?
             Ai-je flatté ses vœux d'une fausse espérance?
             N'éclaircirez-vous point ce front chargé d'ennuis?
Agamemnon: Ah! ma fille!
Iphigénie: Seigneur, poursuivez.
Agamemnon: Je ne puis.
                        (565-68)

A series of six monostichs follow in which Iphigénie just happens to cite the three persons or groups causing Agamemnon's difficulties. Iphigénie misinterprets her father's responses, and the irony of the situation is obvious. After the series of monostichs, a typical pattern of the period called stichomythia, the conversation reverts to more rapid exchanges, which are typically Racinian.

Iphigénie: Périsse le *Troyen* auteur de nos alarmes!
Agamemnon: Sa perte à ses vainqueurs coûtera bien des larmes.
Iphigénie: Les *Dieux* daignent surtout prendre soin de vos jours! '
Agamemnon: Les Dieux depuis un temps me sont cruels et sourds.
Iphigénie: *Calchas,* dit-on, prépare un pompeux sacrifice.
Agamemnon: Puissé-je auparavant fléchir leur injustice!
Iphigénie: L'offrira-t-on bientôt?
Agamemnon: Plus tôt que je ne veux.
Iphigénie: Me sera-t-il permis de me joindre à vos vœux?
             Verra-t-on à l'autel votre heureuse famille?
Agamemnon: Hélas!

Iphigénie: Vous vous taisez?
Agamemnon: Vous y serez, ma fille.
           Adieu.

                                                      (569-79)

In another crucial scene (III, 5) in which rapid exchanges occur, Arcas, who can no longer in good conscience be a party to Agamemnon's project, reveals everything to the interested parties.

Arcas: Vous êtes son amant, et vous êtes sa mère:
                 Gardez-vous d'envoyer la princesse à son père.
Clytemnestre: Pourquoi le craindrons-nous?
Achille: Pourquoi m'en défier?
Arcas: Il l'attend à l'autel pour la sacrifier.
Achille: Lui!
Clytemnestre: Sa fille!
Iphigénie: Mon père!
Ériphile: Ô ciel! quelle nouvelle!

                                                (909-13)

In a single line all four characters react to the announcement. No other rapid exchanges occur in *Iphigénie*. The recital of the denouement itself is composed and expository.

No one character in this tragedy can be singled out as the main character around whom all action revolves or upon whom all action depends. Agamemnon is potentially that person, but he is indecisive. Nowhere is this more apparent than in Act IV, where he is buffeted back and forth by the other characters. As he is buffeted, the frequency of his interrogative sentences increases radically. Facing Clytemnestre and Iphigénie in the third and fourth scenes, the King assumes that they are as yet unaware of the plan to sacrifice Iphigénie. Beginning confidently in a series of questions, he rebukes Clytemnestre for being slow to send their daughter to the altar.

    Agamemnon: A A B E A A B
                ? . ? ? ? ? .

Que faites-vous, Madame? et d'où vient que ces lieux
N'offrent point avec vous votre fille à mes yeux?
Mes ordres par Arcas vous l'avoient demandée.

Qu'attend-elle? Est-ce vous qui l'avez retardée?
A mes justes désirs ne vous rendez-vous pas?
Ne peut-elle à l'autel marcher que sur vos pas?
Parlez.

(1155-61)

Clytemnestre's first reply is also a question. "*S'il faut partir, ma fille est toute prête. / Mais vous, n'avez-vous rien, Seigneur, qui vous arrête?*" (1161-62). Realizing that she has caught her husband offguard, Clytemnestre continues with her questions. "Vos soins ont-ils tout préparé?" (1163). As the Queen pursues this line of questioning and calls Iphigénie the victim and as Iphigénie, in tears, approaches her parents, Agamemnon is unnerved by the realization that Arcas has betrayed his confidence.

> AGAMEMNON: B M EA B E B
>   ? ? . @ . .

Que vois-je? Quel discours? Ma fille, vous pleurez,
Et baissez devant moi vos yeux mal assurés.
Quel trouble. . . . Mais tout pleure, et la fille et la mère.
Ah! malheureux Arcas, tu m'as trahi.

(1171-74)

Iphigénie replies first in her typically submissive manner.[1] Even her single type B sentence emphasizes her submissiveness. "Ma vie est votre bien" (1177).

> IPHIGÉNIE: EA A B EA A A A A A A A A A A A A A
>   . . . .

She does, however, have the foresight to remind her father that neither Clytemnestre nor Achille is willingly going to submit to his plan (vv. 1207-12). These are precisely the two characters who will cause Agamemnon to change his mind several times in this act. In answer to Iphigénie, the King attempts to shift to the Gods all blame and responsibility for this lamentable situation.

Clytemnestre, placing blame squarely on Agamemnon's shoulders, launches a lengthy attack on the King.

CLYTEMNESTRE: A A A A A A A A A A A A A A A A A A A A B E A
A A A A A A B EA A A A A A A A A

....???????..??.?????!.....?.!!!.....

Although incensed, Clytemnestre is in perfect control, as is evident from the series of sarcastic questions (vv. 1255-64) reminiscent of Hermione's sarcasm toward Oreste and Pyrrhus. Clytemnestre then questions the meaning of the oracle and even Agamemnon's involvement in the Trojan venture, leading up to her main point: an accusation that Agamemnon is consumed by ambition (vv. 1289-94). Her final thrust implies that Agamemnon will have to kill her also in order to take their daughter. In the brief monologue that follows (IV, 5) Agamemnon realizes that he could have expected such outbursts and wishes that they were all he had to fear. He begins to weaken in his resolve to follow through on the sacrifice.

Achille's protestations have the opposite effect (IV, 6). Feigning disbelief of all that he has heard, Achille questions the King. "Qu'en dites-vous, Seigneur? Que faut-il que j'en pense? / Ne ferez-vous pas taire un bruit qui vous offense?" (1333-34). The scene is a lively one.

ACHILLE:	A A A B E A	...???
AGAMEMNON:	A A	. .
ACHILLE:	A	
AGAMEMNON:	A	?
ACHILLE:	B EA A A	????
AGAMEMNON:	A	?
ACHILLE:	A	?
AGAMEMNON:	A A B E B	????@
ACHILLE:	E A A A	...?
AGAMEMNON:	A	.
ACHILLE:	B	!
AGAMEMNON:	EA A A A	....
ACHILLE:	B E A A A A A A A B E	!???????????.????
	A A A A A A A A	....
AGAMEMNON:	B E A A A A A A A B EA	....
ACHILLE:	A A A A A	.....

Agamemnon first tries a composed imperial reply to Achille's insinuations
(vv. 1335-38). When Achille answers that he knows only too well
Iphigénie's fate, Agamemnon switches to questions and outrages Achille,
who replies in like manner.

Pourquoi je le demande? Ô ciel! Le puis-je croire,
Qu'on ose des fureurs avouer la plus noire?
Vous pensez qu'approuvant vos desseins odieux,
Je vous laisse immoler votre fille à mes yeux?
Que ma foi, mon amour, mon honneur y consente?

(1341-45)

Agamemnon in turn is outraged at the tone of voice of a young man who
presumes to question the King's right to dispose of his own family. His
questions come as fast as Achille's had.

Et qui vous a chargé du soin de ma famille?
Ne pourrai-je sans vous disposer de ma fille?
Ne suis-je plus son père? Etes-vous son époux?
Et ne peut-elle. . . .

(1349-52)

Agamemnon is clearly more jealous of his position as king than of his
obligations to his family. When Achille returns to a more composed
discourse and reminds Agamemnon that he had given his word on the
marriage of Achille and Iphigénie, Agamemnon's reflex is to blame the
Gods again. Not stopping there, however, Agamemnon accuses Calchas,
the Greeks, Ulysse, Ménélas, and finally Achille himself. Achille's flood of
outraged questions is to no avail; although he stops short of violence,
Achille's parting words, like Clytemnestre's, show that he will defend
Iphigénie's life. Unfortunately, Achille's intervention on Iphigénie's
behalf has just the opposite effect from that which he intends. Although
Agamemnon finds it difficult to continue his bloody plan in the face of
Iphigénie's tender submission and Clytemnestre's outrage, Achille's
prideful threats only make him more determined than ever to sacrifice his
daughter.

   When Eurybate and the guards come to carry out his orders, however,
Agamemnon hesitates once more.

AGAMEMNON: E A A A A A A A A A A A A B EA B EA A A A A A A B
???? . . ??? ?? ?? . . . ? @ ! ? . . . .

His short sentences disclose his new resolve to spare Iphigénie's life. "Non, je ne puis" (1451). "Qu'elle vive" (1453). From this point, where he declares his intention to protect Iphigénie, Agamemnon unwittingly turns the situation over to Ériphile, who will not permit such a denouement.

Subordination: *Pour* + Infinitive

This construction is rather evenly distributed from act to act, although slightly higher in Acts I and V. In terms of characters, Ériphile and Ulysse lead in the use of *pour* + infinitive.[2] Iphigénie also uses the construction significantly more often than the mean for the tragedy. With one exception in each category, all the infinitives are both present infinitives and affirmative. Is it significant that this construction is used more frequently by functional or passive characters? It is not apparent in any case that this feature of sentence structure is linked to characterization in *Iphigénie*.

Conclusion

The features of sentence structure in *Iphigénie* provide an accurate picture of the characters in this tragedy. Unfortunately, the play lacks a central character around whom the action revolves. Agamemnon is simply too indecisive to fulfill that role. His main objective seems to be throwing off all responsibility for the present situation and to avoid making a decision for as long as possible. It would perhaps be more accurate to say that the King makes a series of decisions, each a reaction to his immediate interlocutor. As the interlocutor changes, so does Agamemnon's decision with regard to Iphigénie. Although this process happens continually throughout the play, it is nowhere more evident than in Act IV. Racine has succeeded in preventing Agamemnon from appearing odious. In so doing, however, he has rendered him ineffectual as well. Unlike Mithridate, Agamemnon never redeems himself by a decisive choice; he remains a spectator to the denouement. Iphigénie is entirely too passive to be the central character, except in the sense that her fate must be decided in the denouement.

In other tragedies, contrary to Weinberg's view, one central character is not necessary. A violent rivalry for the possession of a character like Néron can give cohesive force and interest to a tragedy. *Iphigénie* does oppose Clytemnestre and Achille to Agamemnon; in fact, the most successful scenes of the tragedy are the confrontations that in Act IV result from this opposition. Nevertheless, this rivalry is not a viable force, owing primarily to Agamemnon's indecisiveness and inactivity.

Nor do the group dynamics provide sufficient interest. Only Achille and Ériphile participate in the denouement; as carefully as Racine foreshadows the denouement throughout the first four acts, the turn of events is ironic—something of a disappointingly happy ending. This is true in part because three main characters, Agamemnon, Clytemnestre, and Iphigénie, the family group in danger, are mere spectators to the denouement. In another context, Maurice Descotes comments on the difficulties that *Iphigénie* presents to actors: "trop de solennité et, le personnage d'Ériphile mis à part, trop peu d'éclat et de passion" (*Les Grands Rôles*, p. 145). Although Clytemnestre might be included in "éclat" and "passion," this applies only to her verbalizations and not to actions. This critic also notes that *Iphigénie* suffers from the absence of its original set, the Orangerie. That set must have added a spectacular touch that the tragedy otherwise lacks. So it is that, although sentence structure effectively mirrors the characters' thoughts and feelings, those same characters lack the vigor and depth of those in Racine's earlier tragedies.

Notes to Chapter 5

1. Iphigénie does come alive in one scene with Ériphile (II, 5), when she discovers that this captive whom she had befriended is also in love with Achille and that therefore Ériphile's reason for coming to Aulide is not what it had appeared to be.

2. The parallel construction of *pour que* + clause is omitted from the discussion only because it does not occur in *Iphigénie*. By the same token the constructions with *afin que* have not occurred since *Britannicus* (twice) and those with *afin de* not since *Alexandre* (five).

$$\begin{bmatrix} 6 \\ \textit{Phèdre} \end{bmatrix}$$

With *Phèdre* Racine continues his use of Greek source material. In most other ways *Phèdre* resembles earlier plays more, since he here combines some of their most successful elements: violent confrontations between characters as in *Bajazet*; rivalry for the physical possession of a character as in *Britannicus*; tender moments between lovers as in *Bérénice*; a father's confusion about his son's loyalty as in *Mithridate*. This combination of elements might well have been a disjointed mosaic; it is instead a blending of Racine's most successful techniques into a new creation.

While averages for the basic features of sentence structure are not unusual, their distribution among the characters is significant. There are, however, more regular type A sentences (72.6%) than might be anticipated. Three secondary characters are responsible for this phenomenon: Théramène (80.9%), Aricie (77.4%), and Hippolyte (75.5%). These same characters also use longer sentences than do Phèdre and Thésée.

Théramène	23.053
Hippolyte	22.686
---MEAN------	19.569---
Aricie	19.405
confidants	18.528
Thésée	18.383
Phèdre	17.890

It is not surprising to find Phèdre at the lower end of the scale, but Thésée's presence there bears watching. Hippolyte's mean sentence length of 22.686 syllables is deceiving: it includes one sentence of 240 syllables, twice the length of any sentence encountered thus far in Racine's tragedies. When this sentence is excluded because of its extreme length, Hippolyte's mean sentence length drops a full syllable per sentence to 21.518 syllables.

In addition to the statistical effect of the sentence, no actor could hope to deliver it as a single utterance. On the other hand, Racine presumably had a reason for considering this group as a single unit. The sentence occurs in I, 1, and consists of two unequal parts, separated below.

Tu sais combien mon âme, attentive à ta voix,
S'échauffoit au récit de ses nobles exploits,
Quand tu me dépeignois ce héros intrépide
Consolant les mortels de l'absence d'Alcide,
Les monstres étouffés et les brigands punis,
Procruste, Cercyon, et Scirron, et Sinnis,
Et les os dispersés du géant d'Épidaure,
Et la Crête fumant du sang du Minotaure:

Mais *quand tu récitois* des faits moins glorieux,
Sa foi partout offerte et reçue en cent lieux;
Hélène à ses parents dans Sparte dérobée;
Salamine, témoin des pleurs de Péribée;
Tant d'autres, dont les noms lui sont même échappés,
Trop crédules esprits que sa flamme a trompés:
Ariane aux rochers contant ses injustices,
Phèdre enlevée enfin sous de meilleurs auspices;
Tu sais comme à regret écoutant ce discours,
Je te pressois souvent d'en abréger le cours,
Heureux si j'avois pu ravir à la mémoire
Cette indigne moitié d'une si belle histoire.

(75-94)

In the first part Hippolyte reviews for Théramène his admiration for Thésée's exploits against monsters; in the lengthier second part he expresses his negative reaction to his father's amorous pursuits. Each part of the utterance contains a main clause beginning "*Tu sais* . . ." and an elaborate subordinate clause beginning "*quand tu* (me dépeignois) (récitois). . . ." Racine creates a mirror effect by reversing the order of the main and subordinate clauses in the second part. While in reality this can hardly be considered a sentence, a single utterance, it not only possesses unity, but also reveals important information about Thésée and especially about Hippolyte.

The distribution of sentence length from act to act is not particularly informative. Because of exposition, Acts I and V have a level several syllables per sentence above that of the three middle acts.

Act I	21.217
Act II	18.809
Act III	17.787
Act IV	18.561
Act V	21.608

Despite the expository nature of Act I, the level of interrogative sentences is high (32.4% of the sentences in Act I as compared to 23.4% of the total sentences in the tragedy). Both Théramène and Hippolyte are responsible for this. See, for instance, *tirades* in I, 1.

HIPPOLYTE: E A A A A A A A A A A A A A
 ? ? . . . ? ? . ? ? . ? ? @

THÉRAMÈNE: A A A A A A A A A A A A A
 . . ? ? ? ? ? ? ? . . . ?

The impersonal *récits* in Acts I of certain earlier plays are here replaced by a lively discussion between two characters, both of whom are vitally interested and deeply involved in the matters being discussed. This tendency has already been observed in *Iphigénie*, but the opening scene of *Phèdre* is by far the most successful from that point of view. Théramène, in particular, possesses what at first glance is a strange distribution of terminal punctuation. In Act I he uses almost seventy percent questions (68.6%) and in Act V he uses more than ninety percent declaratives (92.9%). This distribution, like that of Ulysse, is based not on character but on function. In Act I Théramène's function is to question Hippolyte regarding the latter's proposed departure as well as his recent neglect of horsemanship, and to suggest through interrogatives the answers to his own questions. At the same time Hippolyte protests through interrogatives.

In Act V Théramène's function is to recite the incidents surrounding Hippolyte's death. With one exception all sentences in the *récit* itself are declarative.

THÉRAMÈNE: A A A A A A A A A A A A A A A AB EA B EA A AB E
A A A A A A A AB EA

. . . . @ .

That exception is an ellipsis that represents Hippolyte's dying words to his father (vv. 1563-67).

Interrogatives are used also by Thésée in Acts II and IV where they convey his bewilderment at the cool reception he has received from his son and his wife as well as his astonishment at OEnone's accusation of Hippolyte. These questions are particularly evident in his irregular sentences. "Quel est l'étrange accueil qu'on fait à votre père, / Mon fils?" (921-22). "Vous, mon fils, me quitter?" (927). "Que dis-je?" (973). "Qui m'a trahi? Pourquoi ne suis-je pas vengé?" (980). "Mon fils, mon propre fils / Est-il d'intelligence avec mes ennemis?" (983-84). In Act IV Phèdre's irregular questions follow the realization that Hippolyte is capable of loving a woman; they betray further loss of control and outrage on Phèdre's part. To her confidante OEnone, Phèdre pours out her despair (vv. 1225-50).

PHÈDRE: E A A B E B M E B E A A A A A A A
!! . !? ? ? ? . ? ? ? ? . . . .

Later in the same scene Phèdre internalizes her questions, expressing her feeling of guilt. "Que fais-je? Où ma raison se va-t-elle égarer?" (1264). "Pour qui? Quel est le cœur où prétendent mes vœux?" (1267). "Misérable! et je vis? et je soutiens la vue / De ce sacré soleil dont je suis descendue?" (1273-74). "Où me cacher?" (1277). Phèdre's interrogatives are almost always here accompanied by irregular sentences, adding to the impression of loss of control. All of the characters use questions in a special way: some reveal character and emotion, others reveal their function. The tragedy as a whole offers nearly the full spectrum of interrogatives. Only sarcasm is missing.

Internal questions and exclamations are fewer in number than in earlier tragedies and belong almost exclusively to Phèdre and to Thésée. Except for four examples in the declaration of love to Hippolyte (II, 5), all of Phèdre's exclamations of this type are addressed to OEnone. Thésée's are restricted to scenes immediately following his return (where they express consternation at his welcome and at OEnone's accusation) and to the final scene of the tragedy (where he learns how effectively Neptune has carried out his wishes).

Taken as a group, subordinations do not reveal general tendencies of any characters. The construction with *sans* + infinitive occurs only seven times and is without interest. The others, although frequent, do not aid in characterization except for isolated examples. Half of Phèdre's twelve conditional clauses occur in the declaration to Hippolyte (II, 5). Two occur early in the scene while Phèdre is still talking to Hippolyte about her son and the throne. The others come up in the declaration. Although these later conditionals may suggest Hippolyte's horror of Phèdre, they more accurately reveal her opinion of herself.

Il suffit de tes yeux pour t'en persuader,
Si tes yeux un moment pouvoient me regarder.

(691-92)

Frappe. Ou *si* tu le crois indigne de tes coups,
Si ta haine m'envie un supplice si doux,
Ou *si* d'un sang trop vil ta main seroit trempée,
Au défaut de ton bras prête-moi ton épée.
Donne.

(707-11)

In her next appearance (III, 1) using *quand/lorsque*, Phèdre repeats the process as OEnone urges the astonished Queen to regain control of herself and to reign.

Moi régner! Moi ranger un État sous ma loi,
Quand ma foible raison ne règne plus sur moi!
Lorsque j'ai de mes sens abandonné l'empire!
Quand sous un joug honteux à peine je respire!
Quand je me meurs!

(759-63)

In this preliminary discussion of the tragedy, it is Phèdre's name that recurs most frequently. And no wonder, since she accounts for nearly one third of the total number of sentences (31.5%). As Jean-Louis Barrault has observed, one of the great difficulties of presenting *Phèdre* is preventing the character of Phèdre from overpowering the others.

Il faudra bien veiller à ce que la représentation ne fasse pas penser à un concerto; à ce que toute l'attention ne se concentre pas sur Phèdre, aux dépens des autres personnages. Nous ne sommes pas devant un personnage entouré de comparses. . . .Mettre en valeur une œuvre d'art, et non "une reine incandescente". . . . Enfin, pour employer un terme d'argot de théâtre: se garder que Phèdre tire à soi la couverture . . . . *Phèdre* n'est pas un concerto pour femme; c'est une symphonie pour orchestre d'acteurs.[1]

The danger is real and difficult to avoid. The sheer volume of the role presents difficulties in itself, and yet quantity is not necessarily a major problem. Mithridate, for instance, utters a full 34.3% of the sentences in the tragedy of the same name and Titus speaks 30.4% of the sentences in *Bérénice*; neither of these roles presents the problems that Phèdre does. Is it because those two roles lack the violent emotion of Phèdre? Roxane surely does not lack violent emotion and at the same time accounts for 29.8% of the sentences in *Bajazet*. But even the role of Roxane does not equal that of Phèdre in difficulty. Thus, the real difficulty of playing Phèdre does not lie entirely in either quantity or in force of emotion. Is Phèdre's opinion of herself part of the key?

Phèdre's first appearance (I, 3) is in the company of her confidante, Œnone. This is a real dialogue, a real encounter, in which Œnone's purpose is to discover Phèdre's secret; for this reason Œnone has the upper hand most of the scene. More and more intensely she presses Phèdre to reveal the cause of her despair. The relatively high frequency of Phèdre's regular sentences (62.9%) is deceiving, because great numbers of them are broken internally by commas or by colons. "Je ne me soutiens plus: ma force m'abandonne" (154). "Que ces vains ornements, que ces voiles me pèsent!" (158). "Je l'ai perdu: les Dieux m'en ont ravi l'usage" (181). "Je le vis, je rougis, je pâlis à sa vue;" (273). Another factor is her use of internal questions and exclamations, mentioned above (see vv. 176, 179, 247, and 249). The broken rhythm of the *alexandrin* conveys Phèdre's weariness in the halting way she speaks. In what she considers Phèdre's best interests, Œnone presses the Queen to divulge her secret. Œnone begins simply by commenting on the situation but moves quickly to questioning Phèdre. Taking advantage of her mistress's bewilderment, Œnone accuses her of being inconsiderate at the same time that she searches for the key to the secret in a series of questions.

Quelle fureur les borne au milieu de leur course?
Quel charme on *quel poison* en a tari la source?
. . . .
À quel affreux dessein vous laissez-vous tenter?
De quel droit sur vous-même osez-vous attenter?

(189-90; 195-96)

ŒEnone is operating on the principle that, despite her weariness, Phèdre
will react when her confidante mentions the forbidden subject. So
ŒEnone reviews the reasons for Phèdre to continue living. Ironically,
ŒEnone mentions just those persons who must in fact be offended by what
Phèdre is concealing; Racine used this technique earlier when Iphigénie
confronts Agamemnon (*Iphigénie*, II, 2).

ŒEnone: Vous offensez les *Dieux* auteurs de votre vie;
          Vous trahissez *l'époux* à qui la foi vous lie;
          Vous trahissez enfin *vos enfants* malheureux,
          Que vous précipitez sous un joug rigoureux.
          Songez qu'un même jour leur ravira leur mère,
          Et rendra l'espérance au fils de l'étrangère,
          A ce fier ennemi de vous, de votre sang,
          Ce fils qu'une Amazone a porté dans son flanc,
          Cet Hippolyte . . .
Phèdre: Ah, Dieux!

(197-205)

Misinterpreting Phèdre's reaction, ŒEnone attempts to capitalize on it by
calling on Phèdre for politically motivated opposition to Hippolyte. Since
Phèdre immediately reverts to her desire to die, ŒEnone, seeing her error,
returns to her questions.

Quoi? *De quelques remords* êtes-vous déchirée?
Quel crime a pu produire un trouble si pressant?
. . . .
Et *quel affreux projet* avez-vous enfanté
Dont votre cœur encor doive être épouvanté?

(218-19; 223-24)

When all else has failed, ŒEnone threatens suicide as she recounts her
past services to her mistress. Even when Phèdre consents to speak,

OEnone must press her hard for each bit of information; Phèdre is particularly reluctant to divulge the name of the person whom she loves.

OEnone: Aimez-vous?
Phèdre: 　　　　　De l'amour j'ai toutes les fureurs.
OEnone: Pour qui?
Phèdre: 　　　　　Tu vas ouïr le comble des horreurs,
　　　　J'aime. . . . À ce nom fatal, je tremble, je frissonne.
　　　　J'aime. . . .
OEnone: 　　　　Qui?
Phèdre: 　　　　　　Tu connois ce fils de l'Amazone,
　　　　Ce prince si longtemps par moi-même opprimé?
OEnone: Hippolyte? Grands Dieux!
Phèdre: 　　　　　C'est toi qui l'as nommé.

(259-64)

This is one of the few rapid-fire exchanges in *Phèdre*. Admitting the fact of her love for Hippolyte frees Phèdre to retrace in a *tirade* the history of her involvement.

PHÈDRE: B EA A A A A A B E A A A A A B E A A A A
　　　　. . . . ! . . ! . . . . . ! ! . . . .

Once again the number of regular type A sentences is deceiving, for the flow of the *alexandrin* is frequently broken by internal punctuation. In addition, nearly every sentence has a first-person-singular subject; many sentences also show other forms of the first person singular — a possessive, an object pronoun, or a disjunctive.

Mon mal vient de plus loin. A peine au fils d'Égée,
Sous les lois de l'hymen *je m*'étois engagée,
Mon repos, *mon* bonheur sembloit être affermi;
Athènes *me* montra *mon* superbe ennemi.
Je le vis, *je* rougis, *je* pâlis à sa vue;
Un trouble s'éleva dans *mon* âme éperdue;
Mes yeux ne voyoient plus, *je* ne pouvois parler;
Je sentis tout *mon* corps et transir et brûler;
Je reconnus Vénus et ses feux redoutables,
D'un sang qu'elle poursuit tourments inévitables.
Par des vœux assidus *je* crus les détourner:
Je lui bâtis un temple, et pris soin de l'orner;

De victimes *moi-même* à toute heure entourée,
Je cherchois dans leurs flancs *ma* raison égarée.
D'un incurable amour remèdes impuissants!
En vain sur les autels *ma* main brûloit l'encens:
Quand *ma* bouche imploroit le nom de la Déesse,
*J'*adorois Hippolyte; et le voyant sans cesse,
Même au pied des autels que *je* faisois fumer,
*J'*offrois tout à ce dieu que *je* n'osois nommer.
Je l'évitois partout. Ô comble de misère!
Mes yeux le retrouvoient dans les traits de son père.
Contre *moi-même* enfin *j'*osai *me* révolter:
*J'*excitai *mon* courage à le persécuter.
Pour bannir l'ennemi dont *j'*étois idolâtre,
*J'*affectai les chagrins d'une injuste marâtre;
Je pressai son exil, et *mes* cris éternels
L'arrachèrent du sein et des bras paternels.
Je respirois, OEnone; et depuis son absence,
Mes jours moins agités couloient dans l'innocence.
Soumise à *mon* époux, et cachant *mes* ennuis,
De son fatal hymen *je* cultivois les fruits.
Vaines précautions! Cruelle destinée!
Par *mon* époux lui-même à Trézène amenée,
*J'*ai revu l'ennemi que *j'*avois éloigné;
Ma blessure trop vive aussitôt a saigné.
Ce n'est plus une ardeur dans *mes* veines cachée:
C'est Vénus toute entière à sa proie attachée.
*J'*ai conçu pour *mon* crime une juste terreur;
*J'*ai pris la vie en haine, et *ma* flamme en horreur.
Je voulois en mourant prendre soin de *ma* gloire,
Et dérober au jour une flamme si noire:
Je n'ai pu soutenir tes larmes, tes combats;
Je t'ai tout avoué; *je* ne *m'*en repens pas,
Pourvu que de *ma* mort respectant les approches,
Tu ne *m'*affliges plus par d'injustes reproches,
Et que tes vains secours cessent de rappeler
Un reste de chaleur tout prêt à s'exhaler.

(269-316)

The obsessive frequency of references to herself (60 in 48 lines) is unprecedented in Racine's theater. While this *tirade* is both a review of past stages in her struggle and a declaration of her love for Hippolyte, it is even more an expression of her guilt and, despite prolonged efforts, of her

inability to cope with the situation. Her unwillingness to push off responsibility and the guilt she feels set Phèdre apart from characters like Hermione and Roxane. Their emotions are no less violent, but Roxane shows
no remorse whatsoever and, in the final analysis, Hermione blames
Oreste for the results of her furors. Here in *Phèdre* are expressed at the
same time Phèdre's preoccupation and her weariness from unsuccessful
struggle. Although basically regular, the *tirade* contains constant repetitions of the first-person-singular forms as well as the broken *alexandrins*
to convey Phèdre's anguished state of mind. OEnone is able to prevent
Phèdre from dominating this scene at least until the closing *tirade*. In the
following short scene (I, 4), Phèdre hardly gets a word in
edgewise — "Ciel!" — as OEnone and Panope discuss the implications of the
reported death of Thésée. OEnone dominates the next scene also as she
adroitly persuades Phèdre to see Hippolyte on behalf of her son's right to
the throne.

Brought face to face with Hippolyte (II, 5), Phèdre dominates the
scene in quantitative terms, but progressively loses control of her utterances. Hippolyte's function in the scene is essentially that of watching
Phèdre destroy herself before his eyes. He does his best to halt the discussion by excusing her past attitudes toward him, encouraging her with
regard to Thésée's safety, and finally removing himself from an in-
tolerable situation. All to no avail. Even in her regular sentences Phèdre
constantly breaks the rhythm of the *alexandrin*. She begins courageously
but loses ground with each exchange to the extent that she combines the
image of Thésée with that of Hippolyte. It is ironic that Hippolyte first
speaks of shame (vv. 669-70). At this point Phèdre loses her last measure
of control and pours out her love for Hippolyte, her long struggle to
dominate her passion, and most prominently, the shame and horror that
she feels in the face of her weakness. Most of her final *tirade* is in broken
rhythm, leading up to the final, violent contrast between the two imperatives and the conditional sentence that separates them (vv. 707-11,
quoted above). In contrast to the earlier scene with OEnone, Phèdre is
more and more vehement, almost to the point of violence. Her weakened
condition is displayed as outbursts when she should have been silent.

Phèdre and OEnone reappear together at the beginning of Act III. The
Queen protests initially, in a series of exclamations based on *quand/lors-
que* (vv. 759-63, quoted above), that she is incapable of governing herself
let alone anyone else. Despite her protestations Phèdre begins to pull

herself together. She admits to some hope, rationalizes Hippolyte's cool
reception as disinterest in all women, and idealizes an attempt to reach
Hippolyte through a political offer. For the first time Phèdre initiates a
plan of action. Her sentences here are regular and declarative. Before
OEnone returns with the distressing news of Thésée's arrival, she has time
only for a short monologue addressed to Venus, suggesting to the goddess
that she subdue Hippolyte (III, 2). Phèdre reverts immediately to accusations against OEnone and to her attitude of despair.

PHÈDRE: E A A A A A B EA A A A B E A A A A A A A
         ? . . ? ? ? . . . . . . ? . . ! . . .

Again the Queen succumbs to one of OEnone's schemes. Thus Act III
possesses a slight détente as Phèdre composes herself and initiates a plan
of action. The plan is aborted by the announcement of Thésée's return;
OEnone substitutes her plan to accuse Hippolyte before Thésée. Interest
still lies with Phèdre, with her willingness to accept OEnone's plan.

The Queen does not return to the stage until midway through Act IV.
In the meantime Thésée and Hippolyte have two lengthy discussions, one
before and one after OEnone accuses Hippolyte. Thésée is badly shaken
by uncertainty as he attempts to get information out of his son regarding
the general coolness surrounding his return (III, 5). A number of these irregular questions are quoted above.

THÉSÉE: B EA A B EA A A A A A AB EA A B E B E A B EA B E A A
        ? ? ? . . . . . . ? . . . . ? ? ? . ? . . . .

Thésée only suspects difficulties; it is not long before OEnone removes all
doubt from his mind. Although, strictly speaking, many sentences are
regular here, internal exclamations help to convey the King's distress.

THÉSÉE: B EA A A A A A A A A A
        ? ? ! . ! ! . . ? ? ?

"Ah! qu'est-ce que j'entends?" (1001). "Ô tendresse! Ô bonté trop mal
récompensée! / Projet audacieux! détestable pensée!" (1005-6). Phèdre
reappears only after Thésée sends Hippolyte to his death. She pleads in
imperatives with her husband to reconsider the decision to condemn his
son.

PHÈDRE: A A A A A
· · · · ·

Phèdre is shocked as Thésée admits that he has assigned the task of killing
Hippolyte to Neptune: "Neptune vous la doit! Quoi? vos vœux irrités . . ."
(1179). She is, however, completely unnerved by the news that Hippolyte
loves Aricie. "Quoi, Seigneur?" (1188).

In the monologue that follows, Phèdre pours out her jealousy. When
OEnone appears, Phèdre literally attacks her confidante with this fact.
Phèdre dominates the scene and it is in vain that OEnone tries to reason
with her mistress. Phèdre's frantic questions first express astonishment
and wonder regarding Aricie and Hippolyte.

Ils s'aiment! Par quel charme ont-ils trompé mes yeux?
Comment se sont-ils vus? Depuis quand? Dans quels lieux?
Tu le savois. Pourquoi me laissois-tu séduire?
De leur furtive ardeur ne pouvois-tu m'instruire?
Les a-t-on vus souvent se parler, se chercher?
Dans le fond des forêts alloient-ils se cacher?
Hélas! ils se voyoient avec pleine licence.

(1231-37)

They also indicate that Phèdre will soon attack OEnone for her involvement. After briefly considering what she could do to Aricie, Phèdre turns
questions and exclamations against herself in a new realization of her
guilt.

Que fais-je? Où ma raison se va-t-elle égarer?
Moi jalouse! et Thésée est celui que j'implore!
Mon époux est vivant, et moi je brûle encore!
Pour qui? Quel est le cœur où prétendent mes vœux?
· ·
Misérable! et je vis? et je soutiens la vue
De ce sacré soleil dont je suis descendue?

(1264-67; 1273-74)

When OEnone dares to excuse Phèdre's love for Hippolyte as common
mortal weakness, Phèdre attacks OEnone, directly accusing her of
perpetuating the agony and causing her to reveal what should have been
eternally concealed. Ironically, these are questions of the same type used
by OEnone on Phèdre in the first act.

Qu'entends-je? Quels conseils ose-t-on me donner?
Ainsi donc jusqu'au bout tu veux m'empoisonner,
Malheureuse?

(1307-9)

De quoi te chargeois-tu? Pourquoi ta bouche impie
A-t-elle, en l'accusant, osé noircir sa vie?

(1313-14)

This is Phèdre at her most irrational. The movement of the scene is from jealousy of Aricie, to horror at her own involvement, and finally to accusation of her confidante. Phèdre's three *tirades* are long; their rhythm again is broken by irregular sentences and by affective punctuation.

PHÈDRE: E Λ Λ B E B M E B E A A A A A A A
!! . ! ? ? ? ? . ? ? ? ? . . . .
E A A A AB EB EA A A B E A A B E A A A A A A
B E A A A A B EA A A
. ! . . . . ? ? ! ! ? ? . . . . ? . ? . . ! ? . . . . .
B E AB E A A A A A B EA A A
? ? ? . . . . ? . . . ! !

The violence of Phèdre's emotion is reminiscent of Hermione. When internal questions and exclamations are counted also, it is not difficult to understand why this scene, even more than the declaration to Hippolyte, is extremely taxing for an actress.

In the final scene (V, 7) Phèdre knows that she will die shortly. She can now tell Thésée what she had intended to tell him in the fourth act. The regularity of her final *tirade* is unmistakable.

PHÈDRE: A A A A A A A A A

. . . .

She uses neither internal questions nor internal exclamations. There are neither colons nor semicolons except at the ends of lines. The first sentence is a monostich, whose purpose is to get Thésée to listen, followed by a series of eight distichs and a final sentence of six lines. This phenomenon of successive distichs is all the more striking in a tragedy in which none of the characters and none of the acts averages more distichs than monostichs. The first distich declares Phèdre's passion for Hippolyte; the next four deal with OEnone's taking advantage of the Queen's

weakened condition and with the confidante's suicide. The final three explain her reason for choosing poison instead of the sword, the need to ex-
pose her crime personally to Thésée. The *sixain* deals with the effects of
the poison as well as the expiation she sees in her death. Based on
sentence structure, it is impossible to conclude anything but complete
composure on the part of Phèdre. After the turmoil of her previous appearances, this final scene shows Phèdre in control of herself and her
destiny at last as a result of her decision to commit suicide, the only effec-
tual act that she personally initiates.

   Early in this chapter two notions regarding the role of Phèdre were
brought forward: the difficulty of the role and its tendency to overpower
the others. These two notions are not unrelated, of course, because part
of the difficulty lies in preventing the role from overpowering the others.
Difficulty lies also in sheer quantity of *tirades* and in Phèdre's violent outbursts (II, 5, and IV, 5-6). These violent scenes alternate with moments
of weakness and despair (I, 3-5 and III, 1-3) and of composure (V, 7).
Adding to this alternation is the difficulty that arises from considerable
numbers of broken *alexandrins*, even in her regular sentences. As if those
difficulties were not enough to challenge any actress, Phèdre can absorb
an overwhelming proportion of the interest in this tragedy. It is particularly evident when Phèdre is on the stage. Only Œnone is able to rival
Phèdre verbally, and then only in the early scenes. Apart from imposing
undue restraint on the actress playing Phèdre, the only possibility of rival-
ing Phèdre is in the scenes from which she is absent.
   There are, of course, confrontations between other characters: Hippolyte versus Théramène (I, 1), Hippolyte versus Aricie (II, 2 and V, 1),
Hippolyte versus Thésée (III, 5, and IV, 2), and Thésée versus Aricie (V,
3). By and large, however, they counterbalance rather than rival Phèdre's
scenes. The animated scenes between other characters occur in the very
acts in which Phèdre's scenes display her weariness; the quieter scenes occur in acts where Phèdre is most upset. This trade-off would be uniformly
true but for Act IV, where the accused Hippolyte faces his outraged
father and where Phèdre explodes in jealousy and rage. This is also the
crucial act, where final decisions are made. If the other characters do
withstand comparison to Phèdre, it is because they counterbalance her
rather than rival her. This delicate balance demands a great deal of all
the actors involved, but in the final analysis depends largely on Phèdre's

willingness to be counterbalanced. Anyone critical of *Iphigénie* for lacking both a central character and good group dynamics should be delighted with *Phèdre*, since this tragedy has both.

Comparison to Pradon's *Phèdre et Hippolyte*

Along with Racine's *Phèdre* comes the opportunity to contrast Racine's sentence structure with that of a lesser playwright, Jacques Pradon, who wrote a rival *Phèdre et Hippolyte* also in 1677. Despite identical source material, Pradon re-creates the Greek story in a distinct fashion. There are differences in the relationships between the characters: Thésée and Phèdre are not married; Aricie is Phèdre's confidante and, while still a princess, is no political threat. No less significant are differences in plot: Phèdre, with her brother's assistance, is planning the imminent demise of the absent Thésée as king in favor of Hippolyte; an oracle has prophesied, albeit inaccurately, the fatal triangle of Thésée, Hippolyte, and Phèdre; Phèdre freely avows her love to Aricie and later to Hippolyte and concocts her own schemes to thwart Thésée, to blackmail Hippolyte, and to destroy Aricie; and finally Phèdre stabs herself over Hippolyte's body.

While these differences are substantial, the truly astonishing ones have to do with techniques of sentence structure and versification. Since seven of Racine's plays have already been studied in depth, it is possible to compare *Phèdre et Hippolyte* to *Phèdre* and also to the normal range of each feature in a sizable portion of the Racinian canon. Only those features in Pradon which lie significantly outside the normal range for Racine are considered important. Significant differences in Racine's other five plays are discussed in the next chapter, but all statistics are summarized for easy reference in Appendix C. Radical differences occur in the basic characteristics so important in Racine's technique. Pradon's mean sentence length in this tragedy, for instance, is an unbelievable 43.505 syllables per sentence (*Phèdre* has 19.569), although the mode is still the monostich.[2] The spread of thirteen syllables among the characters is unusual as well.

Thésée	51.038
Phèdre	43.627
---MEAN------------	43.505---
Hippolyte	41.893
confidants	38.925
Aricie	38.301

The maximum sentence length is an incredible 336 syllables for 28 lines and the minimum is one syllable; the median (30.000) is radically different from the mean, as was the mode (12.000); the standard deviation is in excess of 40 syllables for all characters as compared to a range of 15-18 for Racine. All these statistics point to the same phenomenon, the widely divergent sentence lengths involved. That kind of distribution is simply not correlated to characterization. The distribution from act to act, however, displays a familiar downward trend through Act IV, with a substantial recovery in Act V because of the *récit* of Hippolyte's death by Idas (see Table 4 in Appendix C). This is in fact the only *récit* by the definition advanced early in this study. The lack of *récits* is undoubtedly related to the fact that both declarative sentences (47.0%) and type A sentences (54.5%) occur much less frequently than in Racine. *Phèdre* has 66.0% and 72.6% respectively. This deficit is made up by sentences of types EA, AB, and EAB, all of which occur significantly more often than in Racine, and by an extraordinary number of interrupted sentences marked by the ellipsis (15.4%). These statistics might lead one to expect several rapid-fire exchanges. There are none. On the other hand, it is not surprising to find none of the more common type based on stichomythia, since sentences are so irregular. Not only are regular sentences infrequent, but internal exclamations are extraordinarily numerous (26.7%) as compared to *Phèdre* (5.5%). Pradon's characters simply use three to four times as many interjections as do Racine's characters. The only exception is in constructions beginning with "Ô," which in Racine are often a full hemistich in length, as in "Ô comble de misères!"

	Phèdre et Hippolyte	*Phèdre*
Ah!	66	20
Hélas!	41	10
Dieux!	28	--[3]
Ciel!	17	9
Ô!	2	15

Although the use of internal question marks is not elevated, the specific use of *quoi?* in Pradon is nearly double its use in Racine's play (22 as compared to 13 occurrences). In addition to interjections, Pradon's characters use titles, not to mention proper names, in direct address at a significantly higher rate.

	Phèdre et Hippolyte	*Phèdre*
Madame	83	32
Seigneur	79	51
Princesse	12	--

The net effect of frequent use of internal punctuation and of direct address (sometimes in combination) is excessive choppiness in an *alexandrin* already broken by the high percentage of irregular sentences. Moreover, there is reason to believe that such gratuitous and grammatically unintegrated words are often used by less gifted poets to fill out an *alexandrin* to its full twelve-syllable length. Reinforcing this notion are other statistics, such as the frequency of the conjunction *et* (54.5% of Pradon's sentences contain at least one occurrence of *et*). Or, said another way, there is an average of 30.78 occurrences of *et* per hundred lines in *Phèdre et Hippolyte* as compared to 17.78 in *Phèdre*. The same is true of *mais,* but on a much smaller scale. Pradon's longer sentences are the apparent reason for a higher rate of subordinate constructions introduced by *quand / lorsque* (37 occurrences as compared to 26 used singly except on one occasion), conditional *si* (51 instead of 39), *bien que* (5 instead of 0), and *puisque* (15 instead of 8), but no occurrences of *sans (que)*.

Several conclusions are possible from this necessarily brief comparison of *Phèdre et Hippolyte* to *Phèdre*. Although there were at the time good reasons, political and personal, for Racine's dismay that on two occasions rival playwrights produced plays on similar subject matter to compete with his tragedies, his rivals unwittingly enabled later scholars to make comparisons not often feasible. In controlled experiments one can vary one factor while holding the others constant. It is not often that literary critics get a chance to hold the subject matter and time of composition constant while varying the author. Pradon's sentence structure under those "controlled" conditions is radically different from that of Racine. From all the evidence, these features of sentence structure are author specific, which is to say, differences from author to author are significantly greater than those from subject to subject or from year to year for the same author.

In addition to the statistical differences, it is simply not possible to view characterization in Pradon as a function of sentence structure. Moreover, Pradon uses neither the technique of rapid-fire exchanges between characters nor the technique of distributing *tirades* according to terminal punctuation and sentence type. In fact, affective terminal punctuation, irregular sentence type, and internal exclamations are so much the rule in Pradon's *Phèdre et Hippolyte* as to obviate the differentiating and characterizing function that various *tirades* have in Racine's tragedies. These features, too, are author specific.

In a sense this comparison of two tragedies about Phèdre serves to summarize the distinguishing characteristics of Racine's sentence structure in the tragedies from *Andromaque* to *Phèdre*. While there are trends in certain areas, no clear patterns of evolution emerge from within the group. Racine's five other plays have been considered as distinct in a number of ways from those studied. It is time to ask whether they are significantly different in sentence structure.

Notes to Chapter 6

1. Jean Racine, *Phèdre*: *mise en scène et commentaires de Jean-Louis Barrault* (Paris: Seuil, 1946), p. 21.

2. The computer-readable text is based on *Phèdre et Hippolyte* (Paris: Henry Loyson, 1677), printed in *Les Œuvres de Mr Pradon* (Paris: Jean Ribou, 1682), a copy of which was graciously lent to me by the Library of Congress in Washington, D.C.

3. The four possible cases are actually direct address to the Gods, one imperative, and three questions.

7
Comparative Sentence Structure: The Other Racinian Plays

Two early tragedies based on Greek sources, *La Thébaïde* and *Alexandre*, have been considered quite different from and often inferior to later tragedies for a variety of reasons. The goal of the present chapter is to test their distinctiveness with regard to sentence structure, not through a study in depth but through comparison of specific criteria on which data are now available. The same comparison is then made on two late tragedies of biblical inspiration, *Esther* and *Athalie*. Finally, comparison of *Les Plaideurs* to the entire group of tragedies provides the occasion to verify the magnitude of generic differences in Racine's sentence structure.

La Thébaïde Lathebaide and *Alexandre*

By and large, the basic features of sentence structure are the most reliable criteria in characterization. Terminal punctuation is not appreciably different in these two early plays. (See Tables 1-9 in Appendix C, for easy comparison of the statistics from these two plays with those from the rest of Racine's theater as well as from Corneille's *Tite et Bérénice* and Pradon's *Phèdre et Hippolyte*.) The relative distribution of periods, exclamations, questions, and ellipses is quite similar to that in the seven tragedies studied previously. Distribution from character to character and from act to act varies widely, indicating that this could lead to insights into characterization. With regard to sentence type, there is an unusually high frequency of regular type A sentences.

La Thébaïde	82.0%
Alexandre	76.3

No characters are more responsible for this phenomenon than others. The distribution from act to act is quite uniform. The high proportion of regular sentences indicates that Racine has not yet begun to use exten- sively irregular sentence types as tools of characterization. He appears, however, to be headed in that direction when *Alexandre* is compared to *La Thébaïde*. With *Andromaque*, frequency of type A sentences drops abruptly to 68.6%.

By far the most remarkable difference lies in mean sentence length, which for Racinian tragedies has been in the neighborhood of 19-22 syllables per sentence. In these two early plays the figures are much higher.

La Thébaïde	24.714
Alexandre	26.088

While the range of mean sentence lengths for individual characters is substantially unchanged (a difference of up to seven syllables per sentence from the character with the longest sentences to the character with the shortest ones), the actual numbers associated with each character are significantly higher than in later plays.

La Thébaïde		*Alexandre*	
Étéocle	28.731	Ephestion	30.980
Créon	27.534	Porus	27.364
---MEAN------------ 24.714---		Cléofile	27.331
Antigone	23.899	Taxile	26.168
Hémon	23.707	---MEAN------------ 26.088---	
Jocaste	22.807	Alexandre	25.273
Polynice	22.627	Axiane	23.716
confidants	22.535		

To demonstrate the radical difference between these two tragedies and *Andromaque*, one need simply recall that the shortest average sentence length here (22.535) is more than two syllables per sentence higher than the longest average sentence length in *Andromaque*, in which Pyrrhus averages only 20.197 syllables per sentence. In addition, the distich, rather than the monostich, is the most frequent sentence length in *La Thébaïde* and in *Alexandre*. This is true not only of the plays as a whole but also of most characters: Jocaste, Créon, Hémon, confidants in *La*

Thébaïde, Alexandre, Taxile, Porus, and Axiane. Ephestion and Etéocle actually use the *quatrain* more frequently than any other length, a phenomenon without parallel in Racine's theater. Only three characters use the monostich more often than the distich: Polynice, Antigone, and Cléofile. Likewise, in the various acts, sentence length is almost uniformly high from act to act and the most common sentence length is without exception the distich.

La Thébaïde		Alexandre
25.859	Act I	26.468
25.000	Act II	30.638
27.380	Act III	26.659
21.411	Act IV	24.795
24.556	Act V	22.550

This is the frequent use of the distich hypothesized in chapter 2, where, from the point of view of basic sentence features, the declarative distich was considered the most nearly neutral and most inconspicuous sentence, and therefore the most common. In the seven tragedies studied earlier, the distichs outnumber the monostichs only in isolated cases. In these two early tragedies, however, the distich is not the exception but the rule, a usage similar to Corneille's *Tite et Bérénice*. The change from distich to monostich dominance in *Andromaque* is radical and accompanies the significant increase in irregular, shorter sentences.

Subordination yields little in the way of comparison except for significantly more frequent use of *quand / lorsque* than in any play except *Bérénice*, and significantly more frequent use of conditional *si* than in any play except *Bajazet*. Internal exclamations are at a predictable level, while internal questions are noticeably less frequent than in later tragedies.

In *La Thébaïde* the only departures from the *alexandrin* occur in the reporting of the oracle by Olympe (II, 2) and in the monologue by Antigone (V, 1). This latter contains lines of six, eight, and ten syllables as well as *alexandrins*. There are no such departures in *Alexandre*. At the same time, rapid-fire exchanges between characters are relatively rare. By and large they consist of exchanges of distichs, of monostichs, or of hemistichs (*La Thébaïde*, 1100-1102; *Alexandre*, 217-28). These are not the rapid, affective exchanges of later plays but rather stichomythia, measured exchanges of impersonal *sentences* used to counter arguments. Only one rapid exchange is a foreshadowing of things to come.

Alexandre:	Quoi? Taxile?
Cléofile:	Qu'entends-je?
Éphestion:	Qui, Seigneur, il est mort:

Il s'est livré lui-même aux rigueurs de son sort.

(Alexandre, 1427-28)

In a number of striking ways, *La Thébaïde* and *Alexandre* resemble Corneille's sentence structure in *Tite et Bérénice*: mean sentence length, predominance of the distich and of the regular and declarative sentence, use of stichomythia, and frequency of certain subordinations and of conjunctions *et* and *mais*. Subsequently, Racine modifies his sentence structure, as is first evident in *Andromaque:* by decrease in the number of regular type A sentences, decrease in average length of sentences, increase in use of monostichs in place of distichs, decrease in use of several common methods of subordination, increase in the use of internal questions, and increase and more skillful use of rapid exchanges between characters. With the exception of subordination, all of these changes indicate that Racine is more consistently using the sentence as a tool of characterization than he had in *La Thébaïde* and in *Alexandre*.

Esther and Athalie

The two biblically inspired tragedies of *Esther* and *Athalie* represent a different perspective from early tragedies like *La Thébaïde* and *Alexandre*, if for no other reason than that they follow, and at some years' distance, the seven tragedies studied in earlier chapters. That chronological order is not without significance. Overall distribution of terminal punctuation in *Athalie* is well within the normal range. In *Esther* on the other hand, the frequency of exclamations is abnormally high (10.5% as compared to a range of 5.7-8.2%). This phenomenon is due almost entirely to the Chorus, where one sentence in five is exclamatory. Characteristic apostrophes and lamentations are even repeated as refrains.

Ô rives du Jourdain! ô champs aimés des cieux!
  Sacrés monts, fertiles vallées,
  Par cent miracles signalées!

(Esther, 141-43; 150-52)

Ô mortelles alarmes!

(Esther, 297, 301, 305, 308)

Ô Dieu, que la gloire couronne,
Dieu, que la lumière environne,
Qui voles sur l'aile des vents,
Et dont le trône est porté par les anges!

(Esther, 353-56)

The Chorus in *Athalie* also averages one exclamation every five sentences, although this fact is masked because other characters use exclamations less frequently than normal. Moreover, the level of exclamations is relatively constant from act to act, a fact that reinforces the impression of its essentially functional purpose. The use of internal exclamations is likewise high, because of the Choruses.

In contrast, frequencies for questions and ellipses are unusually low in *Esther*. The Chorus is also responsible in large measure for the high percentage of regular sentences (81.7% in *Esther* and 75.5% in *Athalie*), while at the same time it contributes some of the shortest average sentences. The reasons for this distinctive constellation of features lie in the unusual sentence structure of the Chorus in both tragedies. This is, of course, related to function and not to individual characterization. Although the overwhelming number of the Chorus's sentences are regular (94.2% in *Esther* and 86.0% in *Athalie*), many are not *alexandrins*. Variety is achieved through variation in the length of the poetic line rather than through irregularity within the *alxandrin*. While possessing sentence structure radically different from that of individual characters, the two Choruses are remarkably similar to each other: in use of subordination, of *et*, of internal questions and exclamations, and in average sentence length. The Chorus in *Athalie* is, however, less regular and more affective, especially with regard to interrogatives, than is the Chorus in *Esther*. This progression through time is similar to that observed with respect to individual characters when comparing *La Thébaïde* and *Alexandre* to later tragedies. The range of average sentence length as well as the actual number of characters is much greater than in earlier tragedies. In fact, the functional character Piété, who delivers the almost completely regular and declarative Prologue to *Esther,* has the longest average sentences in the eleven tragedies, whereas in *Athalie* Joas, the only child who speaks, has the shortest (See Appendix C, Table 6).

Esther		Athalie	
Piété	32.308	Abner	24.627
Esther	25.154	Joad	22.660
Aman	22.527	Mathan	21.646
---MEAN----------	20.112---	Zacharie	21.038
confidants	19.720	confidants	20.838
Mardochée	19.421	---MEAN-----------	19.936---
Zarès	19.243	Salomith	18.455
Assuérus	17.239	Josabet	17.634
CHŒUR	15.966	Athalie	17.230
		CHŒUR	17.105
		Joas	14.368

Although there are no rapid exchanges in *Esther*, two well-placed ones occur in *Athalie* (vv. 381-82 regarding the profaning of the temple and vv. 622-38 where Athalie questions Joas about his parentage).

In most other respects *Esther* and *Athalie* have the same type of sentence structure as earlier plays: similar patterns of subordination, similar levels of *et* and *mais*, and predominance of the monostich except in the Prologue to *Esther* and in Act I of *Athalie*. With the exception of modifications related to the introduction of the Chorus and the Prologue then, *Esther* and *Athalie* do not differ significantly in sentence structure from the Racinian tragedies examined in depth in this study. What differences there are do not compare in magnitude with those observed in *La Thébaïde* and *Alexandre*. And even those differences are relatively small when compared to the distinctiveness of Racine's one comedy.

Les Plaideurs

A cursory glance at the tables in Appendix C makes it clear that the premises regarding the specific interrelatedness of language and characterization must apply only to Racine's serious plays. The change of genre in *Les Plaideurs* brings with it radical changes in sentence structure. Taken together, the differences demonstrate the overwhelming distinctiveness of comedy even when written by the same playwright.

Only those features which fall well outside the normal range for Racine, a range established for the eleven tragedies, are considered pertinent to generic distinction. Questions occur approximately half as often while ellipses are noticeably more frequent. Even without the text it is obvious that rapid exchanges are more the rule than the exception, since average sentence length in *Les Plaideurs* plunges to 10.890 syllables per sentence and since the most common sentence length is the hemistich instead of the monostich. The latter statistic is true for the play as a whole as well as for all three acts and for three of the eight characters; four characters still prefer the monostich, while one, *le souffleur*, prefers the two-syllable sentence. Five of the eight characters never say a sentence longer than a quatrain. A mere quarter of the sentences are regular. Nearly fifty percent are either type B or type E; another ten percent are type M. Despite the shortness of the typical sentence, ten percent have internal exclamations (only *Bérénice* is comparable in this respect). Internal questions, on the other hand, are infrequent. Characteristic subordinations are near the bottom of the normal range but still within it. Thus the longer sentences of the tragedies are not accompanied by significantly increased use of subordination by comparison with *Les Plaideurs*; subordination and sentence length are not correlated. Racine's use of subordination is independent of sentence length, just as it is largely unrelated to characterization. Use of *et* is only half as frequent as in the tragedies, a fact that reinforces the earlier hypothesis that use of *et*, unlike subordination, is directly proportional to sentence length.

It has already been demonstrated through comparisons to Corneille and Pradon that sentence structure is author specific. This chapter makes finer distinctions by demonstrating significant differences that occur within the work of Racine. Of the five plays in question, *Esther* and *Athalie* most closely resemble the seven plays from *Andromaque* to *Phèdre*. Distinctiveness results primarily from the introduction of the Chorus. The two early tragedies, *La Thébaïde* and *Alexandre*, are different in enough ways from later plays to posit that Racine begins to use the sentence consistently as a tool for characterization only with *Andromaque*. *Les Plaideurs*, whose sentence structure is radically different from that of the eleven tragedies, confirms the hypothesis that language is genre specific as well as author specific. Moreover, the conclusions of this chapter confirm the intuitive wisdom of beginning the study with *Andromaque*. What remains is to investigate various links to versification that have been alleged from time to time in earlier chapters.

8
Sentence Structure and Versification

Surveying many features of sentence structure in Racine's tragedies has revealed that certain features, definitely not related to characterization, appear to be linked to the structure of the *alexandrin*. The use of *et* for coordination, for instance, defies attempts to correlate it to characterization, despite its variation in direct proportion to sentence length. The conjunction appears on occasion to function as padding, a way of adding a syllable to fill out the *alexandrin*. By the same token, the distribution of *quand* versus *lorsque* seems to be determined by the need in a line for one or two syllables respectively. A more subtle problem is raised by expressions like *pour* + infinitive, a relatively frequent construction that is not correlated to characterization. This construction may also be linked to the structure of the *alexandrin* as a formulaic expression. The basic tool in this search is a computer-generated KWIC concordance. A KWIC (Key Word In Context) concordance, usually generated for prose texts, lists the key word in the center of the page, with context preceding and following the key word. Instead of listing occurrences of the key word sequentially throughout Racine's theater as Bryant Freeman did, I have alphabetized the context that follows the key word in order to bring together similar expressions. The following areas yielded results significant enough to warrant discussion: repetition of whole hemistichs, alternations for metrical compensation, and filler elements for metrical compensation. As in the major portion of this study, Racine's plays from *Andromaque* to *Phèdre* are the principal texts examined and plays by Corneille and Pradon are used as control texts.

Repetition of Whole Hemistichs

The *alexandrin*, the verse line of classical French theater, consists of twelve syllables normally with a caesura after the sixth syllable, which divides the line into two parts of equal length. Since a limited number of syntactical arrangements are possible within this framework, some repetition is inevitable. This is true of all verse lines having a caesura. Repetitions of a hemistich in length, called formulaic style, have been of special interest to medieval scholars studying oral epic poetry. In discussing this aspect of the *Chanson de Roland*, Joseph Duggan defines formulaic style neither as syntactic formulas nor as topoi but rather as "semantically stylized hemistichs,"[1] occurring at least twice and differing lexically only in function words, in terminal words in the case of the second hemistich, or in variations for metrical compensation, that is, singular versus plural, verb tense, etcetera (pp. 10-11). Jacques Cahen in *Le Vocabulaire de Racine* lists myriad examples of the syntactic hemistich that consist of a monosyllabic article, an adjective as epithet, and a noun, not necessarily in that order. His objective is to illustrate the law of metrical compensation whereby a noun of four syllables requires a monosyllabic adjective and vice versa (pp. 199-209). Cahen is careful to add that while this "law" does work against variety of expression, it does not work against density (p. 216). To facilitate comparisons, Duggan's convention has been adopted in this study.[2] According to his findings, the level of repetition for oral epic poetry falls in the neighborhood of 30-40% of all hemistichs. By contrast, the level for written narrative poetry is consistently lower than 20% (p. 25). The level in Racine's seven major tragedies averages 7.49%, a small number of repetitions by comparison with the "limits of tolerance" for written narrative poetry. This difference could, of course, be attributed to several factors: dramatic mode of expression as opposed to narrative; the *alexandrin* with two hemistichs of equal length as opposed to the shorter and less flexible decasyllabic line with hemistichs of four and six syllables respectively; seventeenth-century period style; or even Racine's inventiveness in varying his hemistichs. These possibilities can be considered objectively only after examining Racine's formulaic style in some detail and comparing it to that of Corneille and Pradon.

Several observations about distribution of whole hemistich repetitions are needed to place the 7.49% rate of repetition in proper perspective. In the first place, the longer a text, the more likely a repetition becomes, that is, frequency of repetition is directly proportional to length of text examined. Despite the rate of 7.49% for seven Racinian tragedies as a group, the rate drops radically when only repetitions internal to a particular play are considered. The seven plays then fall clearly into two distinct groups, neither of which approaches the rate for the whole.

Andromaque	2.0%	*Britannicus*	3.3%
Iphigénie	1.7	*Bérénice*	3.4
Phèdre	1.8	*Bajazet*	2.9
		Mithridate	3.1

It is against these individual rates that Pradon's rate of 5.4% in *Phèdre et Hippolyte* and Corneille's rate of 4.8% in *Tite et Bérénice* must be contrasted. Rates that might at first glance appear lower than Racine's rate are in fact nearly double that of a number of Racine's plays and actually triple that of *Phèdre*.

Moreover, the overwhelming majority of repetitions (91.6%) occur five times or fewer. Of the 704 different hemistich repetitions, 507 of them occur only twice in the 11,818 lines of the seven major plays. Another 121 occur only three times, and so on. At the other end of the scale, only three different hemistichs occur ten times or more in 11,818 lines of text, and they are not identical repetitions, as will be seen shortly.

Distribution from act to act is proportional to length of acts and therefore not significant. On the other hand, distribution from play to play appears to be highly significant, with *Bérénice* having more frequent repetitions than the average and *Andromaque* and *Phèdre* having fewer. This statistic may, however, be misleading, since a play's position in the chronological sequence may be an important factor. *Andromaque* might have higher figures if preceding plays, *La Thébaïde* and *Alexandre*, had been included in the analysis; the same could be true with regard to *Phèdre* and the two later plays, *Esther* and *Athalie*. On the other hand, when only internal repetitions are considered, *Andromaque* and *Phèdre* have low rates while *Bérénice* belongs to the group with higher relative rates. When the plays are taken two at a time, it is generally true that chronologically adjacent plays are more likely to share a repetition than ones that are not adjacent. But *Andromaque* and *Britannicus* as well as *Iphigénie* and *Phèdre* share fewer than the mean, whereas *Britannicus* and *Iphigénie* share more than the mean number of occurrences of these repetitions. It is not surprising, however, that *Andromaque* and *Phèdre* share by far the least number of repetitions.

FREQUENCY DISTRIBUTION OF WHOLE HEMISTICH REPETITIONS

Frequency of occurrence	2	3	4	5	6	7	9	10+	total
number of different repetitions	507	121	40	17	12	2	2	3*	704
total number of hemistichs involved	1014	363	160	85	72	14	18	45	1771
	(57.3%)	(20.5)	(9.0)	(4.8)	(4.1)	(0.8)	(1.0)	(2.5)	(100.0)

------77.8%------

------86.8%------

------91.6%------

*one of 10
one of 12
one of 23

	Andromaque	*Britannicus*	*Bérénice*	*Bajazet*	*Mithridate*	*Iphigénie*	*Phèdre*
Andromaque	--	41	42	41	37	39	23
Britannicus	41	--	48	53	43	50	39
Bérénice	42	48	--	62	54	55	39
Bajazet	41	53	62	--	44	42	38
Mithridate	37	43	54	44	--	68	48
Iphigénie	39	50	55	42	68	--	41
Phèdre	23	39	39	38	48	41	--

The distribution of whole hemistich repetitions within the distich is also highly significant. When the seven plays are viewed as a group, the distribution is as follows. It does not vary appreciably for individual plays.

Racine, *Andromaque* to *Phèdre*

	first hemistich	second hemistich	total
first verse	23.5%	30.3	53.8
second verse	16.0	30.3	46.3
total	39.5	60.6	100.0

In other words, a repeated hemistich is more likely to be found at the rhyme than in the first half of a verse, and more likely to be found in the first verse of a distich than in the second. These observations substantiate intuitions that rhyme is a major obstacle. There is also some evidence to support the theory that the second line of a distich is often written first and that the first line is then tailor-made to accompany the second line, hence the more frequent repetitions in the first line. The actual percentages in this latter supposition do not on this evidence alone warrant a strong statement as to their significance. A comparison to the statistics for Pradon's *Phèdre et Hippolyte* lends support to both suppositions, since differences are in the same direction but even more pronounced.

Pradon, *Phèdre et Hippolyte*

	first hemistich	second hemistich	total
first verse	21.3%	37.2	58.5
second verse	10.6	30.9	41.5
total	31.9	68.1	100.0

Corneille's use of whole hemistich repetitions in *Tite et Bérénice* conforms only in part to this tendency. Corneille does reuse a hemistich more often at the rhyme than in the first half of a line, but contrary to the practices of both Racine and Pradon, Corneille more often repeats a hemistich in the second verse of a distich than in the first. This is perhaps because Corneille purposely reuses important hemistichs to underscore parallel situations or developments in a situation more often than do the other two playwrights.

Corneille, *Tite et Bérénice*

	first hemistich	second hemistich	total
first verse	22.2%	24.5	46.7
second verse	20.5	32.8	53.3
total	42.7	57.3	100.0

The vast majority of repetitions do not occur often enough to be of interest in and of themselves, but some general comments are possible. The most prominent repetitions of whole hemistichs involve time expressions.

Pour la { dernière } fois   28 times (17 at rhyme)
         { première }
Dès + a time expression   13
Depuis + a time expression   14
Jusqu(e) + a time expression   5 (5)

All of these expressions occur at least once in either Pradon or Corneille. One other expression occurs frequently enough to deserve special mention (ten occurrences in Racine's seven plays; two in Corneille's play; two in Pradon).

Dans } { l'état   }   { je suis
En   } { le trouble   } où   { vous êtes
                                { nous sommes

Occasionally a repetition is virtually devoid of meaning and therefore can be called "pure filler": "Vous cependant ici" + imperative (*Mithridate*, 625, 1087). Constructions of this type are exceedingly rare in Racine's tragedies.

Only one pattern repetition, mentioned by Cahen as an example of *cheville* (p. 216), emerges: two-syllable unit (often an imperative) + title vocative + similar or identical two-syllable unit.[3]

Venez, Seigneur, venez . . .
On vient, Madame, on vient . . .
Pourquoi, Seigneur, pourquoi . . .

The pattern occurs 38 times, approximately once every 311 lines in Racine; thirty of these occur in the first hemistich of a distich, where literary critics have long said fillers are most likely to be found. The other eight occur in the third hemistich of the distich; none occurs at the rhyme. While a repetition of this type does serve to fill out the hemistich, the effect is emphasis, provided that the construction is used with restraint. Variants show that at least two early patterns of this type (not counted above) were removed by Racine: "Allez, Seigneur, allez" becomes "Que tardez-vous? Allez" (*Bérénice*, 1236); "Venez, Princes, venez" becomes "Approchez, mes enfants" (*Mithridate*, 755). While two examples of this pattern appear in *Phèdre et Hippolyte*, another pattern occurs ten times: interjection + title vocative + imperative.

Ah! Madame, tâchez . . .
Non, Seigneur, croyez . . .

One other pattern of this type occurs three times in Pradon: "Moi, Madame? Oui, vous!" Taken together, the three patterns in Pradon occur 15 times or approximately once every 116 lines. Corneille has 8 occurrences of the above patterns, averaging one every 222 lines. This evidence tends to support the supposition that the less talented poet is more prone to use these patterns as fillers.

Alternations for Metrical Compensation

This type of alternation involves two words of similar meaning, or two forms of a single word, with different number of syllables. Choice of one form over the other may be a function of metrical needs.

Base word *jusque* has three forms in Racine, the first of which is not part of the alternation. Figures for Racine represent the total occurrences for the seven plays, with the average per play in parentheses.

	Racine	Corneille	Pradon
jusque + consonant	24 (3.5)	4	1
jusqu' + vowel	82 (7-)	15	11
jusques + vowel	26 (4-)	2	1

It is clear that *jusqu'* (three times as frequent) is the basic form and that *jusques* is the alternate. Corneille and Pradon both confirm that conclusion.

Base word *encor* also has three forms, the first of which is excluded from alternation for matrical compensation.

	Racine	Corneille	Pradon
encore + vowel	101 (15)	1	6
encore + consonant	6 (1)		--
encor + consonant	140 (20)	32	24

In only six instances is the alternate *encore* chosen by Racine to precede a consonant and thus to add a syllable to the line. Neither Corneille nor Pradon uses the device in the particular plays examined.

Proper names occasionally have alternate forms for metrical reasons (see Cahen, p. 212). These are, however, the only clear-cut cases. A number of possible alternations appear neither in Racine nor in the other two plays: *avec* versus *avecque* (the latter is invariably used before a vowel), *pour que* versus *afin que*, *aussitôt que* versus *dès que*, etcetera. Ironically, the case that led to the original hypothesis of alternation for metrical compensation is ambiguous, despite Cahen's conviction (illustrated by *Bérénice*, 1082-84) that "Racine ne choisit entre *lorsque* et *quand* que pour des raisons exclusivement métriques" (p. 212).

	Racine	Corneille	Pradon
lorsqu' + vowel	13 (2)	-	1
quand + vowel	11 (2-)	9	5

When a vowel follows, the choice between *quand* and *lorsqu'* is clearly motivated by factors other than meter, since the number of syllables remains the same regardless of the choice. That factor is not, however, avoidance of alliteration in *l*, since 6 of the 13 cases of *lorsqu'* are followed by an *l* in the next word as well as 10 of the 11 cases of *quand*. Both Cor-

neille and Pradon seem to choose *quand* over *lorsqu'* almost automatically.

	Racine	Corneille	Pradon
lorsque + consonant	37 (5)	3	6
quand + consonant	110 (16)	30	25

Alternation does appear to be a factor here. Other factors must be at
work since, for example, 11 cases of *quand* are preceded by *et* or *mais*,
presumably as filler in the hemistich. Eight of the 11 cases could have
done without the filler by use of *lorsque*; the other three would involve
lorsqu', which solves nothing in such cases. In seven cases out of the 8,
quand is followed by a monosyllabic word containing a so-called mute *e*.
The most probable explanation for Racine's using *quand* in these cases is
to avoid mute *e* in two successive syllables.

There is also a possible alternation between *dès* and *depuis*, but
overlapping of meaning cannot be demonstrated clearly enough to warrant a claim for alternation based on metrical compensation. Therefore,
while there are clearcut cases of alternation for metrical compensation in
Racine, this study has uncovered a maximum of 69 cases in a total of
nearly 12,000 lines, that is, an average of only one case every 171.3 lines.
Moreover, a number of those cases are ambiguous.

Filler Elements for Metrical Compensation

Words or groups of words that may be used to fill out a hemistich include coordinating conjunctions, adverbs and adverbial phrases, other
formulaic phrases, vocatives, and interjections. Frequent occurrence is
the first clue.

The conjunction *et* is used so frequently in classical French drama that
even the casual reader suspects its use as filler or padding, especially in
sentence initial and hemistich initial position (75.8% of total occurrences), as well as its combination with other words. The same can be said
of *mais*, especially in line initial position.

et quand . . .	*mais* enfin . . .
et si . . .	*mais* cependant . . .

The same may be true for *ou* and *car*, but on a greatly reduced scale.

	Total	Line initial	Other hemistich initial
et	2296	868 (37.8%)	872 (38.0%)
mais	544	423 (77.8%)	53 (9.7%)
ou	177	41 (23.2%)	57 (32.3%)
car	18	14 (77.8%)	1 (5.6%)

Both the total number of occurrences of *et* and the percentage of them in the hemistich initial position are significant. Earlier work on Corneille and Pradon (above) shows that the relative frequency of occurrences of *et* is much lower in Racine. Distribution of position within the *alexandrin* remains more or less constant.

	Total	Line initial	Other hemistich initial
et in Pradon	538	180 (33.5%)	218 (40.5%)
et in Corneille	440	197 (44.8%)	154 (35.0%)

Approximately twenty adverbs and related expressions are used repeatedly (15 times or more) by Racine and serve in part as padding. Evidence of this function in isolated cases is provided in the variants. Having lost a syllable in replacing *leur* by *m'* in the following hemistich from *Bajazet* (281), Racine added *tant* in compensation: "Que leur avoit promise" becomes "Que m'avoit tant promise." In another instance Racine absorbed the syllables of the filler *d'abord* when he changed the verb in a hemistich from *Mithridate* (90). "Virent d'abord Pharnace" becomes "Rencontrèrent Pharnace." In other cases one adverb or adverbial expression is replaced by another of the same length: "Mais puisqu'après cinq ans" becomes "Mais puisqu'en ce moment" (*Bérénice*, 206); "étoit encore unie" becomes "étoit alors unie" (*Mithridate*, 252).

Most of the frequently used adverbs are two syllables in length and choice within the group is subsequently based on meaning and possibly on sound. The most frequent (50-247 occurrences) are the most likely to be utility or all-purpose fillers. Most of these adverbs are combined from time to time with *et*, *mais*, or *car* to provide a three-syllable expression. There are, for instance, 24 cases of *mais enfin* and 10 of *car enfin* in the seven Racinian plays. While *encor(e)* does not have an important role in alternation for metrical compensation, it is the adverb filler of choice for all three playwrights.

	Racine	Corneille	Pradon
encore(e)	247 (35)	33	35
enfin[4]	190 (27)	20	28
toujours	167 (24)	11	13
peut-être	119 (17)	17	17
longtemps	90 (13)	4	9
assez	84 (12)	26	7
déjà	84 (12)	9	6
bientôt	62 (9)	6	6
plutôt	51 (7)	2	6
en vain	50 (7)	11	5

Two other fillers of two syllables are quite common in Pradon but in neither Racine nor Corneille: *du moins* (10 in Pradon) and *sans doute* (14 in Pradon). There is only one significant filler of one syllable in length, *donc* (119 [17] in Racine and a comparable number or fewer in Corneille and Pradon); the three-syllable adverb fillers include *cependant* (57 [8] in Racine but an astounding 19 in Pradon and a mere 4 in Corneille) and *aujourd'hui* (50 [7] in Racine but 16 in Pradon and only 4 in Corneille). These adverbs occur predominantly in the first hemistich, ranging from a low of 57% for *encore* to a high of 94.7% for *cependant* in Racine. Only *encore* is a significant factor in the rhyme scheme (30 occurrences or 28.0%). *Cependant* is hemistich initial more than fifty percent of the time, while *encor(e)*, *enfin*, and *longtemps* tend to be hemistich final, that is, placed directly before the caesura. Others, especially *donc*, are normally hemistich internal. It is clear, in summary, that all three playwrights use adverbs for fillers to a considerable extent; Pradon, however, uses roughly 20 percent more than do either Corneille or Racine. The particular adverbs preferred beyond *encor(e)* and *enfin*, however, do vary markedly from writer to writer. When less frequently occurring adverbs are included (15 or more occurrences), one adverb of this type occurs every 8.2 lines in Racine.

Certain formulaic expressions, while not fillers in the strict sense of padding out a hemistich, fit so conveniently into the metrical pattern of the *alexandrin* that they are used frequently by Racine. A few examples suffice to demonstrate the principle involved.

	Racine	Corneille	Pradon
disjunctive + -*même(s)* pronoun	277 (40)	20	17
À + possessive + *yeux* adjective	118 (17)	11	17
en dans + *ce(s) lieu(x)* de	77 (11)	6	11
que + dis / entends / sais / vois + -*je?*	48 (7)	-	6

On two occasions, Racine replaced the most frequent expression, disjunctive pronoun + -*même(s)*, by a less frequent adverbial expression: "Me fait courir moi-même" becomes "Me fait courir alors" (*Andromaque*, 66); "Si vous-même laissant" becomes "Si laissant en effet" (*Mithridate*, 285). While the figures for Racine may appear unusually high compared to those of Corneille and Pradon, the figures for Racine represent an average over seven plays, which masks variations within his own usage. Moreover, there is no reason to suppose that Racine's favorite formulaic expressions of this nature would be the same ones preferred by other playwrights. They may well have other, more frequent ones.

Significantly, nearly all of these expressions are three syllables in length, exactly half a hemistich; as a group they occur once every 25.8 lines in Racine. This quantitative fact is not meant to obscure either the literary significance or the emotional impact of the expressions. In fact, judicious repetition often enhances dramatic effect. As a prime example with regard to the expression containing *yeux*, I cite Jean Starobinski's remarkable work on "Racine et la poétique du regard" in *L'Œil vivant* (Paris: Gallimard, 1961). The purpose of this present chapter is, however, to underscore typical solutions to metrical exigencies.

While vocatives using personal names do occur, Racinian characters most often address each other by title.

	Racine	Corneille	Pradon
Seigneur	429 (61)	85	79
Madame	386 (55)	62	83
Prince	50 (7)	6	3
total	865 (123)	153	165

Thus a title vocative occurs on the average of once every 13.7 lines in Racine. The distribution from play to play depends, however, on developments not adequately represented by the averages given above. The relative frequencies of *Seigneur* and *Madame* vary, depending on the number of principal male and female roles in a given play. In *Bérénice* the fact of twice as many *Seigneurs* (83) as *Madames* (41) can be accounted for by appearance of two principal male roles and one principal female role. For comparisons between plays, therefore, all title vocatives are grouped together. Taking the length of individual plays into account, title vocatives in *Andromaque* and *Mithridate* approach the average for the group, while in *Britannicus* and *Bérénice* they are significantly more frequent, and in *Bajazet*, *Iphigénie* and *Phèdre* they are significantly less frequent. While the decrease in use is by no means constant, Racine does tend to use fewer and fewer title vocatives after *Bérénice*. This makes the contrast all the more striking between *Phèdre* (88 title vocatives) and *Phèdre et Hippolyte* (165). Pradon's use of title vocatives is, however, not significantly different from Racine's in *Britannicus* (168). Nevertheless, the variants record 14 cases in which Racine removed a title vocative; no fewer than 7 of the fourteen changes were made in *Bérénice*. Thus it seems plausible to suppose that after reaching a maximum level in *Britannicus*, Racine consciously reduced the number of title vocatives in *Bérénice*, whose rate would otherwise have exceeded even that of *Britannicus*. Thereafter, Racine used the title vocative to a lesser and lesser degree.

These title vocatives are invariably set apart by intonation from the rest of a line and thus perceptibly affect the rhythm of the line;[5] they do not necessarily have any emotional force. On the other hand, interjections, often combined with the title vocatives, do have emotional force, ranging from surprise to dismay, despair, or terror. As was seen in earlier chapters, these interjections are frequently accompanied by internal punctuation and in this respect were discussed in relation to characterization. There are of course numerous combinations, such as *Ah! Dieux!* and *ô ciel!*, for a total of 807 separate interjections or one every 14.6 lines in Racine.

	Racine	Corneille	Pradon
ah	244 (35)	11	66
quoi	177 (25)	6	22
ô	142 (20)	3	2
hélas	102 (15)	8	41
hé	95 (15-)	5	3
ciel	61 (9)	1	15
Dieux	48 (7)	2	29
total	869 (127)	36	178

By this criterion the three playwrights differ radically. Corneille characteristically uses the fewest interjections, a fact that could be inferred from his infrequent use of internal punctuation. Corneille's use of individual interjections in *Tite et Bérénice* is within the range provided by Racine's seven tragedies, with the single exception of *ah* (11) compared to Racine's low in *Phèdre* (20). On the other hand, Pradon's use of four specific interjections is far outside Racine's range, and his total exceeds Racine's average by roughly forty percent.

	Racine's range	*Phèdre*	Pradon
ah	20-42	20	66
hélas	7-27	11	41
Dieux	0-15	12	29
ciel	0-13	9	15

In conclusion, Corneille uses the interjection rarely, about thirty percent as often as Racine or once every 49.3 lines. At the other end of the scale, Pradon uses an interjection once every 9.8 lines. This contrast is particularly striking in the cases of *ah* and *hélas* as compared to Racine's range; it is astounding when contrasted to *Phèdre* individually. In fact, Pradon uses those two interjections so frequently that any possibility of contrastive characterization within the play is obliterated. They are, on the contrary, very convenient one- and two-syllable fillers.

Conclusion

The combined results from the various areas of investigation can be summarized as follows in order of decreasing frequency.

	Racine	Corneille	Pradon
	once every		
*et	5.1 lines	3.9	3.3
All adverbs	8.2	10.8	8.3
Title vocatives	13.7	11.6	10.5
Interjections	14.6	49.3	9.8
Whole hemistichs	20.4	10.4	9.2
*mais	21.7	18.5	18.2
Formulaic expressions	25.8	47.9	34.1
*Alternations for metrical compensation	171.3	295.7	216.8

NOTE: An asterisk precedes any entry that unavoidably contains occurrences of the construction unrelated to metrical considerations. It is to be presumed in such cases that compensation occurs less frequently than indicated in the table.

These statistics describe a number of features of the *alexandrin* in three seventeenth-century writers of serious dramatic poetry. They permit generalizations as well as distinctions in the genre in the 1660s and 1670s. Alternations for metrical compensation, the impetus in part for this chapter on versification, are of minimal importance from a quantitative perspective. Corneille and Pradon show a negligible frequency and Racine profits from the possibilities only infrequently. Moreover, many alleged examples of alternation for metrical compensation proved to be ambiguous at best.

Use of *et* and *mais* for metrical considerations is generalized, although Racine employs both *et* and *mais* significantly less often than do Corneille and Pradon. Title vocatives are an important factor in dramatic poetry but are subject to abuse, since they can provide free and syntactically independent syllables to the *alexandrin*. Racine resorts to title vocatives less frequently on the average than either Corneille or Pradon. The latter is the greatest offender in this regard. Moreover, Racine replaces numerous title vocatives in later editions of early plays and tends to use title vocatives less and less frequently. Interjections, like title vocatives, are syntactically independent units and as such are easy to add to a short *alexandrin*. Used with restraint they can contribute to characterization, but used excessively as fillers they work against both the density and the fluidity of the *alexandrin*. Racine seems to have found a happy medium between Corneille's relative avoidance of interjections and Pradon's proliferation.

Rate of repetition of whole hemistichs may be the most general indicator of a writer's skill and ingenuity in composing long series of *alexandrins*. The rate is clearly linked to the length of a text; for that reason the figure given for Racine in the summary table above represents the average of the rates for individual plays rather than the composite rate, since only the former could be comparable to rates for Corneille and Pradon. The differences are enormous: Racine's rate is roughly half that of both Corneille and Pradon. In fact, what distinguishes Racine from Pradon objectively is restraint: restraint in the use of title vocatives, of interjections, and of *et* and *mais,* and restraint in repetition of whole hemistichs. What distinguishes Racine from Corneille is more frequent use of adverbs and of interjections, slightly less frequent use of title vocatives, *et* and *mais,* and dramatically fewer repetitions of whole hemistichs.

In one sense this chapter on versification is a digression from the main purpose of the study, although it deals with questions raised by the study of techniques of characterization. The results both confirm and refute certain intuitions about features of sentence structure not related to characterization. A number of these features, but not all, are in fact related to versification and can even be used to distinguish the *alexandrin* of three contemporary playwrights. Several features are widely employed in similar ways, but others are author specific and permit objective and concrete distinctions among authors whose *alexandrins* have intuitively been considered distinctive by literary critics. This chapter provides a preliminary yardstick in distinctive versification and obtains results impressive enough to encourage further quantitative investigation into the technical aspects of the *alexandrin*.

Notes to Chapter 8

1. *The Song of Roland: Formulaic Style and Poetic Craft* (Berkeley: University of California Press, 1973), p. 7.

2. For work on the syntactically styled hemistich, see Ricardo Casterán, "Les Rapports de la syntaxe et de la versification dans *Phèdre*," *Langue et Littérature: Actes du VIIIe Congrès de la Fédération Internationale des Langues et Littératures Modernes* (Paris: Société d'Edition "Les Belles Lettres," 1961), pp. 271-74. For summary of the views of seventeenth-century theoreticians, see Yves Le Hir, *Esthétique et structure du vers français d'après les théoriciens du XVIe siècle à nos jours* (Paris: Presses Universitaires de France, 1956).

3. See also Philip Wexler, "On the Grammetrics of the Classical Alexandrine," *Cahiers de Lexicologie* 4 (1964): 63.

4. Alain Seznec makes sweeping claims on the interpretative level about the distribution of *enfin* in *Andromaque:* "In fact, it is possible, by noting the appearances of this word, to follow the progress and change of a character or a situation and, in part, delineate the dramatic structure of a scene or of the play as a whole" ("The Uses of *enfin* in Racine's *Andromaque*," *French Review* 45, Special Issue 4 [1972]: 62).

5. See Théophile Spoerri, "Le Rythme tragique," *Trivium* 3 (1945): 161-84.

Conclusion

The basic features with which the study began in *Andromaque* are by far
the most consistently useful in understanding characterization. Other
features tend to give only momentary insights rather than consistent ones.
Still others have little or no bearing on characterization but are linked to
function or to verse structure. A balance must be struck between quantitative and qualitative considerations with regard to the primary
sentence features: terminal punctuation, internal questions and exclamations, sentence type, and sentence length. Quantity is particularly important in variations of sentence length. In the seven tragedies discussed in
depth, the variations of mean sentence length from play to play are
minimal; from a high in *Mithridate* (21.928 syllables per sentence) to a
low in *Bérénice* (18.941), there is less than a three-syllable-per-sentence
range (see Appendix C, Table 3). The variations from act to act are more
pronounced. The only overall pattern that emerges is a tendency to
longer sentences in Act I than in the other acts of a given play, and to
decreasing sentence length from act to act with a possible resurgence in
the third or fourth act. A reversal of the trend to decreasing mean
sentence length from act to act invariably indicates a détente in the action, while a marked decrease indicates a crisis. Each play presents a
special configuration within the basic pattern.

The differences from character to character within a single play are
more radical. There may be up to nine syllables per sentence separating
the character with the longest average sentences from the character with
the shortest ones, as in *Iphigénie*, or this difference may be as little as
three syllables per sentence, as in *Andromaque*. Sentences longer or
shorter than these occur only in the early tragedies, *La Thébaïde* and
Alexandre, or in the later ones, *Esther* and *Athalie*. Table 6 in Appendix
C arranges all the characters in Racine's tragedies in order of decreasing
mean sentence length. Groupings are apparent from this table. In the
17-18 syllable-per-sentence range are the characters most likely to be
emotionally oriented, those most commonly given to outrage and to loss
of control. As the mean sentence length increases, characters are more
and more likely to be in control of themselves, until toward the top of the

scale appear royal counselors and functional characters who invariably have the longest sentences. This is an approximate and relative criterion that indicates tendencies and not absolute or precise rules. It is particularly dangerous to claim distinctions with respect to closely ranked characters or even to oppose the characters with seventeen-odd syllables per sentence to those of eighteen-odd syllables. The breaks in Table 6 are placed primarily for legibility and as such are not hard-and-fast boundaries. With *Andromaque* the monostich permanently replaces the distich as the most common sentence length for all tragedies and for the vast majority of characters.

The distribution of terminal punctuation is surprisingly consistent from play to play: for each feature the range from most frequent use to least frequent is on the order of 2 to 7 percent (see Appendix C, Table 1). Thus variations from play to play are not significant in a quantitative sense and do not show any evolution with regard to terminal punctuation. Variations between characters, however, are highly significant; a number of generalizations are possible. The period has several functions, one of which marks simple narration. The *récit* typically contains sentences all or most of which end in periods. Declarative sentences can reveal what is on a character's mind, but usually only when that character intends to reveal his thoughts (Néron to Narcisse about his mother; Phèdre to Thésée in the final scene). More often, a character is controlling or attempting to control a situation: threats (Pyrrhus, Roxane), imperatives (Mithridate), and sometimes sarcasm are expressed through sentences ending in periods. Characters often attempt to hide their feelings in declarative sentences (Junie, Pyrrhus), which can result in ironic overtones (Agamemnon, Roxane). Thus while sentences ending in periods might appear neutral, closer examination reveals a wide variation in their applications. Real questions, posed in order to gain information, are rare in Racinian tragedy and are used primarily by functional characters. A character can control his questions for a variety of purposes: suggestion that something may or may not be true (Hermione, Achille), internal debate and uncertainty (Andromaque, Titus, Mithridate, and numerous others), reproaches directed at oneself or at others (Titus, Bérénice), sarcasm (Hermione, Clytemnestre), anger, and attack upon another character. The range of controlled uses runs from calm suggestion to bitter sarcasm and anger. On the other hand, characters also express loss of control through questions. Milder forms consist of wondering and confu-

sion, whereas more extreme forms result in attack, outrage, and derangement. Examination of the specific questions in a tragedy leads invariably
to insights into characterization. Exclamations express surprise and occasionally sarcasm; they appear for apostrophe and lamentation in later
tragedies. Their distribution, however, does not lead to important
discoveries about characters. The same is true of ellipses or unfinished
sentences. Except for isolated cases like Oreste, no patterns can be
established. Individual occurrences can be significant, for instance,
Phèdre's comment to Œnone, "J'aime. . . ," as well as breaks in
monologues when a character realizes errors in his reasoning (Titus).

Unlike terminal punctuation, internal questions and exclamations are
not consistently useful for gaining insight into characterization. Evolution
in internal questions is apparent, since they occur less and less frequently
in the chronological sequence of tragedies (see Appendix C, Table 7). Expressions like "Hé quoi?" and "Mais quoi?" tend to indicate a character
caught offguard, expressing surprise and confusion (Britannicus), or
outrage (Clytemnestre). Internal exclamations are more frequent than internal questions in all of Racine's tragedies. They consist of such expressions as "Ah!", "Ô . . . !", "Hé (bien)!" and "Hélas!". Occasionally a
character like Hermione gives them more content: "Le perfide!" Internal
exclamations, most commonly associated with emotionally oriented
characters, further break the flow of their typically short and irregular
sentences.

The other important factor in basic sentence structure is sentence type,
a measure of the extent to which the physical limits of a sentence coincide
with the physical limits of the *alexandrin*. When they coincide, a sentence
is termed regular. When they do not, it is irregular. At least sixty percent
of the sentences in a Racinian tragedy are regular; this figure may reach a
level of almost 75 percent, as it does in *Phèdre* (see Appendix C, Table 2).
The basic trend is a considerable drop in regular sentences from the two
early plays to *Andromaque*, slight fluctuation for several plays, then a rise
again in *Iphigénie* and *Phèdre* The type B sentences that stand out prominently within a series of type A sentences invariably reveal the
character's main preoccupation.

It is difficult to discuss sentence type without discussing terminal punctuation as well, for they so often combine to characterize the larger units
of Racinian tragedy: *récits, tirades,* and rapid exchanges between
characters. The *récit* is narrative, and in its purest form it consists of a

series of regular and declarative sentences. *Récits* occur most often in Act I for exposition of background information and in Act V for recounting that part of the denouement which occurs offstage. The expository material is particularly evident in *Bajazet* and *Mithridate*, but as early as *Bérénice* Racine presents in the first act characters so deeply involved in the situation at hand that they talk in animated terms and thus in affective terminal punctuation and irregular sentences rather than in *récits*. Long *récits* of the denouement become more and more the rule as with Arbate, Ulysse, and Théramène in the last three tragedies studied. *Bajazet* is a notable exception, where a number of characters appear in sequence, each adding a bit of information about the denouement. Because of its predominantly expository nature, the *récit* is not related to characterization but is a functional activity of the chosen characters. When the activity is more than functional, sentence type and terminal punctuation are modified. The *tirades* examined in the chapter on *Mithridate* show how sentence type and terminal punctuation combine in interesting ways as characters reveal and conceal their thoughts and feelings. Sometimes working together, they convey control or loss of control; at other times working at cross purposes, they represent imperfect control or imminent loss of control. Rapid exchanges between characters, when they are more than conventional stichomythia, occur for the first time in *Andromaque*, where only two such exchanges take place. By contrast, there are six or more in *Britannicus* (II, 2 and 4; III, 6; V, 1, 4, and 6). It is curious that this development should directly follow Racine's experiment in comedy, *Les Plaideurs*, where rapid exchanges are the rule rather than the exception. Racine continues to use rapid exchanges in the rest of the tragedies at crucial points of revelation, but never again to the extent that he does in *Britannicus* and *Bérénice*.

Other sentence features are only marginally useful for the study of characterization. Many forms of subordination used rarely by Racine cannot be studied, since it is impossible to draw conclusions from only a few cases. One frequent construction, *pour* + infinitive, is simply not linked to characterization. Study of three other forms of subordination involving conjunctions or prepositions that introduce infinitives, conditional *si*, *quand* and *lorsque*, and *sans* + infinitive, are potentially interesting but ultimately disappointing. They offer only occasional and isolated insights. A very curious increase in their use in *Bérénice* (*quand/lorsque*) and in *Bajazet* and *Mithridate* (conditional *si* and *sans*

+ infinitive) is followed by an equally curious tapering off thereafter (see Appendix C, Table 8). In the final analysis Roxane is the only Racinian character to appropriate one of these constructions as the expression of her customary way of dealing with others. She uses the conditional *si* as a weapon, especially on Bajazet. Threatening people is a definite character trait here, and the violence of Roxane's threats increases as the play progresses and as Bajazet resists. In no other case is subordination used consistently as a mark of character rather than as a momentary expression of an idea or a function.

Comparison to other plays of the period permits conclusions about the specificity of all features of sentence structure studied in Racinian tragedy. Happily, a major and a minor playwright wrote works treating the same subjects as Racine, thereby eliminating a possibly significant variable in subject matter. Corneille's *Tite et Bérénice* discussed in chapter 3 is quite different from Racine's *Bérénice*: sentences are consistently longer and more regular; the distich predominates; subordinations are more frequent and internal punctuation less so. In fact, Corneille's sentence structure is remarkably similar to Racine's early style in *La Thébaïde* and *Alexandre*, before he developed consistent techniques for characterization through language. Pradon's *Phèdre et Hippolyte* presents truly astonishing differences in sentence structure as well; sentences are more than twice as long, on the average; the range of sentence length between characters is much greater; affective and irregular sentences are half again as frequent as in Racine; no rapid exchanges occur, but internal exclamations and interjections are three to four times as frequent. In short, Corneille and Pradon demonstrate that Racine's techniques of sentence structure are author specific: they represent neither some vague period style nor a style derived from the subject matter. Moreover, *Les Plaideurs* shows that the techniques in question are even more genre specific, for Racine's only comedy differs more radically from his tragedies than do the tragedies of other contemporary playwrights: in radically shortened sentences and greatly increased use of irregular and affective sentences as well as internal punctuation (Pradon does resemble *Les Plaideurs* in this respect). Subordination, however, is within the expected range for Racine.

The chapter on versification grew naturally out of questions raised about sentence structure. Obviously, the latter is limited in part by the metrical requirements of the *alexandrin*. Once again comparisons to Corneille and Pradon are instructive. One basic intuition involving alternations for metrical compensation proved of minimal importance, whereas others regarding filler elements and formulaic expressions were productive. The three contemporary playwrights have distinctive styles in this regard also. Pradon in particular, as the least skilled poet, resorts most frequently to compensatory devices: conjunctions *et* and *mais*, adverbial expressions, and especially interjections and title vocatives appear so frequently as filler elements that they regularly interfere with both the fluidity and the density of Pradon's *alexandrin*. Repetition of whole hemistichs occurs at a level that confirms suspicions about Pradon's lack of poetic flexibility. Corneille and Racine are not so different from each other as they are from Pradon. Nevertheless, Racine does use fewer fillers, such as *et* and *mais*, and title vocatives than does Corneille. He uses internal punctuation and interjections more frequently than Corneille, but as a tool for characterization. While the work on the *alexandrin* in this context is far from definitive, it clearly demonstrates that objective and verifiable distinctions can be found to undergird or to refute intuitions about "good" and "bad" verse, at least in dramatic poetry.

A study of this magnitude cannot be accomplished in a reasonable length of time or with reasonable accuracy without the assistance of a computer. The IBM 370/165 has performed three essential functions: (1) breaking the text of the plays into sentences and associating with each sentence a number of variables; (2) cross-tabulating great masses of data into usable and manageable tables; and (3) generating concordances and word-frequency lists. The results of the computer phase are, of course, purely quantitative; it has been the purpose of this study to interpret those data. Despite obvious limitations, literary critics should not disparage the quantitative aspect of computer-assisted research. Although quantitative results must always be analyzed and interpreted to determine their literary significance, they have the distinct advantage of being tangible and verifiable, something that everyone can see. They are not impressionistic, but provide the critic with a concrete point of departure. I had supposed that distichs are more common in Racinian tragedy than are monostichs, but in fact they are not. I had thought that certain characters like Phèdre have an affinity for conditional sentences, when in fact they do not. On the other hand, I was able to verify a number of impressions and actually stumbled onto unexpected discoveries. It is the interplay between the concreteness of the data and its interpretation that has produced this study. A critic must never be satisfied to stop with tables and statistics, but rather must move beyond that stage to make inferences. These inferences lead from the perspective of language to the perspective of poetics, in a movement whose rationale was stated in my preliminary remarks about tragedy.

It is now clear just how the movement was accomplished and what its results have been. Tragedy is serious drama. The dramatic nature of Racine's work is a basic principle of characterization, since the characters in large measure reveal themselves through what they say. The seriousness of it has been borne out in the attitudes of the characters and in the consequences of their words and deeds. Tragedy must be carefully constructed. This abstract assumption has been verified by the high degree of success in investigating specific aspects of that careful construction, that is, patterns of sentence structure. In tragedy a high level of inference is demanded on the part of the audience. Although true for a number of aspects, setting, gestures, action, and language, I chose to examine only language and, in particular, the sentence. The inferences made from language are inferences about characterization. One important function of language in Racine's tragedies, then, is to furnish consistent and relevant clues to characterization, clues to the thoughts, desires, and motives of the characters presented on the stage. Reviewing the features of sentence structure topically earlier in this conclusion produced a list of specific clues to characterization furnished by specific features of sentence structure. The general tendencies of characterization can be seen in a series of oppositions.

The first opposes characters in confrontation to characters alone. A peaceful confrontation may involve two characters, normally sympathetic to each other, who need to resolve a misunderstanding or a conflict of interest (Junie and Britannicus, Xipharès and Monime). In most confrontations, however, at least one of the characters is hostile. This situation produces either a purely verbal conflict (Clytemnestre and Agamemnon) or one that ultimately results in physical violence (Roxane and Bajazet, Néron and Agrippine). The scenes of confrontation are by and large the most interesting and informative for making inferences about character. The other scenes show characters alone or with their confidants. Some monologues are useful. More often than not they reveal uncertainty on the part of the character about his or her proposed plan of action (Titus, Andromaque, Roxane). Careful differentiation among scenes with confidants is crucial. In tragedies like *Andromaque*, the confidants serve primarily as a sounding board for their master or mistress, whereas in *Britannicus*, for instance, confidants are royal counselors, and in *Phèdre* the heroine's conversations with her confidante Œnone are clearly confrontations.

In scenes of reflection and decision-making, characters usually reveal what they are thinking and feeling. In scenes of confrontation, however, they may either reveal or conceal those thoughts and emotions. Involved also in this alternation is the notion of control and loss of control. Characters may voluntarily reveal or conceal their desires. By the same token, they may involuntarily reveal desires when placed in a particularly stressful situation (Phèdre, Hermione). Only when they are not sure of what they want do characters conceal involuntarily. Control of the situation and thus of language usually manifests itself when a character proposes a course of action (Mithridate, Néron) or actually embarks on it (Roxane). Control can also show itself when a character manipulates another character (Atalide, Hermione) or when he willfully shifts the responsibility for action and for consequences onto the shoulders of another. Pyrrhus shifts responsibility to Andromaque, Agamemnon shifts it to the Greeks, Calchas, and the gods.

The notion of control versus loss of control leads to another set of opposing terms: emotionally directed and rationally directed characters. This opposition has been evident in distinctive patterns of sentence structure throughout the study. It is not to be confused with the preceding opposition, for emotionally directed characters are as capable of control as rationally directed ones are of loss of control. These, then, are the basic alternations uncovered in Racine's characterizations: situations of confrontation versus situations of solitude, reflection, and decision-making; concealment versus revelation of inner thoughts and feelings; control of oneself and of the situation through language versus loss of that control; and emotionally directed versus rationally directed characters. In all cases these generalized oppositions have been brought to light through examination of specific patterns of sentence structure and of their relationship to characterization.

Discussion of characterization in tragedy has invariably led to special insight into the denouement. This is in keeping with preliminary assumptions about tragedy, namely, that the outcome is of the utmost importance and of the utmost significance. Looking back over individual denouements reveals a wide variety. The one constant is destruction, although the level of violence differs considerably. *Bérénice* bears witness to the destruction of the relationship between Titus and Bérénice, whereas the other tragedies present different combinations of murder and suicide, where the number of fatalities varies, as does the condition of the survivors. The presentation of the denouement differs also from tragedy to tragedy. The denouement may occur entirely offstage with a functional character arriving on the scene to narrate it in a *récit*, as in *Iphigénie* and in *Bajazet*, or the denouement may occur entirely before the eyes of the audience as in *Bérénice*. The other tragedies combine the two procedures: Hippolyte's death is recited by Théramène, and Phèdre herself appears to confess her guilt before Thésée; Pylade relates the assassination of Pyrrhus, but both Oreste and Hermione appear on stage to demonstrate the extent of their despair.

In most of these tragedies one main character makes a decision that precipitates the denouement (Roxane, Thésée) or actually takes an active part in it (Oreste, Mithridate). Only in *Iphigénie* are the main characters mere spectators to the denouement. It is relatively easy to categorize the denouements by these three criteria: level of destructive violence, presentation of the denouement, participation of characters in the denouement. It is more difficult to classify them by type. Several consist of the culmination of a contest for the possession of one character: *Britannicus* ends in a temporary victory for the forces opposing Agrippine for the possession of Néron's soul; *Bajazet* ends in annihilation of the interested parties. *Andromaque* would fit this category except that each character seeks possession of another, so that the dynamics of the situation are different. *Bérénice* can be opposed to *Iphigénie* and *Mithridate*, since the first ends in separation while the other two end in some degree of reconciliation, although the reconciliation in *Iphigénie* is less satisfying. *Phèdre* is conspicuously different from the others, since the tragedy ends on a note of revelation and some degree of inner peace achieved by Phèdre. Nuances make each denouement unique, and similarities relate them to each other. In every case the denouement is an important factor in tragedy, as originally supposed.

Thus certain features of sentence structure reliably portray character in Racine's tragedies. In combination these features enable the critical reader or spectator to understand more fully the characters themselves and the dynamics of their predicaments and thus to appreciate more fully and more concretely Racine's masterful use of language. This study of sentence structure leads invariably beyond characterization to insights into each tragedy as an organic whole, particularly with reference to the denouements. Study of tangible and verifiable details of the relationships among sentence structure, characterization, and versification, valuable in and of itself, has wider implications, since it sheds light on that poetic unity which is a Racinian tragedy.

APPENDIX A.
The Computer-Readable Texts

The texts of Racine's tragedies used in this study are those of the Mesnard edition of 1885; this edition is based on the edition of 1697, the last to be published during Racine's lifetime. The computer-readable texts are based on the ones prepared by Bryant C. Freeman and Alan Batson and used to generate the *Concordance du théâtre et des poésies de Jean Racine*. I have, however, altered the format and some of the symbols to suit the purposes of this particular study and to facilitate future use of these texts. The text of Corneille's *Tite et Bérénice* is that of the Marty-Laveaux edition of 1862; Pradon's *Phèdre et Hippolyte* is a seventeenth-century edition published in 1677 by Henry Loyson and printed in *Les Œuvres de Mr Pradon* in 1682 by Jean Ribou. I prepared computer-readable texts for both on punched cards especially for this study in the same format as the Racine texts.

The texts are contained on one 9-track, 2400-foot, 1600 BPI, standard-label IBM tape. Each play is a separate file, so that each can be read individually. The DSN (data set name) for each play consists of the first six letters of its title, excluding the definite article and conjunctions. The only exception is Pradon's play, whose DSN is HIPPOL in order to distinguish it from *Phèdre*. The records are in fixed and blocked format with an LRECL (logical record length) of 100 characters and a BLKSIZE (blocksize) of 4000.

The basic disposition of the text is as follows: the text of the edition of 1697 (one line per LRECL) + one line of 'XXXXXXXXXX' (to separate text from variants) + the variants. The disposition of a given line is as follows: six columns reserved for sequential numbering of the LRECLs for file maintenance purposes + sixteen column ID + line of text. The breakdown of the ID is as follows: 'ANORESTE 1 1   1 '

'AN'	'ORESTE'	'l'	' l'	' l'	' '	
Play	Character	Act	Scene	Line	Variant	
7	9	15	16	18	22	column

Since it is of fixed length, the ID is placed to the left of the line of text. This eliminates the need to justify the left-hand margin of an ID, which follows a text of irregular length and facilitates file maintenance procedures. The play is identified by the first two letters of its title, excluding the definite article (Corneille's play by 'TB' and Pradon's play by 'HP'); the character by the first six letters. The only exceptions are La Comtesse and Petit Jean in *Les Plaideurs* whose names appear in the ID as 'CTESSE' and 'JEAN' respectively and Domitian in *Tite et Bérénice*, whose name appears as 'DOMITN'. The act, scene, and line numbers are in Arabic numerals to facilitate cross-tabulations. For the same reason, the Prologue to *Esther* is listed as '0 1' (Act 0, scene 1) + line number; with Act I, the line numbers begin with one again, as in the Mesnard edition. The variant column is either blank for a line of the text of 1697 or it contains 'V' for a variant.

Nonstandard symbols are reproduced in the following table.

Symbol	Equivalent
$	precedes a capital letter
>	marks end of line of text
5	´ (accent aigu)
=	` (accent grave)
*	^ (accent circonflexe)
3	¨ (tréma)
#	˛ (cédille)
/	marks a change of character within a line

APPENDIX B.
The Computer Programs

Except for the SPSS package discussion in section 4 below, all programs for this study are written in SPITBOL,[1] a programming language designed specifically for natural language processing, that is, for processing strings of alphabetical, numerical, and related characters. SPITBOL is similar to SNOBOL4,[2] but has additional built-in capabilities like REVERSE (used to spell a work backwards), is faster in terms of computer usage time, and requires much less computer core than does SNOBOL4. I personally wrote all SPITBOL programs in consultation with Thomas Whitney on special problems. Most of the data for this study were generated at the Instructional and Research Computer Center of the Ohio State University on the IBM 370/165. Computer time was provided by the IRCC as part of the allocation to the Department of Romance Languages for research purposes. Some data, including KWIC concordances, work on plays by Corneille and Pradon, and versification research, were generated at the University of Kentucky Computing Center on the IBM 360 and 370 machines. Computer time was provided by the College of Arts and Sciences and released time for research was funded by a Summer Faculty Research Grant from the University of Kentucky.

1. Breakdown of Text into Sentences

The complete program is listed following this discussion. For clarity each section of the program is preceded by comments (identified by the asterisk in column 1) that describe the function of the section immediately following the comments.

A. Main Program

This program breaks the text into sentences and associates with each sentence its type, its terminal punctuation, and a number that identifies its sequential position in the play. The program also flags any change of speaker within a line of a play and lists separately those which cannot be adjusted by the computer itself. The three subroutines to be discussed later count syllables in irregular sentences, search sentences for certain features of sentence structure, and print out the sentences. After the subroutines have been performed, the main program stores in a separate tape file the data associated with each sentence.

A sentence is identified as a string of characters and blanks beginning with a capital letter, a letter preceded by '$', and ending with a terminal punctuation mark, PUNCT = '.?!'. The program distinguishes internal question marks and exclamation points from terminal ones by (1) determining whether or not the punctuation mark is followed by a capital letter; if not, it has to be internal; if it is followed by a capital letter an additional check is necessary (2) to determine whether it is preceded by PATTERN as defined in the Preliminaries of the program. The vertical bar means *or*.

PATTERN = '$AH' | ' AH' | 'O*' | ' HE5LAS' | '$ HE5' | 'HE5' | ' QUOI' | ' QUOI'

The presence of the constant, PATTERN, is determined by pattern matching. If one of the forms included in PATTERN is present, the PUNCT is considered internal, since a capital after one of these expressions is almost invariably a proper name or a title, such as "Seigneur," "Madame," or "Prince."

The program also detects the presence of ellipses, which must be differentiated from the period. This punctuation is subsequently designated as @ because a one-character symbol is needed. Internal ellipses are also distinguished from terminal ones by the same procedure as that used on question marks and exclamation points.

Change of character speaking is recognized by ' / ' when the change is internal to a line of text. The name of the new speaker is identified by the computer whenever possible.

1) One '/' in the line

a. No terminal punctuation after '/': change is done automatically since ID for a sentence will always be based on its last line, whose ID will contain the name of the new character speaking.

b. Terminal punctuation after '/': if the sentence is type M, the character's identity cannot be determined and that information is listed on a disk for correction by hand. Otherwise, comparison is made between character's name for the line in question and for the following line; if identical, the identity of the new character speaking cannot be determined since only that partial line belongs to the character in question. List on disk. If the character of the next line is different from that of the line in question, the new speaker is substituted for the old. There is, of course, a remote possibility that the character whose name appears in the next line is actually a third character. That situation can be uncovered only by actually examining the text. In fact, it occurs only rarely in the tragedies, but with alarming frequency in *Les Plaideurs*.

2) Two '/' in the line

a. The name of the character who says the middle sentence of type M cannot be determined. List on disk.
b. The final sentence or beginning of a sentence is treated as above in paragraph 1).

Built into the main program is a mechanism for assigning type to each sentence. (See chapter 2, for a discussion of types.)

KP1 saves an entire line when it is only part of a sentence and assigns an 'A' as its type if one has not already been assigned.
KP2 saves the end of a line and assigns an 'E' as its type.
CT.A, CT.B, CT.M, and CT.E assign the appropriate types to sentences, concatenating it to any type already stored in TYPE. For instance, CT.B might add 'B' to the null string giving 'B', to 'A' giving 'AB' or to 'EA' giving 'EAB'.

B. Subroutine One: COUNT (Syllable Count)

The subroutine is used to count syllables only in sentences containing partial lines of text; complete lines and multiples thereof are assumed to be *alexandrins*, twelve syllables in length. In several plays this is not strictly the case. Where this problem is limited in scope, such as letters in *Bajazet* or Antigone's monologue in *La Thébaïde*, the limited adjustments necessary are made by hand. In *Esther* and *Athalie* the Chorus speaks in verses of other lengths. In these two tragedies, therefore, the number of syllables is counted in all lines spoken by the Chorus as well as in all partial lines; the remaining lines can be assumed to be *alexandrins*.

The subroutine logic for counting syllables is based on the alternation of vowels and consonants as defined in the Preliminaries: VOWEL = 'AEIOUY' and CONS = 'BCDFGHJKLMNPQRSTVWXZ'. Mute *e* is handled as it would be manually. If the next word begins with a consonant or aspirate *h*, the mute *e* is counted; otherwise, it is not. Aspirate *h* is identified by pattern matching of the word in question against a string of characters representing the beginning of all words in Racine with an initial aspirate *h*. The list is drawn from the Freeman concordance.

ASPIRATED = 'HAI'|'HARDI'|'HASARD'|'HA*T'|'HAUT'|'HE5RIS'|'HONTE'|
'HORS'|'HE5RAU'|'HE5ROS'

Later in the subroutine NO.SYLL1 compensates for *-es* at the end of a line, where it must not be counted.

In several cases vowels representing two different syllables are not separated by consonants as defined in the Preliminaries of the program. These cases are identified by a series of pattern matchings and, when they are present, one syllable is added to the count.

TWO.SYLL1 takes care of words like *essayer, essuyer, nettoyer*, in all forms involving *y*.

TWO.SYLL2 takes care of *cruel(le)(s)* and *mutuel(le)(s)*.

TWO.SYLL3 takes care of *prier, crier, expier, oublier, lier*, in all cases where a syllable must be added. By using the Freeman concordance, I was able to determine that these combinations in *-ier* always have the higher of two possible syllable counts in Racine.

TWO.SYLL4 takes care of *é* + vowel as in *obéir, Créon*.

TWO.SYLL5 takes care of *violen(t)(ce)*.

PL.SYLL1 takes care of proper names in a particular play that are not already taken care of above, such as *Hermione, Antiochus*.

This subroutine counts syllables accurately to the extent that problems can be predetermined. Those words where syllable count may vary in Racine cannot be predetermined. As is the case when syllable counting is done manually, the only indication of an error comes from an eleven- or thirteen-syllable total for a twelve-syllable line. Only then can adjustment be made. Such cases are rare. The count in any case is never in error by more than one syllable in either direction.

C. Subroutine Two: STRUCTURE

This subroutine searches each sentence for morphological patterns, strings of characters, that identify features of sentence structure. In order to find multiple occurrences of a structure in a given sentence, once a structure is found it is replaced by the null string and the sentence is reexamined. The data are stored on a separate tape file, which looks like this for the first few sentences of *Andromaque:*

```
1ANORESTE1    1 4 48A . 31000 40010A0 10B001000
2ANORESTE1    1 6 24A ? 10000 10000A0 01B000000
3ANORESTE1    1 8 24A ? 10000 10000A0 00B000000
```

The comments that precede this subroutine list the data contained in this file.

D. Subroutine Three: PRINT

This subroutine simply prints out the sentences in sequence to permit cross-checking of the data file generated in Subroutine Two against the numbered sentences. For legibility, the maximum line length is seventy characters and the text is indented after the first line of a sentence.

When this process has been repeated for all lines of the text, control is passed to the final phase of the main program, DSK.DATA and following. Here the 'UNCORRECTABLE CHANGES OF SPEAKER' are printed out from the disk for manual correction and the newly generated data on sentence structure are printed out in the 'TABLE OF PARAMETERS.'

```
//      8191,CLASS=E
/*SETUP          UNIT=TAPE9,ID=(RACINE,F058)
/*SETUP          UNIT=TAPE9,ID=(CC2462,C051,WRITE)
//      EXEC  SPITRUN,TIME=3,PARM.GO='R=30K,T=240'
//GO.TAPIN  DD  DSN=BERENI,UNIT=TAPE9,DISP=(OLD,KEEP),LABEL=(5,SL),
//              VOL=SER=RACINE     F058
//GO.DSK  DD  DSN=TEMP,UNIT=SYSDA,DISP=(NEW,DELETE),
//      SPACE=(CYL,(3,2)),DCB=(RECFM=FB,LRECL=22,BLKSIZE=440)
//GO.TOUT  DD  DSN=BESTR,UNIT=TAPE9,LABEL=(5,SL),DISP=(NEW,KEEP),
//      DCB=(RECFM=FB,LRECL=60,BLKSIZE=2400),VOL=SER=CC2462     C051
//GO.SYSIN    DD  *




        INPUT(.IN,'TAPIN')
        OUTPUT(.TOTAPE,'TOUT')
        OUTPUT(.DISK,'DSK')
        OUTPUT('HEADING',6,'(1H1,50A1)')
        &STLIMIT = 200000
*                                                               *
*                    PRELIMINARIES                              *
*                                                               *
*       DEFINITION OF ALL OF THE CONSTANTS IN THE PROGRAM;  DEFINITION  *
*       ALSO OF THE THREE SUBROUTINES.                          *
*                                                               *
        PLAY = 'BERENICE'
        RECORD.LAYOUT = LEN(6) LEN(16) . ID REM . ALINE
        DEFINE('COUNT()')
        DEFINE('STRUCTURE()')
        DEFINE('PRINT()')
        PUNCT = '.!?'
        PATTERN = '$AH' | ' AH' | 'O*' | 'HE5LAS' | 'H5ELAS' | '$HE5' |
    . '$H5E' | ' HE5' | ' H5E' | '$QUOI' | ' QUOI'
        VOWEL = 'AEIOUY'
        CONS = 'BCDFGHJKLMNPQRSTVWXZ'
        ALPHA = VOWEL CONS
        ACCENT = '*=5'
        NON.CADUC = ACCENT VOWEL
        TWO.SYLL1 = ('A' | 'O' | 'U') ('Y') ('ER' | 'EZ' | 'E5' | 'E=' |
    . 'O' | 'A')
        TWO.SYLL2 = 'CRUEL' | 'MUTUEL'
        TWO.SYLL3 = ('PR' | 'CR' | 'EXP' | 'OUBL' | ' L') ('I') ('ER' |
    . 'EZ' | 'E5' | 'E=' | 'O' | 'A')
        TWO.SYLL4 = ('E5') ('I' | 'O' | 'A' | 'U')
        TWO.SYLL5 = 'VIOLEN'
        NO.SYLL1 = ('ES') ('>' | ';>' | ':>' | '.>' | ',>' | '?>' | '!>')
        PL.SYLL1 = '$ANTIOCHUS'
        ASPIRATED = 'HAI' | 'HARDI' | 'HASARD' | 'HA*T' | 'HAUT' |
    . 'HE5RIS' | 'HE5ROS' | 'HONTE' | 'HORS' | 'HE5RAU'
        SI.PATTERN = "JE" | "J'" | "VOUS " | "TU " | "LE " | "L'" |
    . "LA " | "LES " | "L'ON " | "NOUS " | " ELLE"
        ET.PATTERN = (' ' | '$') ('ET') (' ' | ',')
        OU.PATTERN = (' ' | '$') ('OU') (' ' | ',')
        MAIS.PATTERN = (' ' | '$') ('MAIS') (' ' | ',')
        I = 0
```

```
*                                                              *
*                    THE MAIN PROGRAM                          *
*                                                              *
*     THIS PROGRAM BREAKS THE TEXT INTO SENTENCES AND ASSOCIATES  *
*     WITH EACH SENTENCE ITS TYPE, ITS TERMINAL PUNCTUATION, AND  *
*     A NUMBER WHICH IDENTIFIES ITS SEQUENTIAL POSITION IN THE PLAY,  *
*     I.E., FIRST (1), SECOND (2), ETC.                        *
*                                                              *
*     THE PROGRAM ALSO FLAGS ANY CHANGE OF SPEAKER WITHIN A LINE OF  *
*     OF THE PLAY AND LISTS SEPARATELY THOSE WHICH CANNOT BE CHANGED  *
*     BY THE COMPUTER.                                         *
*                                                              *
*     AFTER THE TWO SUBROUTINES HAVE BEEN PERFORMED, THE MAIN PRO-  *
*     GRAM LISTS ON A SEPARATE TAPE ALL THE FEATURES TO BE ASSOCI-  *
*     ATED WITH THAT PARTICULAR SENTENCE.                      *
*                                                              *
        OUTPUT = 'LIST OF SENTENCES FROM ' PLAY
        OUTPUT =
BEGIN       S = 0
        SAVED = NULL
        TYPE = NULL
READ1     RECORD = IN              :F(DSK.DATA)
        RECORD RECORD.LAYOUT
        ID 'XX'                     :S(DSK.DATA)
        TEXT = TRIM(ALINE)
CONT1   TEXT BREAK(PUNCT) . SENTENCE LEN(1) . TERM REM . TEXT   :F(KP1)
        HOLD = TEXT
        HOLD LEN(1) . FINAL REM . HOLD
        IDENT(FINAL,'>')            :S(CT.A)
        IDENT(TERM,'.')                  :F(CH1)
        IDENT(FINAL,'.')            :S(IRR1)F(CT.B)
READ2     S = 0
        SAVED = NULL
        TYPE = NULL
CONT2   TEXT LEN(1) BREAK(PUNCT) . SENTENCE LEN(1) . TERM
.       REM . TEXT              :F(KP2)
        HOLD = TEXT
        HOLD LEN(1) . FINAL REM . HOLD
        IDENT(FINAL,'>')           :S(CT.E)
        IDENT(TERM,'.')                  :F(CH2)
        IDENT(FINAL,'.')             :S(IRR2)F(CT.M)
KP1     SAVED = SAVED TEXT ' '
        S = S + 12
        TYPE 'A'                   :S(READ1)
        TYPE = TYPE 'A'            :(READ1)
KP2     SAVED = SAVED TEXT ' '
        SAVED BREAK('$') REM . SAVED
        STUFF = SAVED
         COUNT()
        TYPE = TYPE 'E'            :(READ1)
*                                                              *
*     DETERMINE WHETHER QUESTION MARK OR EXCLAMATION POINT IS      *
*     INTERNAL OR TERMINAL PUNCTUATION.                        *
*                                                              *
CH1     HOLD LEN(2) . CAP
        CAP '$'                     :S(CH1A)
        CAP '/'                     :S(CT.B)F(CH1B)
CH1A    SENTENCE PATTERN           :F(CT.B)
CH1B    TEXT LEN(1) REM . TEXT
        SAVED = SAVED SENTENCE TERM ' '   :(CONT1)
CH2     HOLD LEN(2) . CAP
        CAP '$'                     :S(CH2A)
```

```
         CAP '/'                      :S(CT.M)F(CH2B)
CH2A  SENTENCE PATTERN              :F(CT.M)
CH2B  SAVED = SAVED SENTENCE TERM ' '    :(CONT2)
*                                                                    *
*     TAKE INTO ACCOUNT THE ELLIPSIS ('...') AS INTERNAL OR          *
*     TERMINAL PUNCTUATION.                                          *
*                                                                    *
IRR1    HOLD LEN(1) LEN(1) . XTR REM . HOLD
        TERM = '@'
        IDENT(XTR,'>')               :S(CT.A)
        XX = HOLD
        XX LEN(1) . CAP
        IDENT(CAP,'$')               :S(IRR1A)
        IDENT(CAP,'/')               :S(IRR1A)F(IRR1B)
IRR1A   TEXT = ' ' HOLD              :(CT.B)
IRR1B     SAVED = SENTENCE '...'
        TEXT = HOLD                  :(CONT1)
IRR2    HOLD LEN(1) LEN(1) . XTR REM . HOLD
        TERM = '@'
        IDENT(XTR,'>')               :S(CT.E)
        XX = HOLD
        XX LEN(1) . CAP
        IDENT(CAP,'$')               :S(IRR2A)
        IDENT(CAP,'/')               :S(IRR2A)F(IRR2B)
IRR2A   TEXT = ' ' HOLD              :(CT.M)
IRR2B     SAVED = SENTENCE '...'
        TEXT = ' ' HOLD              :(CONT2)
CT.A   S = S + 12
        TYPE 'A'                     :S(SKIPA)
        TYPE = TYPE 'A'
SKIPA    WHOLE = SAVED SENTENCE TERM '>'
        I = I + 1
        STRUCTURE()
        PRINT()
             :(BEGIN)
CT.B   TYPE = TYPE 'B'
        I = I + 1
        STUFF = SAVED SENTENCE TERM ' '
B1     STUFF BREAK('>') LEN(2) REM . STUFF      :S(B1)
        COUNT()
        WHOLE = SAVED SENTENCE TERM
        STRUCTURE()
        PRINT()
             :(READ2)
CT.E   TYPE = 'E'
        I = I + 1
        STUFF = SAVED SENTENCE TERM '> '
        COUNT()
        WHOLE = SAVED SENTENCE TERM '>'
        ALL = WHOLE
        ALL BREAK('$') . BEG REM . ALL
        BEG '/'                      :F(E2)
        ALINE BREAK('/') LEN(1) BREAK('/')      :F(CHG.SP)
        WHOLE = ALL
E2     STRUCTURE()
        OUTPUT = LPAD(I,4) '. ' WHOLE
        OUTPUT =                    :(BEGIN)
CT.M   TYPE = 'M'
        I = I + 1
        ALL = SAVED SENTENCE TERM ' '
        ALL BREAK('$') . BEG REM . STUFF
        BEG '/'                      :S(CHG)
```

```
      COUNT()
      WHOLE = TRIM(STUFF)
M2    OUTPUT = LPAD(I,4) '. ' WHOLE
      OUTPUT =
      STRUCTURE()
            :(READ2)
CHG   DISK = LPAD(I,4) ' ' ID
      COUNT()
      WHOLE = TRIM(STUFF)        :(M2)
*                                                                    *
*     ADJUST FOR CHANGE OF SPEAKER WITHIN A LINE WHENEVER POSSIBLE;   *
*     OTHERWISE, NOTE THAT IT WAS NOT POSSIBLE FOR THE COMPUTER TO    *
*     DETERMINE THE IDENTITY OF THE OTHER SPEAKER.                    *
*                                                                    *
CHG.SP  ID LEN(2) . AA LEN(6) . OLD REM . CC
      RECORD = IN
      RECORD RECORD.LAYOUT
      ZZ = ID
      ZZ LEN(2) LEN(6) . BB
      IDENT(OLD,BB)              :F(CHG.SP2)
      DISK = LPAD(I,4) ' ' ID
CHG.SP2  OUTPUT = LPAD(I,4) '. ' ALL
      OUTPUT =
      ID = AA BB CC
      STRUCTURE()
      S = 0
      SAVED = NULL
      TYPE = NULL
      ID = ZZ
      ID 'XX'                    :S(DSK.DATA)
      TEXT = TRIM(ALINE)         :(CONT1)
```

```
*                                                                      *
*                 SUBROUTINE ONE :  SYLLABLE COUNT                     *
*                                                                      *
*      THIS SUBROUTINE COUNTS THE NUMBER OF SYLLABLES OF ANY PARTIAL   *
*      LINE OF TEXT INCLUDED IN A SENTENCE, SINCE WITH VERY FEW        *
*      EXCEPTIONS FULL LINES ARE ALEXANDRINS AND, THEREFORE, CONTAIN   *
*      TWELVE SYLLABLES.                                               *
*                                                                      *
COUNT    COUNTER = 0
         COLLECT(2)
      STUFF BREAK(' ') . WORD LEN(1) REM . REST
FIRST  AWORD = WORD ' '
       AWORD BREAK(VOWEL) LEN(1) REM . AWORD    :F(SECOND)
COUNT1  COUNTER = COUNTER + 1
       AWORD BREAK(CONS) LEN(1) REM . AWORD     :F(SECOND)
THIRD  AWORD BREAK(VOWEL) LEN(1) . LET REM . AWORD      :F(SECOND)
       AWORD BREAK(CONS) LEN(1) REM . AWORD     :S(COUNT2)
       IDENT(LET,'E')            :F(COUNT3)
       AWORD LEN(1) . SYMB
       NON.CADUC SYMB            :S(COUNT3)
       IDENT(SYMB,' ')           :S(CHECK)
       AWORD '>'                 :S(RECORD)
       IDENT(REST,NULL)          :S(TRL)
       CONTROL = REST            :(CK2)
TRL    CONTROL = TEXT            :(CK2)
SECOND   REST BREAK(' ') . WORD LEN(1) REM . REST    :S(FIRST)F(RECORD)
CHECK   CONTROL = REST
CK2  CONTROL BREAK(ALPHA) . JUNK LEN(1) . NEXT REM . LAST.PART
 .       :F(RECORD)
       IDENT(NEXT,'H')           :S(CHECK.H)
       VOWEL NEXT                :S(SECOND)F(COUNT3)
CHECK.H  HWORD = NEXT LAST.PART
       HWORD LEN(6) . H.PART
       H.PART ASPIRATED          :S(COUNT3)F(SECOND)
COUNT2  COUNTER = COUNTER + 1      :(THIRD)
COUNT3  COUNTER = COUNTER + 1      :(SECOND)
RECORD STUFF '3'                 :F(ADJT1)
       COUNTER = COUNTER + 1
ADJT1   STUFF TWO.SYLL1          :F(ADJT2)
       COUNTER = COUNTER + 1
ADJT2   STUFF TWO.SYLL2          :F(ADJT3)
       COUNTER = COUNTER + 1
ADJT3   STUFF TWO.SYLL3          :F(ADJ4)
       COUNTER = COUNTER + 1      :(ADJ4)
ADJ4    STUFF NO.SYLL1           :F(ADJT5)
       COUNTER = COUNTER - 1      :(ADJT5)
ADJT5   STUFF TWO.SYLL4          :F(ADJT6)
       COUNTER = COUNTER + 1      :(ADJT6)
ADJT6   STUFF TWO.SYLL5          :F(ADJT7)
       COUNTER = COUNTER + 1      :(ADJT7)
ADJT7   STUFF PL.SYLL1           :F(TOTAL)
       COUNTER = COUNTER + 1      :(TOTAL)
TOTAL    S = COUNTER  + S
       :(RETURN)
```

```
*******************************************************************
*                                                                 *
*     IDENTIFICATION OF DATA ON SENTENCE STRUCTURE TAPE           *
*                                                                 *
*     COLUMNS 1-4:          SENTENCE NUMBER                       *
*     COLUMNS 5-20:         ID OF FINAL LINE OF SENTENCE          *
*                           5-6:     PLAY                         *
*                           7-12:    SPEAKER                      *
*                           13:      ACT                          *
*                           14-15:   SCENE                        *
*                           16-19:   LINE                         *
*                           20:      VARIANT (OR BLANK)           *
*                                                                 *
*     COLUMNS 21-23:        NUMBER OF SYLLABLES IN SENTENCE       *
*     COLUMNS 24-26:        SENTENCE TYPE                         *
*                           B = BEGINNING OF LINE                 *
*                           M = MIDDLE OF LINE                    *
*                           E = END OF LINE                       *
*                           A = ALL OF LINE                       *
*                                                                 *
*     COLUMN 27:            TERMINAL PUNCTUATION   ('@' = '...')   *
*     COLUMNS 28-29:        NUMBER OF COMMAS                      *
*     COLUMN 30:            NUMBER OF SEMI-COLONS                 *
*     COLUMN 31:            NUMBER OF COLONS                      *
*     COLUMN 32:            NUMBER OF INTERNAL QUESTION MARKS     *
*     COLUMN 33:            NUMBER OF INTERNAL EXCLAMATION POINTS *
*     COLUMNS 34-35:        SUM OF INTERNAL PUNCTUATION MARKS     *
*                                                                 *
*     COLUMN 36:            NUMBER OF 'QUAND'                     *
*     COLUMN 37:            NUMBER OF 'LORSQU'                    *
*     COLUMN 38:            NUMBER OF 'PUISQU'                    *
*     COLUMN 39:            NUMBER OF 'TANDIS QU'                 *
*     COLUMN 40:            'A' (LOCATOR FOR ADDING 'SANS' TO COLUMN 41) *
*     COLUMN 41:            NUMBER OF 'SANS QU'                   *
*     COLUMNS 42-43:        SUM OF SUBORDINATING CONJUNCTIONS LISTED *
*     COLUMN 44:            NUMBER OF 'QUI'                       *
*     COLUMN 45:            'B' (LOCATOR FOR ADJUSTING 'SI')      *
*     COLUMN 46:            NUMBER OF CONDITIONAL 'SI'            *
*     COLUMN 47:            NUMBER OF 'SI' = 'WHETHER'            *
*     COLUMN 48:            NUMBER OF 'ET'                        *
*     COLUMN 49:            NUMBER OF 'OU'                        *
*     COLUMN 50:            NUMBER OF 'MAIS'                      *
*     COLUMN 51:            NUMBER OF 'FALLOIR' (ALL FORMS)       *
*                                                                 *
*******************************************************************
```

```
*                                                                    *
*                  SUBROUTINE TWO:   STRUCTURE                       *
*                                                                    *
*     THIS SUBROUTINE SEARCHES EACH SENTENCE FOR PATTERNS (STRINGS   *
*     OF LETTERS) WHICH IDENTIFY FEATURES OF SENTENCE STRUCTURE.     *
*                                                                    *
*     IN ORDER TO FIND MULTIPLE OCCURRENCES OF A STRUCTURE IN A      *
*     GIVEN SENTENCE, ONCE A STRUCTURE IS FOUND IT IS REPLACED BY    *
*     A NULL STRING.                                                 *
*                                                                    *
STRUCTURE      DATA = WHOLE
          QD = 0;   LORS = 0;   PS = 0;   TDS = 0;   SN = 0;   SUBORD = 0;
          COMMA = 0;   SEMI = 0;   COLON = 0;   QUEST = 0;   EXCL = 0;
          INTERNAL = 0;   REL = 0;   SI = 0;   ET = 0;   OU = 0;   MAIS = 0;
          IMP = 0;
QD        DATA 'QUAND' = NULL       :F(LORS)
          QD = QD + 1               :(QD)
LORS   DATA 'LORSQU' = NULL      :F(PS)
          LORS = LORS + 1           :(LORS)
PS      DATA 'PUISQU' = NULL     :F(TDS)
          PS = PS + 1               :(PS)
TDS      DATA 'TANDIS QU' = NULL     :F(SN)
          TDS = TDS + 1             :(TDS)
SN      DATA 'SANS QU' = NULL    :F(SUBORD)
          SN = SN + 1               :(SN)
SUBORD          SUBORD = QD + LORS + TDS + SN + PS
COMMA    DATA ',' = NULL         :F(SEMI)
          COMMA = COMMA + 1         :(COMMA)
SEMI    DATA ';' = NULL          :F(COLON)
          SEMI = SEMI + 1           :(SEMI)
COLON       DATA ':' = NULL        :F(QST)
          COLON = COLON + 1         :(COLON)
QST      DATA '? ' = NULL        :F(XCL)
          QUEST = QUEST + 1         :(QST)
XCL      DATA '! ' = NULL        :F(PUNCTS)
          EXCL = EXCL + 1           :(XCL)
PUNCTS      INTERNAL = COMMA + SEMI + COLON + QUEST + EXCL
RELATIVE        DATA 'QUI' = NULL       :F(S1)
          REL = REL + 1             :(RELATIVE)
S1      DATA "S'IL " = NULL      :F(S2)
          SI = SI + 1               :(S1)
S2      DATA "S'ILS " = NULL     :F(S3)
          SI = SI + 1               :(S2)
S3      DATA @SPOT 'SI '         :F(CO.OR1)
          DATA LEN(SPOT) LEN(3) . IT LEN(6) . BIT
          BIT SI.PATTERN               :F(S4)
          SI = SI + 1
S4      DATA 'SI ' = NULL        :(S3)
CO.OR1    DATA ET.PATTERN = NULL      :F(CO.OR2)
          ET = ET + 1               :(CO.OR1)
CO.OR2    DATA OU.PATTERN = NULL      :F(CO.OR3)
          OU = OU + 1               :(CO.OR2)
CO.OR3    DATA MAIS.PATTERN = NULL    :F(IMP1)
          MAIS = MAIS + 1           :(CO.OR3)
IMP1    DATA 'FAUT' = NULL          :F(IMP2)
          IMP = IMP + 1             :(IMP1)
IMP2    DATA 'FAUDRA' = NULL        :F(IMP3)
          IMP = IMP + 1             :(IMP2)
IMP3    DATA ('FALL') ('U' | 'AIT') = NULL    :F(IMP4)
          IMP = IMP + 1             :(IMP3)
IMP4     DATA 'FALLOIR' = NULL      :F(DATA.OUT)
          IMP = IMP + 1             :(IMP4)
```

```
DATA.OUT        PADT = DUPL(' ',3 - SIZE(TYPE))
        TOTAPE = LPAD(I,4) ID LPAD(S,3) TYPE PADT TERM LPAD(COMMA,2) SEMI
. COLON QUEST EXCL LPAD(INTERNAL,2) QD LQRS PS TDS 'A' SN
. LPAD(SUBORD,2) REL 'B' SI 'Q' ET OU MAIS IMP
        :(RETURN)
*                                                                      *
*                   SUBROUTINE THREE:  PRINTOUT OF SENTENCES           *
*                                                                      *
*       THIS SUBROUTINE SIMPLY PRINTS OUT THE SENTENCES IN SEQUENCE    *
*       AND ALLOWS A MAXIMUM LINE-LENGTH OF SEVENTY CHARACTERS;        *
*       AFTER THE FIRST LINE OF A SENTENCE, THE TEXT IS INDENTED TO    *
*       CORRESPOND TO THE FIRST CHARACTER OF TEXT IN THE FIRST LINE.   *
*                                                                      *
PRINT   WHOLE BREAK('$') REM . WHOLE
        Z = SIZE(WHOLE)
        OUTPUT = LT(Z,70) LPAD(I,4) '. ' WHOLE     :F(CRCT1)S(CRCT4)
CRCT1   WHOLE LEN(55) . LEFT BREAK(' ') . MIDDLE REM . WHOLE
        OUTPUT = LPAD(I,4) '. ' LEFT MIDDLE
CRCT2   Z = SIZE(WHOLE)
        OUTPUT = LT(Z,70) '       ' WHOLE     :F(CRCT3)S(CRCT4)
CRCT3   WHOLE LEN(55) . LEFT BREAK(' ') . MIDDLE REM . WHOLE
        OUTPUT = '       ' LEFT MIDDLE         :(CRCT2)
CRCT4   OUTPUT =
        :(RETURN)
*                                                                      *
*                   RETURN TO MAIN PROGRAM                             *
*                                                                      *
*       PRINT INFORMATION OF 'UNCORRECTABLE CHANGES OF SPEAKER';       *
*       PRINT NEWLY GENERATED DATA IN 'TABLE OF PARAMETERS'.           *
*                                                                      *
DSK.DATA    REWIND('DSK')
        INPUT(.IN,'DSK')
        HEADING = 'THE UNCORRECTABLE CHANGES OF SPEAKER'
        OUTPUT =
DSKOUT      OUTPUT = IN            :S(DSKOUT)F(TP.DATA)
TP.DATA    REWIND('TOUT')
        INPUT(.IN,'TOUT')
        HEADING = 'TABLE OF PARAMETERS'
        OUTPUT =
TPOUT       REC = TIN              :F(END)
        REC LEN(4) . NUM LEN(16) . ID REM . JAZZ
        OUTPUT = NUM '     ' ID '     ' JAZZ     :(TPOUT)
END
//
```

2. The Diagrams

This is a simple program that prints out two variables, sentence type and terminal punctuation, in graphic format. Each scene of a play is identified at the top of a separate page. For each series of sentences spoken by a particular character, the sentences types are concatenated, separated by blanks for ease in reading, as are the terminal punctuation marks, without blanks and using '@' to represent the ellipsis. When the speaker changes, the data are printed out in parallel columns and concatenation begins again. Numerous examples of these diagrams are found throughout this study.

```
//    1023,CLASS=B
/*SETUP        UNIT=TAPE9,ID=(CC1450,J170)
//    EXEC    SPITRUN,TIME=(,30),PARM.GO='R=20K'
//GO.TPIN  DD  DSN=PHSTR2,UNIT=TAPE9,DISP=(OLD,KEEP),LABEL=(3,SL),
//       VOL=SER=CC1450    J170
//GO.SYSIN DD  *


      INPUT(.IN,'TPIN')
      OUTPUT('HEADING',6,'(1H1,40A1)')
      PLAY = 'PHEDRE'
      RECORD.LAYOUT = LEN(6) LEN(6) . SPEAKER LEN(1) . ACT
. LEN(2) . SCENE LEN(8) LEN(3) . TYPE LEN(1) . TERM
      SAVED = NULL
      KEPT = NULL


R1    RECORD = IN              :F(END)
      RECORD RECORD.LAYOUT
      TYPE = TRIM(TYPE)
PRT1  HEADING = PLAY ', ACT ' ACT ', SCENE ' SCENE
      OUTPUT =
SV1   SAVED = SPEAKER ': ' TYPE ' '
      KEPT = SPEAKER ': ' TERM
      SAVE.SP = SPEAKER
      SAVE.SC = ACT SCENE      :(R2)
R2    RECORD = IN              :F(PRT4)
      RECORD RECORD.LAYOUT
      TYPE = TRIM(TYPE)
      SC = ACT SCENE
      IDENT(SAVE.SC,SC)        :F(PRT3)
      IDENT(SAVE.SP,SPEAKER)   :F(PRT2)
      KEPT = KEPT TERM
      SAVED = SAVED TYPE ' '        :(R2)
PRT2  PAD = DUPL(' ',80 - SIZE(SAVED))
      OUTPUT = SAVED PAD KEPT
      OUTPUT =
      KEPT = NULL
      SAVED = NULL             :(SV1)
PRT3  PAD = DUPL(' ',80 - SIZE(SAVED))
      OUTPUT = SAVED PAD KEPT
      OUTPUT =
      KEPT = NULL
      SAVED = NULL             :(PRT1)
PRT4  PAD = DUPL(' ',80 - SIZE(SAVED))
      OUTPUT = SAVED PAD KEPT      :(END)
END
//
```

3. Specific Features of Sentence Structure

Occasionally one feature of sentence structure must be examined in context to determine all legitimate cases or to study its possible relationship to characterization. This is accomplished by pattern matching. The program that follows is one used to isolate cases of *pour* + infinitive and *pour qu(e)* + subjunctive. This basic program can easily be modified to search for any feature identifiable by lexical elements. First an occurrence of *pour* is located; then the program must determine whether it is followed by an infinitive or *que*. Each line of text is examined for PATTERN = 'POUR '. If this succeeds, the next word is examined to determine first if it is *qu(e)* and then if it is an infinitive as defined in the program.

INFIN = ('ER' | 'IR' | 'RE') (' ' | ',' | '?' | '.' | ';' | ':' | '!' | ' ')

This pattern matches words ending in *-er, -ir,* or *-re* and followed by a blank or a mark of punctuation. Any time that the pattern matching is successful, the line is printed out. If it is unsuccessful, the next word is examined and the process is repeated for up to three words. The program is not perfect, for some of the lines printed out are not actually examples of *pour* + infinitive. A certain number of words ending in *-er, -ir,* or *-re* are not infinitives: *fier, plaisir, gendre.* The common problems are, however, solved by another pattern matching:

ELIM = 'VOTRE' | 'AUTRE' | 'E = RE'

While the program may list extraneous lines, it does not miss any of the possible occurrences of *pour* + infinitive. Extraneous lines can easily be eliminated by hand. The accuracy of the program could have been improved further by supplying the computer with a dictionary of infinitives for comparison to the word in question. For the present study this was deemed impractical from the standpoint of program writing time, since the problem arises less than five times per play and the faulty lines can be deleted by hand. The other problem is more delicate, if not so frequent, because it involves *pour* followed by an infinitive that the *pour* does not govern.

Seigneur, je viens pour elle implorer votre appui.

(Iphigénie, 900)

Again a more elaborate program could automatically reject such occurrences, but it was deemed too time-consuming and unnecessary for the present study.

```
// 255,CLASS=B
/*SETUP          UNIT=TAPE9,ID=(RACINE,F058)
//       EXEC        SPITRUN
//GO.TAPE   DD   DSN=IPHIGE,UNIT=TAPE9,DISP=(OLD,KEEP),LABEL=(8,SL),
//         VOL=SER=RACINE      F058
//GO.SYSIN DD   *



       INPUT(.IN,'TAPE')
       &DUMP = 2
       PLAY = 'IPHIGENIE'
       PATTERN = 'POUR '
       INFIN = ('ER' | 'IR' | 'RE') (' ' | ',' | '?' | '.' | ';' | ':' |
  '!' | '>')
       ELIM = 'VOTRE' | 'AUTRE' | 'E=RE'
       CONJ = ("QU") ("E " | '"')
       RECORD.LAYOUT = LEN(6) LEN(16) . ID REM . TEXT
       I = 0


       OUTPUT = 'OCCURRENCES OF ' PATTERN ' IN ' PLAY
       OUTPUT =
READ      RECORD = IN            :F(END)
       RECORD RECORD.LAYOUT
       ID 'XX'                   :S(END)
       TEXT = TRIM(TEXT) ' '
       TEXT @SPOT PATTERN        :F(READ)
       TEXT LEN(SPOT) LEN(5) REM . REST      :F(READ)
       REST BREAK(' ') . WORD LEN(1) REM . REST      :F(READ)
       WORD = WORD ' '
       WORD CONJ                 :S(PRINT)
       WORD INFIN                :S(PRINT)
       REST BREAK(' ') . WORD LEN(1) REM . REST      :F(READ)
       WORD = WORD ' '
       WORD INFIN                :S(PRINT)
       REST BREAK(' ') . WORD LEN(1) REM . REST      :F(READ)
       WORD = WORD ' '
       WORD INFIN                :S(PRINT)F(READ)
PRINT     WORD ELIM               :S(READ)
       I = I + 1
       OUTPUT = LPAD(I,3) '. ' ID '    ' TEXT      :(READ)
END
//
```

4. The SPSS Package for Cross-Tabulations and Marginals

SPSS or Statistical Package for the Social Sciences[3] has the particular advantage of being capable of handling data composed of alphanumeric characters. This characteristic is important for analyzing distribution of nonparametric and discrete data like sentence type (A, B, M, etc.) and terminal punctuation (.?!@).

This study made extensive use of two routines from SPSS, CROSSTABS, and MARGINALS. CROSSTABS analyzes data and arranges the results in tabular format where one variable is plotted against another. For instance, I plotted speaker against terminal punctuation to determine which characters show an affinity for declarative, interrogative, exclamatory, and incomplete sentences. I also plotted act against terminal punctuation to determine what variation is due to the change from act to act. This was my primary tool in SPSS, since all variables except syllable count were handled with CROSSTABS. Samples of the computer-generated tables for *Andromaque* are reproduced at the end of this appendix as illustrations of this procedure. The tables in Appendix C show these cross-tabulations in summary form.

Syllable count was analyzed with MARGINALS, a routine designed to handle parametric data and to compute mean, median, mode, standard error, standard deviation, variance, kurtosis, skewness, range, minimum, and maximum. This count was done for each play as a whole and then for each of the characters and for each of the acts.

The basic SPSS control cards needed to generate the tables used in this study are reproduced following this discussion to facilitate further applications of the technique.

```
//      4095,CLASS=C
/*SETUP          UNIT=TAPE9,ID=(CC1450,J170,READ)
//   EXEC  PGM=SPSS,PARM=80000,REGION=252K,TIME=(,45)
//STEPLIB   DD   DSN=SYS4.PROGLIB,DISP=SHR
//FT01F001   DD   UNIT=SYSDA,SPACE=(CYL,(1,1))
//FT02F001   DD   UNIT=SYSDA,SPACE=(CYL,(2,2))
//FT06F001   DD   SYSOUT=A
//FT08F001   DD   DSN=MISTR2,UNIT=TAPE9,DISP=(OLD,KEEP),VOL=SER=CC1450          J170
//FT05F001   DD   *
```

```
RUN NAME          CROSSTABULATION OF RACINE DATA AND MARGINALS RUNS
FILE NAME         RACMI,RACINE'S MITHRIDATE
VARIABLE LIST     SPEAKER,ACT,SYLCT,SENTTYPE,TERMPUNC,QUEST,EXCLAM,QUAND,LORSQUE,
                  SANS,IF,ET,OU,MAIS
INPUT FORMAT      FIXED (6X,A4,2X,F1.0,7X,F3.0,A3,A1,4X,F1.0,F1.0,2X,F1.0,F1.0,3X,
                  F1.0,4X,F1.0,1X,F1.0,F1.0,F1.0)
PRINT FORMATS     SPEAKER,SENTTYPE,TERMPUNC(A)/ACT,SYLCT,QUEST,EXCLAM,SANS,IF,ET,
                  OU,MAIS(0)
# OF CASES        929
INPUT MEDIUM      TAPE
VALUE LABELS      ACT (1)ACT I(2)ACT II(3)ACT III(4)ACT IV(5)ACT V
RECODE            SPEAKER ('ARBA','PHOE','ARCA' = 'CONF')
VALUE LABELS      SPEAKER ('CONF')CONFIDENTS('MITH')MITHRIDATE('MONI')MONIME
                  ('XIPH')XIPHARES('PHAR')PHARNACE
COMPUTE           CHARNO = SPEAKER
RECODE            CHARNO ('MITH' = 1)('MONI' = 2)('XIPH' = 3)('PHAR' = 4)
                  ('CONF' = 5)
CROSSTABS         SPEAKER BY ACT/
                  SPEAKER BY TERMPUNC,SENTTYPE/
                  ACT BY TERMPUNC,SENTTYPE/
                  ACT BY SENTTYPE BY SPEAKER/
                  ACT BY TERMPUNC BY SPEAKER/
                  SPEAKER BY QUEST,EXCLAM,IF,QUAND,LORSQUE,SANS,ET,OU,MAIS/
                  ACT BY QUEST,EXCLAM,IF,QUAND,LORSQUE,SANS,ET,OU,MAIS
STATISTICS        1,2,3
READ INPUT DATA
MARGINALS         SYLCT
OPTIONS           5
STATISTICS        ALL
*SELECT IF        (CHARNO EQ 1)
MARGINALS         SYLCT
OPTIONS           5
STATISTICS        ALL
*SELECT IF        (CHARNO EQ 2)
MARGINALS         SYLCT
OPTIONS           5
STATISTICS        ALL
*SELECT IF        (CHARNO EQ 3)
MARGINALS         SYLCT
OPTIONS           5
STATISTICS        ALL
*SELECT IF        (CHARNO EQ 4)
MARGINALS         SYLCT
STATISTICS        ALL
OPTIONS           5
*SELECT IF        (CHARNO EQ 5)
MARGINALS         SYLCT
OPTIONS           5
STATISTICS        ALL
*SELECT IF        (ACT EQ 1)
MARGINALS         SYLCT
```

```
OPTIONS         5
STATISTICS      ALL
*SELECT IF      (ACT EQ 2)
MARGINALS       SYLCT
OPTIONS         5
STATISTICS      ALL
*SELECT IF      (ACT EQ 3)
MARGINALS       SYLCT
OPTIONS         5
STATISTICS      ALL
*SELECT IF      (ACT EQ 4)
MARGINALS       SYLCT
OPTIONS         5
STATISTICS      ALL
*SELECT IF      (ACT EQ 5)
MARGINALS       SYLCT
OPTIONS         5
STATISTICS      ALL
FINISH
//
```

```
CROSSTABULATION OF RACINE DATA                                    06/19/73    PAGE 2

FILE   RACAN   (CREATION DATE = 06/19/73)   RACINE'S ANDROMAQUE

* * * * * * * * * * * * * * *   C R O S S T A B U L A T I O N   O F   * * * * * * * * * * * * * * *
          SPEAKER                              BY  TERMPUNC
* * * * * * * * * * * * * * * * * * * * * * * * * * * * * * * * * * * * *   PAGE 1 OF 1
```

	TERMPUNC				
COUNT ROW PCT COL PCT TOT PCT	.	!	?	@	ROW TOTAL
SPEAKER					
PYRR	136 72.3 21.2 13.1	10 5.3 14.3 1.0	40 21.3 13.7 3.8	2 1.1 5.6 0.2	188 18.1
DRES	151 80.4 23.5 14.5	17 6.8 24.3 1.6	69 27.6 23.6 6.6	13 5.2 36.1 1.3	250 24.0
HERM	134 51.0 20.9 12.9	18 6.8 25.7 1.7	105 39.9 36.0 10.1	6 2.3 16.7 0.6	263 25.3
CONF	135 67.8 21.0 13.0	12 6.0 17.1 1.2	40 20.1 13.7 3.8	12 6.0 33.3 1.2	199 19.1
ANDR	86 61.4 13.4 8.3	13 9.3 18.6 1.3	38 27.1 13.0 3.7	3 2.1 8.3 0.3	140 13.5
COLUMN TOTAL	642 61.7	70 6.7	292 28.1	36 3.5	1040 100.0

```
CHI SQUARE = 43.39832 WITH 12 DEGREES OF FREEDOM
CRAMER'S V =  0.11794
CONTINGENCY COEFFICIENT =   0.20014
```

CROSSTABULATION OF RACINE DATA   06/19/73   PAGE 3

FILE   RACAN   (CREATION DATE = 06/19/73)   RACINE'S ANDROMAQUE

* * * * * * * * * * * * * * *   C R O S S T A B U L A T I O N   O F   *** * * * * * * * * * * * * * ***
SPEAKER   BY SENITYPE
*   PAGE 2 OF 1

SENITYPE

Cell key: COUNT / ROW PCT / COL PCT / TOT PCT

SPEAKER	M	EB	EAB	EA	E	B	AE	A	ROW TOTAL
PYRR	2 / 1.1 / 16.7 / 0.2	1 / 0.5 / 14.3 / 0.1	1 / 0.5 / 50.0 / 0.1	11 / 5.9 / 15.9 / 1.1	16 / 8.5 / 19.0 / 1.5	21 / 11.2 / 15.9 / 2.0	1 / 0.5 / 4.8 / 0.1	135 / 71.8 / 18.9 / 13.0	188 / 18.1
ORES	3 / 1.2 / 25.0 / 0.3	1 / 0.4 / 14.3 / 0.1	1 / 0.4 / 50.0 / 0.1	22 / 8.8 / 31.9 / 2.1	16 / 6.4 / 19.0 / 1.5	32 / 12.8 / 24.2 / 3.1	6 / 2.4 / 28.6 / 0.6	169 / 67.6 / 23.7 / 16.3	250 / 24.0
HERM	5 / 1.9 / 41.7 / 0.5	3 / 1.1 / 42.9 / 0.3	0 / 0.0 / 0.0 / 0.0	17 / 6.5 / 24.6 / 1.6	21 / 8.0 / 25.0 / 2.0	36 / 13.7 / 27.3 / 3.5	5 / 1.9 / 23.8 / 0.5	176 / 66.9 / 24.7 / 16.9	263 / 25.3
CONF	2 / 1.0 / 16.7 / 0.2	1 / 0.5 / 14.3 / 0.1	0 / 0.0 / 0.0 / 0.0	12 / 6.0 / 17.4 / 1.2	21 / 10.6 / 25.0 / 2.0	29 / 14.6 / 22.0 / 2.8	7 / 3.5 / 33.3 / 0.7	127 / 63.8 / 17.8 / 12.2	199 / 19.1
ANDR	0 / 0.0 / 0.0 / 0.0	1 / 0.7 / 14.3 / 0.1	0 / 0.0 / 0.0 / 0.0	7 / 5.0 / 10.1 / 0.7	10 / 7.1 / 11.9 / 1.0	14 / 10.0 / 10.6 / 1.3	2 / 1.4 / 9.5 / 0.2	106 / 75.7 / 14.9 / 10.2	140 / 13.5
COLUMN TOTAL	12 / 1.2	7 / 0.7	2 / 0.2	69 / 6.6	84 / 8.1	132 / 12.7	21 / 2.0	713 / 68.6	1040 / 100.0

CHI SQUARE =   21.01140 WITH   28 DEGREES OF FREEDOM
CRAMER'S V =   0.07107
CONTINGENCY COEFFICIENT =   0.14072

CROSSTABULATION OF RACINE DATA   06/19/73   PAGE   4

FILE RACAN   (CREATION DATE = 06/19/73)   RACINE'S ANDROMAQUE

* * * * * * * * * * * * * * * * * *   C R O S S T A B U L A T I O N   O F   * * * * * * * * * * * * * * * * * *
          ACT   BY TERMPUNC
*   PAGE   1 OF 1

                    TERMPUNC

COUNT ROW PCT COL PCT TOT PCT	.	!	?	@	ROW TOTAL
ACT					
ACT I 1.	126 65.6 19.6 12.1	13 6.6 18.6 1.3	55 27.8 18.8 5.3	4 2.0 11.1 0.4	198 19.0
ACT II 2.	135 61.6 21.0 13.0	21 9.6 30.0 2.0	54 24.7 18.5 5.2	9 4.1 25.0 0.9	219 21.1
ACT III 3.	156 82.9 24.3 15.0	13 5.2 18.6 1.3	67 27.0 22.9 6.4	12 4.8 33.3 1.2	248 23.8
ACT IV 4.	133 69.6 20.7 12.8	11 3.8 15.7 1.1	38 19.9 13.0 3.7	9 4.7 25.0 0.9	191 18.4
ACT V 5.	92 50.0 14.3 8.8	12 6.5 17.1 1.2	78 42.4 26.7 7.5	2 1.1 5.6 0.2	184 17.7
COLUMN TOTAL	642 61.7	70 6.7	292 28.1	36 3.5	1040 100.0

CHI SQUARE =   35.64117 WITH 12 DEGREES OF FREEDOM
CRAMER'S V =   0.10688
CONTINGENCY COEFFICIENT =   0.18203

CROSSTABULATION OF RACINE DATA

FILE RACAN (CREATION DATE = 06/19/73) RACINE'S ANDROMAQUE 06/19/73 PAGE 5

* * * * * * * * * * * * * * CROSSTABULATION OF *
ACT1 BY SENTTYPE
* PAGE 1 OF 1

Cell legend: COUNT / ROW PCT / COL PCT / TOT PCT

ACT	SENTTYPE M	EB	EAB	EA	E	B	EB	A	ROW TOTAL
ACT I — 1.	1 / 0.5 / 8.3 / 0.1	1 / 0.5 / 14.3 / 0.1	0 / 0.0 / 0.0 / 0.0	8 / 4.0 / 11.6 / 0.8	9 / 4.5 / 10.7 / 0.9	13 / 6.6 / 9.8 / 1.3	4 / 2.0 / 19.0 / 0.4	162 / 81.8 / 22.7 / 15.6	198 / 19.0
ACT II — 2.	1 / 0.5 / 8.3 / 0.1	1 / 0.5 / 14.3 / 0.1	1 / 0.5 / 50.0 / 0.1	19 / 8.7 / 27.5 / 1.8	19 / 8.7 / 22.6 / 1.8	31 / 14.2 / 23.5 / 3.0	7 / 3.2 / 33.3 / 0.7	140 / 63.9 / 19.6 / 13.5	219 / 21.1
ACT III — 3.	1 / 0.4 / 8.3 / 0.1	4 / 1.6 / 57.1 / 0.4	0 / 0.0 / 0.0 / 0.0	10 / 4.0 / 14.5 / 1.0	28 / 11.3 / 33.3 / 2.7	33 / 13.3 / 25.0 / 3.2	5 / 2.0 / 23.8 / 0.5	167 / 67.3 / 23.4 / 16.1	248 / 23.8
ACT IV — 4.	3 / 1.6 / 25.0 / 0.3	0 / 0.0 / 0.0 / 0.0	0 / 0.0 / 0.0 / 0.0	16 / 8.4 / 23.2 / 1.5	13 / 6.8 / 15.5 / 1.3	25 / 13.1 / 18.9 / 2.4	4 / 2.1 / 19.0 / 0.4	130 / 68.1 / 18.2 / 12.5	191 / 18.4
ACT V — 5.	6 / 3.3 / 50.0 / 0.6	1 / 0.5 / 14.3 / 0.1	1 / 0.5 / 50.0 / 0.1	16 / 8.7 / 23.2 / 1.5	15 / 8.2 / 17.9 / 1.4	30 / 16.3 / 22.1 / 2.9	1 / 0.5 / 4.8 / 0.1	114 / 62.0 / 16.0 / 11.0	184 / 17.7
COLUMN TOTAL	12 / 1.2	7 / 0.7	2 / 0.2	69 / 6.6	84 / 8.1	132 / 12.7	21 / 2.0	713 / 68.6	1040 / 100.0

CHI SQUARE = 51.82010 WITH 28 DEGREES OF FREEDOM
CRAMER'S V = 0.11139
CONTINGENCY COEFFICIENT = 0.21746

Appendix B

205

Notes for Appendix B

1. Robert B. K. Dewar, *SPITBOL, Version 2.0,* Illinois Institute of Technology, 1971.

2. R. E. Griswold, et al., *The SNOBOL4 Programming Language* (Englewood Cliffs, N.J.: Prentice-Hall, 1968).

3. Norman H. Nie, et al., *SPSS: Statistical Package for the Social Sciences,* 2d ed. (New York: McGraw-Hill, 1975).

APPENDIX C.
Tables

The tables that follow are summaries of those generated by the IBM 370/165 for this study using SPSS. Tables 1-4 and 7-9 present the distribution from play to play of basic features of sentence structure. Table 5 presents mean sentence length for characters in each play and Table 6 is a cumulative presentation of all the characters in order of decreasing sentence length. Characters from the seven plays from *Andromaque* to *Phèdre* are on the left and characters from the other plays are on the right. The blank lines in Table 6 are primarily for legibility and should not be construed as boundaries separating groups of characters.

Racine's only comedy, *Les Plaideurs,* Corneille's *Tite et Bérénice,* and Pradon's *Phèdre et Hippolyte* are included in all tables except Table 6 in order to demonstrate significant differences in sentence structure.

TABLE 1
DISTRIBUTION OF TERMINAL PUNCTUATION
(percentage of sentences)

	.	!	?	. . .
La Thébaïde	68.2	7.6	20.7	3.4
Alexandre	66.9	3.5	24.7	4.9
Andromaque	61.7	6.7	28.1	3.5
Britannicus	68.1	6.5	22.9	2.5
Bérénice	63.6	7.7	26.6	2.1
Bajazet	66.5	5.7	24.6	3.2
Mithridate	65.6	7.2	23.3	4.0
Iphigénie	63.0	6.8	27.1	3.1
Phèdre	66.0	8.2	23.4	2.5
Esther	68.5	10.5	20.0	1.1
Athalie	64.3	6.3	26.5	3.0
Les Plaideurs	67.3	11.2	14.6	6.9
Tite et Bérénice	67.8	4.5	22.7	4.9
Phèdre et Hippolyte	47.0	10.6	26.9	15.4

TABLE 2
DISTRIBUTION OF SENTENCE TYPES
(percentage of sentences)

	A	B	E	EA	AB	M	EB	EAB
La Thébaïde	82.0	6.5	5.0	3.4	1.9	1.0	---	0.1
Alexandre	76.3	7.9	3.4	7.7	3.2	1.3	0.1	0.1
Andromaque	68.6	12.7	8.1	6.6	2.0	1.2	0.7	0.2
Britannicus	68.2	11.7	7.5	7.1	2.8	1.9	0.7	0.1
Bérénice	63.2	13.9	9.4	7.2	2.7	2.6	0.4	0.4
Bajazet	65.1	13.8	8.9	7.2	2.3	2.2	0.4	0.1
Mithridate	67.3	13.2	7.5	7.8	2.0	1.9	0.2	---
Iphigénie	71.7	11.9	6.9	6.4	1.4	1.5	0.1	0.1
Phèdre	72.6	10.7	7.1	5.8	2.2	1.1	0.4	0.1
Esther	81.7	7.9	4.7	3.8	0.7	1.1	0.1	---
Athalie	75.5	9.3	6.0	5.1	1.8	1.6	0.7	0.1
Les Plaideurs	26.2	26.0	22.6	6.7	3.3	10.1	4.1	0.9
Tite et Bérénice	82.2	6.5	4.0	4.4	1.9	0.5	0.3	0.1
Phèdre et Hippolyte	54.5	8.4	5.0	14.0	10.6	1.9	1.9	3.8

TABLE 3
SENTENCE LENGTH: MEAN, MODE, MEDIAN
(syllables)

	Mean	Mode	Median
La Thébaïde	24.714	24.000	23.649
Alexandre	26.088	24.000	23.664
Andromaque	19.012	12.000	12.776
Britannicus	21.403	12.000	15.667
Bérénice	18.941	12.000	12.615
Bajazet	19.966	12.000	12.331
Mithridate	21.928	12.000	17.733
Iphigénie	20.170	12.000	12.797
Phèdre	19.569	12.000	12.377
Esther	20.112	12.000	12.432
Athalie	19.936	12.000	12.312
Les Plaideurs	10.890	6.000	6.500
Tite et Bérénice	28.421	24.000	23.909
Phèdre et Hippolyte	43.505	12.000	30.000

TABLE 4
DISTRIBUTION OF MEAN SENTENCE LENGTH BY ACTS
(syllables)

	Act I	Act II	Act III	Act IV	Act V
La Thébaïde	25.859	25.000	27.380	21.411	24.556
Alexandre	26.468	30.638	26.659	24.795	22.550
Andromaque	23.273	17.744	16.452	21.607	16.690
Britannicus	22.600	20.961	19.132	24.249	20.329
Bérénice	21.377	20.816	16.655	17.252	19.019
Bajazet	23.009	20.758	19.701	15.853	20.870
Mithridate	23.365	22.029	21.556	19.853	23.429
Iphigénie	24.712	20.958	18.980	18.333	18.612
Phèdre	21.217	18.809	17.787	18.561	21.608
Esther*	21.778	19.799	18.163	------	------
Athalie	25.579	16.740	19.285	20.636	20.581
Les Plaideurs	11.337	10.459	11.000	------	------
Tite et Bérénice	30.435	32.231	27.755	26.963	25.714
Phèdre et Hippolyte	49.079	44.727	42.810	36.923	46.500

*Esther, unlike the other tragedies, contains a Prologue. Its mean sentence length is 32.308.

TABLE 5
DISTRIBUTION OF MEAN SENTENCE LENGTH BY CHARACTERS
Grouped by Play
(syllables)

La Thébaïde			*Alexandre*		
Étéocle	28.731		Éphestion	30.980	
Créon	27.534		Porus	27.364	
----------MEAN----------24.714----			Cléofile	27.331	
Antigone	23.899		Taxile	26.168	
Hémon	23.707		----------MEAN----------26.088----		
Jocaste	22.807		Alexandre	25.273	
Polynice	22.627		Axiane	23.716	
confidants	22.535				

Andromaque			*Britannicus*		
Pyrrhus	20.197		Burrhus	23.847	
Oreste	19.884		Agrippine	22.688	
Andromaque	19.421		Narcisse	21,857	
----------MEAN----------19.012----			Néron	21.493	
Hermione	18.327		----------MEAN----------21.403 ----		
confidants	17.412		Albine	21.300	
			Junie	18.796	
			Britannicus	18.606	

Bérénice			*Bajazet*		
Paulin	24.460		Bajazet	24.177	
Titus	20.548		Acomat	22.103	
confidants	18.972		confidants	20.924	
----------MEAN----------18.941----			----------MEAN----------19.966----		
Bérénice	17.703		Atalide	18.533	
Antiochus	17.333		Roxane	17.770	

Mithridate			*Iphigénie*		
Xipharès	23.246		Ulysse	26.746	
confidants	22.991		Ériphile	25.109	
Pharnace	22.000		Iphigénie	20.337	

---------MEAN -------21.928----		---------MEAN--------20.170----	
Mithridate	21.777	Achille	19.804
Monime	20.692	Agamemnon	19.085
		confidants	17.867
		Clytemnestre	17.701

Phèdre

Esther

Théramène	23.053	Piété	32.308
Hippolyte	22.686	Esther	25.154
---------MEAN--------19.569----		Aman	22.527
Aricie	19.405	---------MEAN--------20.112----	
confidants	18.528	confidants	19.720
Thésée	18.383	Mardochée	19.421
Phèdre	17.890	Zarès	19.243
		Assuérus	17.239
		Chœur	15.966

Athalie

Les Plaideurs

Abner	24.627	L'Intimé	13.908
Joad	22.660	Petit Jean	11.958
Mathan	21.646	---------MEAN--------10.890----	
Zacharie	21.038	Léandre	10.648
confidants	20.838	Chicanneau	10.423
---------MEAN--------19.936----		Dandin	9.533
Salomith	18.455	La Comtesse	9.425
Josabet	17.634	Isabelle	9.091
Athalie	17.230	Souffleur	3.615
Chœur	17.105		
Joas	14.368		

Tite et Bérénice	(Corneille)	*Phèdre et Hippolyte*	(Pradon)
Tite	29.467	Thésée	51.038
confidants	28.810	Phèdre	43.627
---------MEAN--------28.421----		---------MEAN--------43.505----	
Bérénice	28.404	Hippolyte	41.893
Domitie	28.117	confidants	38.925
Domitian	27.304	Aricie	38.301

TABLE 6
DISTRIBUTION OF MEAN SENTENCE LENGTH BY CHARACTERS
in Descending Order
(syllables)

	32.308	Piété (ES)
	30.980	Éphestion (AL)
	28.731	Étéocle (TH)
	27.534	Créon (TH)
	27.364	Porus (AL)
	27.331	Cléofile (AL)
Ulysse (IP)	26.746	
	26.168	Taxile (AL)
	25.273	Alexandre (AL)
	25.154	Esther (ES)
Ériphile (IP)	25.109	
	24.627	Abner (AT)
Paulin (BE)	24.460	
Bajazet (BA)	24.177	
	23.899	Antigone (TH)
Burrhus (BR)	23.847	
	23.716	Axiane (AL)
	23.707	Hémon (TH)
Xipharès (MI)	23.246	
Théramène (PH)	23.053	
confidants (MI)	22.991	
	22.807	Jocaste (TH)
Agrippine (BR)	22.688	
Hippolyte (PH)	22.686	
	22.660	Joad (AT)
	22.627	Polynice (TH)
	22.535	confidants (TH)
	22.527	Aman (ES)
Acomat (BA)	22.103	
Pharnace (MI)	22.000	
Narcisse (BR)	21,857	
Mithridate (MI)	21.777	
	21.646	Mathan (AT)
Néron (BR)	21.493	
Albine (BR)	21.300	
	21.038	Zacharie (AT)
confidants (BA)	20.924	
	20.838	confidants (AT)

Monime (MI)	20.692	
Titus (BE)	20.548	
Iphigénie (IP)	20.337	
Pyrrhus (AN)	20.197	
Oreste (AN)	19.884	
Achille (IP)	19.804	
	19.720	confidants (ES)
Andromaque (AN)	19.421	Mardochée (ES)
Aricie (PH)	19.405	
	19.243	Zarès (ES)
Agamemnon (IP)	19.085	
confidants (BE)	18.972	
Junie (BR)	18.796	
Britannicus (BR)	18.606	
Atalide (BA)	18.533	
confidants (PH)	18.528	
	18.455	Salomith (AT)
Thésée (PH)	18.383	
Hermione (AN)	18.327	
Phèdre (PH)	17.890	
confidants (IP)	17.867	
Roxane (BA)	17.770	
Bérénice (BE)	17.703	
Clytemnestre (IP)	17.701	
	17.634	Josabet (AT)
confidants (AN)	17.412	
Antiochus (BE)	17.333	
	17.239	Assuérus (ES)
	17.230	Athalie (AT)
	17.105	Chœur (AT)
	15.966	Chœur (ES)
	14.368	Joas (AT)
	13.908	L'Intimé (PL)
	11.958	Petit Jean (PL)
	10.648	Léandre (PL)
	10.423	Chicanneau (PL)
	9.533	Dandin (PL)
	9.425	La Comtesse (PL)
	9.091	Isabelle (PL)
	3.615	Souffleur (PL)

TABLE 7

DISTRIBUTION OF INTERNAL PUNCTUATION

(percentage of sentences)

	Questions			Exclamations		
	0	1	2	0	1	2
La Thébaïde	97.0	3.0	--	92.0	8.0	--
Alexandre	97.1	2.7	0.3	93.3	6.7	--
Andromaque	92.5	7.2	0.3	91.3	8.6	0.2
Britannicus	90.7	8.7	0.6	92.3	7.6	0.1
Bérénice	89.2	10.2	0.6	90.5	9.0	0.5
Bajazet	96.9	3.0	0.1	93.2	6.8	--
Mithridate	95.4	4.4	0.2	92.5	7.3	0.2
Iphigénie	96.3	3.5	0.3	92.4	7.5	0.1
Phèdre	98.0	2.0	--	94.5	5.2	0.3
Esther	98.7	1.3	--	94.0	6.0	--
Athalie	97.7	2.3	--	96.1	3.8	0.1
Les Plaideurs	97.9	2.0	0.1	90.3	9.3	0.4
Tite et Bérénice	98.4	1.6	--	96.4	3.3	0.3
Phèdre et Hippolyte	94.6	5.2	0.2	73.3	24.0	2.7

TABLE 8
DISTRIBUTION OF FREQUENT SUBORDINATIONS
(percentage of sentences)

	Quand/lorsque	Conditional *si*	Sans *(que)*
La Thébaïde	3.9	9.1	2.0
Alexandre	2.9	7.4	2.9
Andromaque	1.2	5.6	1.4
Britannicus	2.1	5.3	2.0
Bérénice	3.3	4.4	2.5
Bajazet	2.4	7.2	3.4
Mithridate	2.6	6.1	3.1
Iphigénie	1.9	4.6	2.2
Phèdre	2.5	3.4	0.9
Esther	2.9	3.1	0.9
Athalie	1.9	3.2	0.8
Les Plaideurs	1.6	3.2	1.2
Tite et Bérénice	5.4	18.8	2.9
Phèdre et Hippolyte	7.5	9.0	---

TABLE 9
DISTRIBUTION OF COORDINATION
(percentage of sentences)

	et			*ou*		*mais*	
	0	1	2+	0	1	0	1+
La Thébaïde	58.4	30.8	10.8	96.3	3.7	89.9	10.1
Alexandre	66.9	25.8	7.3	96.9	3.1	87.9	12.1
Andromaque	74.4	21.7	3.9	97.3	2.7	91.3	8.7
Britannicus	75.8	20.0	4.2	97.1	2.9	90.6	9.4
Bérénice	77.0	19.2	3.8	98.2	1.8	94.7	5.3
Bajazet	73.5	21.7	4.8	97.3	2.7	90.8	9.2
Mithridate	66.5	26.8	6.7	98.1	1.9	92.4	7.6
Iphigénie	72.0	22.0	6.0	98.4	1.6	93.5	6.5
Phèdre	75.6	20.9	3.5	98.6	1.4	93.9	6.1
Esther	74.0	20.9	5.1	99.5	0.5	95.9	4.1
Athalie	74.2	20.7	5.1	99.1	0.9	94.5	5.5
Les Plaideurs	87.6	10.7	1.7	98.5	1.5	93.9	6.1
Tite et Bérénice	57.0	30.8	12.2	93.9	6.1	87.3	12.7
Phèdre et Hippolyte	45.5	23.8	30.7	96.9	3.1	82.0	18.0

Bibliography

I. Primary Texts

Corneille, Pierre. *Tite et Bérénice*. In *Œuvres de P. Corneille*, edited by Ch. Marty-Laveaux. Paris: Hachette, 1862. 10: 201-76.

Pradon, Jacques. *Phèdre et Hippolyte*. Paris: Henry Loyson, 1677. Printed as part of *Les Œuvres de Mr Pradon*. Paris: Jean Ribou, 1682.

Racine, Jean. *Œuvres*. 8 vols. Edited by Paul Mesnard. Paris: Hachette, 1885.

———. *Iphigenia / Phaedra / Athaliah*. Translated by John Cairncross. Baltimore, Md.: Penguin Classics, 1968.

———. *Phaedra*. English Version by Robert Lowell. In *The Classical Theatre. Vol. IV: Six French Plays*. Edited by Eric Bentley. Garden City, N.Y.: Doubleday Anchor Books, 1961.

———. *Phèdre*. Translated by Margaret Rawlings. New York: E. P. Dutton Co., 1961.

II. Works on Racine

A. On Tragedy and Racine's Theater

Descotes, Maurice. *Les Grands Rôles du théâtre de Jean Racine*. Paris: Presses Universitaires de France, 1957.

Goldmann, Lucien. *Le Dieu caché*. Paris: Gallimard, 1955.

———. "The Structure of Racinian Tragedy." In *Racine: Modern Judgments*. Edited by R. C. Knight. London: Macmillan and Company, 1969. Pp. 101-16.

Hubert, Judd David. *Essai d'exégèse racinienne: les secrets témoins*. Paris: Nizet, 1956.

Knight, Roy C. "Evolution of Racine's Poétique." *Modern Language Review* 35 (1940): 19-39.

Kohler, Pierre. "Racine et la Tragédie française." *Revue des cours et des conférences* 41 (1939-40): 449-58; 520-30.

Lapp, John C. *Aspects of Racinian Tragedy*. University of Toronto Romance Series, 2. Toronto: Toronto University Press, 1955.

Mauron, Charles. *L'Inconscient dans l'œuvre et la vie de Racine*. Aix-en-Provence: Publications des Annales de la Faculté des Lettres, n.s. 16 (1957).

May, Georges. "Comment Racine distribuait ses rôles." *French Studies* 4 (1950): 306-12.

— — —. "Connaissance préalable de la matière tragique." In his *Dramaturgie cornélienne, dramaturgie racinienne.* Illinois Studies in Language and Literature 32, no. 4. Urbana: University of Illinois Press, 1948. Pp. 116-91.

Nurse, Peter H. "Towards a Definition of 'Le Tragique Racinien.'" *Symposium* 21 (1967): 197-221.

Picard, Raymond. *La Carrière de Jean Racine.* 2d ed. Paris: Gallimard, 1956.

Racine, Jean. *Bajazet: Mise en scène et commentaires de Xavier de Courville.* Paris: Seuil, 1947.

— — —. *Phèdre: Mise en scène et commentaires de Jean-Louis Barrault.* Paris: Seuil, 1946.

Starobinski, Jean. "Racine et la Poétique du regard." *L' Œil vivant.* Paris: Gallimard, 1961.

Vinaver, Eugene. "Action and Poetry in Racine's Tragedies." In *Racine: Modern Judgments,* edited by R. C. Knight. London: Macmillan and Company, 1969. Pp. 147-60.

— — —. *Racine et la Poésie tragique.* Paris: Nizet, 1951; 1963.

Weinberg, Bernard. *The Art of Jean Racine.* Chicago: University of Chicago Press, 1963.

B. On Racine's Language and Style

Barthes, Roland. *Sur Racine.* Paris: Seuil, 1963.

Cahen, Jacques G. *Le Vocabulaire de Racine.* Revue de Linguistique Romane 16 (1940-45). Paris: Droz, 1946.

Casterán, Ricardo. "Les Rapports de la syntaxe et de la versification dans *Phèdre.*" *Langue et Littérature: Actes du VIIIe Congrès de la Fédération Internationale des Langues et Littératures Modernes.* Bibliothèque de la Faculté de Philosophie et de Lettres de l'Université de Liège, fascicule 161. Paris: Société d'Edition "Les Belles Lettres," 1961. Pp. 271-74.

France, Peter. *Racine's Rhetoric.* Oxford: Clarendon Press, 1965.

Freeman, Bryant C., and Batson, Alan. *Concordance du théâtre et des poésies de Jean Racine.* 2 vols. Ithaca, N.Y.: Cornell University Press, 1968.

Giraudoux, Jean. "Racine." *Nouvelle Revue Française* 33 (1929): 733-56.

Pommier, Jean. "Langage et poésie." In his *Aspects de Racine.* Paris: Nizet, 1954. Pp. 241-309.

Sayce, R. A. "Racine's Style: Periphrasis and Direct Statement." In *Racine: Modern Judgments,* edited by R. C. Knight. London: Macmillan and Company, 1969. Pp. 132-46.

Seznec, Alain. "The Uses of *enfin* in Racine's *Andromaque.*" *French Review* 45, Special Issue, no. 4 (1972): 61-64.

Spitzer, Leo. "The Muting Effect of Classical Style in Racine." In *Racine: Modern Judgments*, Edited by R. C. Knight. London: Macmillan and Company, 1969. Pp. 117-31.

Spœrri, Théophile. "Le Rythme tragique." *Trivium* 3 (1945): 161-84.

Strachey, Giles Lytton. *Literary Essays*. New York: Harcourt, Brace, 1949.

Wexler, Philip J. "Distich and Sentence in Corneille and Racine." In *Essays on Style and Language*, edited by Roger Fowler. London: Routledge, and Kegan Paul, 1966. Pp. 100-117.

— — — . "On the Grammetrics of the Classical Alexandrine." *Cahiers de Lexicologie* 4 (1964): 61-72.

III. General Work on Theater and Tragedy

Aubignac, L'Abbé François d'. *La Pratique du théâtre*. Edited by Pierre Martino. Paris: Champion, 1927.

Barrault, Jean-Louis. *Réflexions sur le théâtre*. Paris: Jacques Vautrin, 1949.

Boileau-Despréaux, Nicolas. "L'Art poétique." In *Œuvres*, edited by Georges Mongrédien. Paris: Garnier, 1961.

Corneille, Pierre. *Le Discours de l'utilité et des parties du poème dramatique*. In *Œuvres de P. Corneille*, edited by Ch. Marty-Laveaux. Paris: Hachette, 1862. 1: 13-51.

— — — . *Le Discours de la tragédie et des moyens de la traiter selon le vraisemblable ou le nécessaire*. In *Œuvres de P. Corneille*, edited by Ch. Marty-Laveaux. Paris: Hachette, 1862. 1: 52-97.

— — — . *Le Discours des trois unités d'action, de jour et de lieu*. In *Œuvres de P. Corneille*, edited by Ch. Marty-Laveaux. Paris: Hachette, 1862. 1: 98-122.

Lancaster, Henry Carrington. *A History of French Dramatic Literature in the Seventeenth Century*. 5 pts. in 9 vols. Baltimore, Md.: Johns Hopkins Press, 1929-42.

Olson, Elder. *Tragedy and the Theory of Drama*. Detroit, Mich.: Wayne State University Press, 1966.

Schérer, Jacques. *La Dramaturgie classique en France*. Paris: Nizet, 1950.

Vilar, Jean. *De la tradition théâtrale*. Paris: Gallimard, 1963.

IV. General Works on Language and Style

A. Traditional Approaches

Cressot, Marcel. *Le Style et ses techniques*. 4th ed. Paris: Presses Universitaires de France, 1959.

Deloffre, Frédéric. *Stylistique et poétique françaises*. Paris: SEDES, 1970.

Grammont, Maurice. *Petit Traité de versification française*. Collection U. Paris: Armand Colin, 1965.

Guiraud, Pierre, and Kuentz, Pierre. *La Stylistique: Lectures.* Initiation à la linguistique, série A: Lectures, 1. Paris: Klincksieck, 1970.

Le Hir, Yves. *Analyses stylistiques.* Collection U. Paris: Armand Colin, 1965.

Rousset, Jean. *Forme et signification: essais sur les structures littéraires de Corneille à Claudel.* Paris: José Corti, 1964.

Sayce, R. A. *Style in French Prose: A Method of Analysis.* Oxford: Clarendon Press, 1958.

Spitzer, Leo *Linguistics and Literary History: Essays in Stylistics.* Princeton, N.J.: Princeton University Press, 1948.

———. "Language—The Basis of Science, Philosophy and Poetry." In *Studies in Intellectual History,* edited by George Boas. Baltimore, Md.: Johns Hopkins Press, 1953. Pp. 67-93.

———. "Stylistique et critique littéraire." *Critique* 98 (July 1955): 595-609.

B. Computer-Assisted Approaches

Dolezel, Lubomír, and Bailey, Richard, eds. *Statistics and Style.* Mathematical Linguistics and Automatic Language Processing 6. New York: Elsevier, 1969.

Duggan, Joseph. *The Song of Roland: Formulaic Style and Poetic Craft.* Berkeley: University of California Press, 1973.

Francis, Ivor S. "An Exposition of a Statistical Approach to the *Federalist* Dispute." In *The Computer and Literary Style,* edited by Jacob Leed. Kent, Ohio: Kent State University Press, 1966. Pp. 38-78.

Haskel, Peggy I. "Collocations as a measure of stylistic variety." In *The Computer in Literary and Linguistic Research: Papers from a Cambridge Symposium.* Cambridge: Cambridge University Press, 1971. Pp. 159-68.

Radday, Yehuda T. *The Unity of Isaiah in the Light of Statistical Linguistics.* Gerstenberg: Hildersheim, 1973.

Wachal, Robert S. "On Using a Computer." In *The Computer and Literary Style,* edited by Jacob Leed. Kent, Ohio: Kent State University Press, 1966. Pp. 14-37.

Widmann, R. L. "Recent Scholarship in Literary and Linguistic Studies." *Computers and the Humanities* 7 (1972-73): 3-27.

V. General Works on Grammar and History of the Language

Brunot, Ferdinand. *Histoire de la langue française des origines à 1900, IV, ii: La Langue classique (1660-1715).* Paris: Armand Colin, 1924.

Chevalier, Jean-Claude. *Histoire de la syntaxe: naissance de la notion de complément dans la grammaire française (1530-1750).* Publications romanes et françaises, 100. Genève: Droz, 1968.

Cohen, Marcel Samuel Raphael. *Grammaire et style, 1450-1950: cinq cents ans de phrase française.* Paris: Editions sociales, 1954.

Deloffre, Frédéric. *La Phrase française*. Paris: SEDES, 1967.

Dubois, Jean. *Grammaire structurale du français, III: La Phrase et ses transformations*. Langue et langage. Paris: Larousse, 1969.

Dubois, Jean; Lagane, René; and Lerond, Alain. *Dictionnaire du français classique*. Paris: Larousse, 1971.

Grand Dictionnaire de l'Académie Françoise. 2 vols. 2d ed., 1695. Reprint. Genève: Slatkine, 1972.

Haase, A. *Syntaxe française du XVIIe siècle*. 5th ed. Paris: Delagrave, 1965.

Le Hir, Yves. *Esthétique et structure du vers français d'après les théoriciens du XVIe siècle à nos jours*. Paris: Presses Universitaires de France, 1956.

VI. Computer-Programming Materials

Dewar, Robert B. K. *SPITBOL, Version 2.0*. Illinois Institute of Technology, 1971.

Griswold, R.E.; Poage, J.F.; and Polonsky, I.P. *The SNOBOL4 Programming Language*. Englewood Cliffs, N.J.: Prentice-Hall, 1968.

Nie, Norman H.; Bent, Dale H.; and Hull, C. Hadlai. *SPSS: Statistical Package for the Social Sciences*. 2d ed. New York: McGraw-Hill, 1975.

[Index]

221